Survival

GLOBAL POLITICS AND STRATEGY

Volume 64 Number 1 | February–March 2022

'A key question is why Putin has chosen this time to intensify his hostility and pressure on Ukraine, NATO and the West in general. The most plausible explanation is that he has bided his time until Russia has recovered from its debilitated post-Soviet condition.'

Robert Hunter, The Ukraine Crisis: Why and What Now?, p. 19.

'In intelligence, most treatments of confidence are little more than hand-waves: at one point, NIC products came with a footnote saying something to the effect that, unless otherwise noted, all the judgements in the document were of medium confidence. Had that been a comment in a student paper, I would have marked it NSS (for 'No S*** Sherlock') in large letters in the margin.'

Gregory F. Treverton, Connecting Intelligence and Policy, p. 47.

'Here, as in Vietnam and Iraq, it seems that senior US military officials did not objectively assess the capability of the forces they trained and equipped. And as in Iraq, they were surprised by the [Afghan Army's] quick collapse.'

Julia Santucci, After Afghanistan: Intelligence Analysis and US Military Missions, p. 167.

T0191119

Survival
GLOBAL POLITICS AND STRATEGY
Volume 64 Number 1 | February–March 2022

Contents

The Reckoning: Russia, NATO and Ukraine

7 **The Ukraine Crisis: Why and What Now?** *Robert Hunter*
However the crisis plays out, the most important requirement of successful US-led negotiations with Russia is that Moscow demonstrate that it is prepared to be a responsible international actor.

29 **Hope Deferred: Russia from 1991 to 2021** *Rodric Braithwaite*
Vladimir Putin's military posturing around Ukraine may be intended to force the Americans to provide written assurance about NATO enlargement. But the US can hardly accept Putin's ultimatum.

Commentary

45 **Connecting Intelligence and Policy** *Gregory F. Treverton*
The intelligence profession has much to learn from private-sector, open-source intelligence analysts who operate crowdsourcing networks.

51 **Geopolitical Forecasting and Actionable Intelligence** *Ian S. Lustick*
Only when political scientists and sociologists play a prominent role in the design and assessment of forecasting tools will geopolitical forecasting become an effective tool for policymakers.

57 **War with China: Five Scenarios** *Stacie L. Pettyjohn*
The United States needs to demonstrate that it has the capability and willingness to stop Chinese aggression without accidentally precipitating a conflict.

67 **National Security and Climate Change: The Attention It Deserves?** *Erin Sikorsky*
In practice, despite high-level proclamations, climate change still occupies little of the United States' and others' day-to-day national-security agendas.

74 **Noteworthy**

Deterrence and Stability

77 **Alliances and Nuclear Risk: Strengthening US Extended Deterrence** *Stephan Frühling and Andrew O'Neil*
Current US debates regarding no first use tend to underplay the broader alliance implications of any shift in US nuclear policy.

99 **Disruptive Technologies and Nuclear Risks: What's New and What Matters** *Andrew Futter*
Technological challenges to nuclear stability are concerning but not insurmountable, and will often – though not always – have political remedies.

On the cover
A Ukrainian soldier patrols in a trench near the town of Zolote-4, Ukraine, in January 2022.

On the web
Visit www.iiss.org/ publications/survival for brief notices on new books on Africa, Russia and Eurasia, Latin America and Asia-Pacific.

Survival **editors' blog**
For ideas and commentary from *Survival* editors and contributors, visit www.iiss.org/blogs/ survival-blog.

Survival
GLOBAL POLITICS AND STRATEGY

The International Institute for Strategic Studies

2121 K Street, NW | Suite 600 | Washington DC 20037 | USA
Tel +1 202 659 1490   Fax +1 202 659 1499   E-mail survival@iiss.org   Web www.iiss.org

Arundel House | 6 Temple Place | London | WC2R 2PG | UK
Tel +44 (0)20 7379 7676   Fax +44 (0)20 7836 3108   E-mail iiss@iiss.org

14th Floor, GBCorp Tower | Bahrain Financial Harbour | Manama | Kingdom of Bahrain
Tel +973 1718 1155   Fax +973 1710 0155   E-mail iiss-middleeast@iiss.org

9 Raffles Place | #49-01 Republic Plaza | Singapore 048619
Tel +65 6499 0055   Fax +65 6499 0059   E-mail iiss-asia@iiss.org

Pariser Platz 6A | 10117 Berlin | Germany
Tel +49 30 311 99 300   E-mail iiss-europe@iiss.org

Survival Online www.tandfonline.com/survival and www.iiss.org/publications/survival

Aims and Scope *Survival* is one of the world's leading forums for analysis and debate of international and strategic affairs. Shaped by its editors to be both timely and forward thinking, the journal encourages writers to challenge conventional wisdom and bring fresh, often controversial, perspectives to bear on the strategic issues of the moment. With a diverse range of authors, *Survival* aims to be scholarly in depth while vivid, well written and policy-relevant in approach. Through commentary, analytical articles, case studies, forums, review essays, reviews and letters to the editor, the journal promotes lively, critical debate on issues of international politics and strategy.

Editor **Dana Allin**
Managing Editor **Jonathan Stevenson**
Associate Editor **Carolyn West**
Assistant Editor **Jessica Watson**
Production and Cartography **Kelly Verity**

Contributing Editors

Mälfrid Braut-Hegghammer	**Russell Crandall**	**Melissa K. Griffith**	**Jeffrey Mazo**	**Ray Takeyh**
Ian Bremmer	**Toby Dodge**	**John L. Harper**	**Teresita C. Schaffer**	**David C. Unger**
Rosa Brooks	**Bill Emmott**	**Matthew Harries**	**Steven Simon**	**Lanxin Xiang**
David P. Calleo	**Mark Fitzpatrick**	**Erik Jones**	**Karen Smith**	
	John A. Gans, Jr	**Hanns W. Maull**	**Angela Stent**	

Published for the IISS by
Routledge Journals, an imprint of Taylor & Francis, an Informa business.

About the IISS The IISS, a registered charity with offices in Washington, London, Manama, Singapore and Berlin, is the world's leading authority on political–military conflict. It is the primary independent source of accurate, objective information on international strategic issues. Publications include *The Military Balance*, an annual reference work on each nation's defence capabilities; *Strategic Survey*, an annual review of world affairs; *Survival*, a bimonthly journal on international affairs; *Strategic Comments*, an online analysis of topical issues in international affairs; and the *Adelphi* series of books on issues of international security.

SUBMISSIONS

To submit an article, authors are advised to follow these guidelines:

- *Survival* articles are around 4,000–10,000 words long including endnotes. A word count should be included with a draft.
- All text, including endnotes, should be double-spaced with wide margins.
- Any tables or artwork should be supplied in separate files, ideally not embedded in the document or linked to text around it.
- All *Survival* articles are expected to include endnote references. These should be complete and include first and last names of authors, titles of articles (even from newspapers), place of publication, publisher, exact publication dates, volume and issue number (if from a journal) and page numbers. Web sources should include complete URLs and DOIs if available.
- A summary of up to 150 words should be included with the article. The summary should state the main argument clearly and concisely, not simply say what the article is about.

- A short author's biography of one or two lines should also be included. This information will appear at the foot of the first page of the article.

Please note that *Survival* has a strict policy of listing multiple authors in alphabetical order.

Submissions should be made by email, in Microsoft Word format, to survival@iiss.org. Alternatively, hard copies may be sent to *Survival*, IISS–US, 2121 K Street NW, Suite 801, Washington, DC 20037, USA.

The editorial review process can take up to three months. *Survival*'s acceptance rate for unsolicited manuscripts is less than ·20%. *Survival* does not normally provide referees' comments in the event of rejection. Authors are permitted to submit simultaneously elsewhere so long as this is consistent with the policy of the other publication and the Editors of *Survival* are informed of the dual submission.

Readers are encouraged to comment on articles from the previous issue. Letters should be concise, no longer than 750 words and relate directly to the argument or points made in the original article.

ADVERTISING AND PERMISSIONS
For advertising rates and schedules
USA/Canada: The Advertising Manager, Taylor & Francis Inc., 530 Walnut Street, Suite 850, Philadelphia, PA 19106, USA Tel +1 (800) 354 1420 Fax +1 (215) 207 0050.

UK/Europe/Rest of World: The Advertising Manager, Routledge Journals, Taylor & Francis, 4 Park Square, Milton Park, Abingdon, Oxfordshire OX14 4RN, UK Tel +44 (0) 207 017 6000 Fax +44 (0) 207 017 6336.

SUBSCRIPTIONS
Survival is published bimonthly in February, April, June, August, October and December by Routledge Journals, an imprint of Taylor & Francis, an Informa Business.

Annual Subscription 2022

	UK, RoI	US, Canada Mexico	Europe	Rest of world
Individual	£180	$303	€ 243	$303
Institution (print and online)	£648	$1,113	€ 951	$1,194
Institution (online only)	£551	$963	€ 808	$1,015

Taylor & Francis has a flexible approach to subscriptions, enabling us to match individual libraries' requirements. This journal is available via a traditional institutional subscription (either print with online access, or online only at a discount) or as part of our libraries, subject collections or archives. For more information on our sales packages please visit http://www.tandfonline.com/page/librarians.

All current institutional subscriptions include online access for any number of concurrent users across a local area network to the currently available backfile and articles posted online ahead of publication.

Subscriptions purchased at the personal rate are strictly for personal, non-commercial use only. The reselling of personal subscriptions is prohibited. Personal subscriptions must be purchased with a personal cheque or credit card. Proof of personal status may be requested.

Dollar rates apply to all subscribers outside Europe. Euro rates apply to all subscribers in Europe, except the UK and the Republic of Ireland where the pound sterling rate applies. If you are unsure which rate applies to you please contact Customer Services in the UK. All subscriptions are payable in advance and all rates include postage. Journals are sent by air to the USA, Canada, Mexico, India, Japan and Australasia. Subscriptions are entered on an annual basis, i.e. January to December. Payment may be made by sterling cheque, dollar cheque, euro cheque, international money order, National Giro or credit cards (Amex, Visa and Mastercard).

Survival (USPS 013095) is published bimonthly (in Feb, Apr, Jun, Aug, Oct and Dec) by Routledge Journals, Taylor & Francis, 4 Park Square, Milton Park, Abingdon, OX14 4RN, United Kingdom.

The US annual subscription price is $1,085. Airfreight and mailing in the USA by agent named WN Shipping USA, 156-15, 146th Avenue, 2nd Floor, Jamaica, NY 11434, USA. Periodicals postage paid at Jamaica NY 11431.

US Postmaster: Send address changes to Survival, C/O Air Business Ltd / 156-15 146th Avenue, Jamaica, New York, NY11434.

Subscription records are maintained at Taylor & Francis Group, 4 Park Square, Milton Park, Abingdon, OX14 4RN, United Kingdom.

ORDERING INFORMATION
Please contact your local Customer Service Department to take out a subscription to the Journal: **USA, Canada:** Taylor & Francis, Inc., 530 Walnut Street, Suite 850, Philadelphia, PA 19106, USA. Tel: +1 800 354 1420; Fax: +1 215 207 0050. **UK/ Europe/Rest of World:** T&F Customer Services, Informa UK Ltd, Sheepen Place, Colchester, Essex, CO3 3LP, United Kingdom. Tel: +44 (0) 20 7017 5544; Fax: +44 (0) 20 7017 5198; Email: subscriptions@tandf.co.uk.

Back issues: Taylor & Francis retains a two-year back issue stock of journals. Older volumes are held by our official stockists: Periodicals Service Company, 351 Fairview Ave., Suite 300, Hudson, New York 12534, USA to whom all orders and enquiries should be addressed. *Tel* +1 518 537 4700 *Fax* +1 518 537 5899 *e-mail* psc@periodicals.com *web* http://www.periodicals.com/tandf.html.

The International Institute for Strategic Studies (IISS) and our publisher Taylor & Francis make every effort to ensure the accuracy of all the information (the "Content") contained in our publications. However, the IISS and our publisher Taylor & Francis, our agents, and our licensors make no representations or warranties whatsoever as to the accuracy, completeness, or suitability for any purpose of the Content. Any opinions and views expressed in this publication are the opinions and views of the authors, and are not the views of or endorsed by the IISS and our publisher Taylor & Francis. The accuracy of the Content should not be relied upon and should be independently verified with primary sources of information. The IISS and our publisher Taylor & Francis shall not be liable for any losses, actions, claims, proceedings, demands, costs, expenses, damages, and other liabilities whatsoever or howsoever caused arising directly or indirectly in connection with, in relation to or arising out of the use of the Content. Terms & Conditions of access and use can be found at http://www.tandfonline.com/page/terms-and-conditions.

The issue date is February–March 2022.

The print edition of this journal is printed on ANSI-conforming acid-free paper.

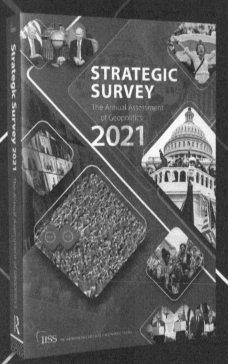
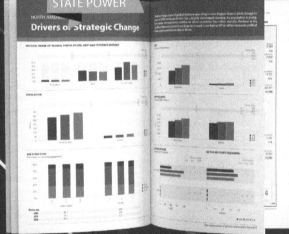

The Ukraine Crisis: Why and What Now?

Robert Hunter

The current crisis over Ukraine has deep roots and, of course, is not limited to Ukraine. The view prevailing in the United States and most of Western and Central Europe is that Russian President Vladimir Putin has selected Ukraine, on account of its strategic location in Central Europe, to be the leading edge of an attempt to reconstitute the Soviet Union or at least to establish a new sphere of influence in Russia's near abroad. Russian machinations in the energy, cyber and political realms, with a special focus on the Baltic states, appear to be part of his overall game plan. An alternative view is that Putin is seeking a major role for Russia in European security, given that in the last two decades the United States and most NATO allies have sought to subordinate Russian influence in Europe. Whichever view of Putin's motives is correct – perhaps both are to some extent – it is important to consider the current Ukraine crisis as a point of departure in long-term relations between Russia and the West. The crisis is crucial to understanding Russia's effort to revive its great-power status, to shaping Western efforts to channel Russia's ambitions in non-threatening ways and to avoiding a new cold war.[1]

Roots of crisis

Historians, as well as Putin, might argue that the modern Ukraine crisis began with Nikita Khrushchev's 1954 transfer of Crimea from the Russian Socialist Federal Republic to the Ukrainian Socialist Federal Republic to commemorate

Robert Hunter was US Ambassador to NATO from 1993 to 1998.

Survival | vol. 64 no. 1 | February–March 2022 | pp. 7–28   https://doi.org/10.1080/00396338.2022.2032953

the 300th anniversary of Ukrainian–Russian unification.[2] Since both republics were within the Soviet Union, this was a symbolic event, until the 1991 collapse of the Soviet Union, when the location of Crimea in newly independent Ukraine became significant. For contemporary purposes, the starting point was Christmas night in 1991, when the Soviet Union formally ceased to exist. Since then, the key geopolitical challenge in Europe has been to create security for all of its countries and, at the same time, to accommodate Russia to the political evolution of the continent without isolating Moscow or seeing it threaten Europe. The latter objective in particular remains elusive.

For the US and its main NATO allies, a key post-Cold War goal was to prevent a reprise of the First World War's aftermath, when a defeated Germany was stigmatised in the Treaty of Versailles as the sole cause of the conflict, subjected to reparations and broadly treated as a pariah state. This treatment was a significant factor in Adolf Hitler's rise to power. At the end of the 1980s, Western leaders understood that Russia must not be cast as a defeated state. Both George H.W. Bush and his successor, Bill Clinton, were careful not to do so. Even though Russia was then supine and no longer a major factor in continental politics, economics and security, it was likely that in time it would recover a measure of national power sufficient to threaten European security and stability if it chose to do so.

The West sought to move beyond the balance of power

A critical task for the West was therefore to develop post-Cold War structures, processes, perceptions and activities that preserved each European nation's legitimate interests and promoted democratic and liberal values – if possible, in Russia as well – without alienating any country or, worse, nurturing or validating Russian revanchism. In the process, the West sought to move beyond classical themes of statecraft in Europe, notably spheres of influence and the balance of power. Success or failure would help determine whether the goal of a 'Europe whole and free' and at peace, enunciated by George H.W. Bush in May 1989, could be secured. This was a tall order. Unlike Germany and Japan following the Second World War, Russia was not occupied and, unlike Germany, it did not have a democratic tradition.

The initial focus was on the future of Germany. Notably, in the so-called 'Two Plus Four Agreement' – the 1990 treaty signed by East and West Germany and the post-Second World War occupying countries: France, the Soviet Union, the United Kingdom and the United States – it was agreed that there should be one Germany that would become part of NATO.[3] Moscow's acquiescence was not entirely self-abnegation: it could recognise that a united Germany embedded in the viable institution of NATO, subject to American oversight, would discourage revived German militarism – a prospect which, however unlikely, also worried other NATO members. Debate continues about whether, in reaching the agreement about a united Germany's membership, the United States made promises – explicit or implied – not to expand NATO to other countries.[4]

Under US leadership, NATO developed an architecture of several interlocking and mutually dependent elements: the United States would remain a European power; NATO's integrated military command structure would be preserved; the German question that first arose in the late 1860s would remain solved; Central Europe would be removed from the geopolitical chessboard; and NATO would try to develop close working relations with the European Communities (which would become the European Union). At no point, however, did the United States and other NATO allies take seriously the declared Russian preference that NATO itself be dissolved as the Warsaw Pact had been, and that Russia would play an equal part in creating a new institution to provide for security across the continent. Here the West's acquiescence to the palliative notion that Russia did not lose the Cold War hit a hard and virtually unanimous stop.

Various instruments were created at NATO under US leadership. Most significant for promoting European security was undoubtedly the Partnership for Peace (PfP). It has served four purposes: to advance the Western aspirations of most of the member countries; to help promote democracy in former Warsaw Pact states; to foster common military standards and practices, potentially as steps for some of those countries eventually to join NATO; and to forge lasting institutional connections to NATO for countries that would not join it. All members of the Organization for Security and Co-operation in Europe (OSCE) and Euro-Atlantic

Partnership Council (EAPC) were eligible for PfP membership. Notably, after some coaxing, Russia agreed to join both the PfP and the EAPC.

During what in retrospect was a halcyon period, NATO–Russia cooperation became possible. Indeed, at one point, in a bilateral discussion at which I was present, the Russian defence minister told the US secretary of defense that Moscow had no problem with NATO other than its Cold War-vintage name. When NATO resolved to use airpower to end the Bosnian war in summer 1995, Russia supported Western diplomacy and, following the Dayton Accords, joined the Implementation Force – notably under formal US rather than NATO command – designed to keep the peace.[5] Difficulties began when NATO, led by Washington, moved towards expansion, acceding to the desires of prospective new members to gain protection from possible Russian revanchism as they reformed internally.[6] Also operating was a belief that NATO membership would foster development of Western-tilting domestic institutions and engagement, as well as Western economic investment.

Several allies were sceptical about enlargement, basically on two grounds. Firstly, enlargement could dilute the Alliance and its military capabilities. Secondly, the political requirements for triggering collective NATO response to aggression under Article 5 could become too onerous, diminishing the provision's credibility. Antagonising Russia and thus creating new divisions in Europe was a real though secondary concern for some NATO members.

When the allies agreed on enlargement at the January 1994 NATO summit in Brussels, they did so in a statement whose every word was carefully chosen after intense bargaining: 'We expect and would welcome NATO expansion that would reach to democratic states to our East, as part of an evolutionary process, taking into account political and security developments in the whole of Europe.'[7] The last two clauses were designed to minimise friction with Russia and to avoid rushing some allies into security commitments that they were not then, and might not later be, prepared to make.

Even this conditional statement met with Russian objections, including from the often-compliant Boris Yeltsin, and objections have continued to this day. Nevertheless, while Moscow in principle continued to see NATO enlargement as breaking what it believed to be commitments dating from the unification of Germany, as well as ignoring what it argued were its legitimate political and security prerogatives, Russia tolerated NATO's admission of the first three invitees: the Czech Republic, Poland and Hungary. The first two surrounded Germany with NATO and indicated American engagement. Helmut Kohl, the German chancellor, stressed this aspect of the enlargement project, understanding that Germany's relationships in Central Europe and with Russia would depend on reassurances about Germany's future behaviour, even though the younger generation of Germans had discarded geopolitical or nationalist ambitions.

Before NATO formally invited the first Central European countries to join the Alliance at the July 1997 NATO summit in Madrid, the US and allies recognised that much more substantial consideration of Russia was required in terms not only of its involvement in European security but also its political role in the future of Europe. The NATO–Russia Founding Act of May 1997 contains a set of broad principles and notes 19 specific areas for cooperation.[8] Embedded within the Act were unilateral NATO statements, studiously inserted without negotiation with Russia, declaring limits on deployment of nuclear weapons in Central Europe as well as limits on conventional forces. Institutionally, the Founding Act created a NATO–Russia Permanent Joint Council, which in 2002 became the NATO–Russia Council, with Russia accorded equal status with the allies.

This left one major matter to resolve: what to do about Ukraine. One of the major achievements during the period of relative comity between Russia and NATO was the December 1994 Budapest Memorandum agreed by Russia, the UK and the US (with China and France separately concurring) regarding nuclear weapons that continued to be deployed in three new countries that emerged from the Soviet Union: Belarus, Kazakhstan and Ukraine. Their nuclear weapons were removed to Russia, while with respect to Ukraine, Russia, the UK and the US committed

> to respect the Independence and Sovereignty and the existing borders of Ukraine … to refrain from the threat or use of force against the territorial integrity or political independence of Ukraine, and that none of their weapons will ever be used against Ukraine except in self-defense or

> otherwise in accordance with the Charter of the United Nations ... [and]
> to refrain from economic coercion designed to subordinate to their own
> interest the exercise by Ukraine of the rights inherent in its sovereignty
> and thus to secure advantages of any kind.[9]

There was nothing ambiguous about this commitment. In seizing Crimea in February 2014 and taking other military actions against Ukraine, Russia was clearly in breach of it, as well as the 1975 Helsinki Final Act.

As NATO was about to invite the first three Central European countries to join NATO at its 1997 summit, following conclusion of the NATO–Russia Founding Act, Russia deeply opposed any idea that Ukraine might be considered for NATO membership. NATO allies almost unanimously took the point, as did the Kyiv government, which did not seek membership at that time. But given its strategic location and its history as part of the Soviet Union, Ukraine could not just be treated like any other Central European country. These concerns led to the NATO–Ukraine Charter, including creation of a NATO–Ukraine Commission and a robust list of areas for NATO–Ukrainian cooperation. It also called for the development of 'a crisis consultative mechanism to consult together whenever Ukraine perceives a direct threat to its territorial integrity, political independence, or security'.[10] Thus, Ukraine gained a special relationship with the Alliance. But even though the charter did note 'the inherent right of all states ... to be free to choose or change their security arrangements, including treaties of alliance', the West and Kyiv understood that Ukraine would not become a member of NATO.

Even though the NATO–Russia Founding Act was designed to cushion the impact of the first NATO expansion on Moscow, other developments soon indicated that Russia would not be truly included as part of a 'Europe whole and free', assuming that it had any such aspiration. NATO has often not been inclined to consult Moscow even when Russia has believed its interests were involved. Following Russia's acquiescence to the first NATO expansion, and its positive role in the Implementation Force for Bosnia, the issue came to a head with the US-led NATO decision in 1998 to use airpower against Serbia over Kosovo. To Russia, Serbia's humanitarian transgressions were not as important as the West's ignoring Russian concerns about attacks on Serbia in light of the special ethnic and religious relationship between Russia and Serbia, the provocations of the ethnic-Albanian Kosovo Liberation Army and the absence of a UN Security Council resolution. From Russia's perspective, stopping aggression against Bosnia-Herzegovina, a sovereign state, had been one thing; attacking Serbia over Kosovo, which was part of Serbia, was quite another.

Even before the enlargement question was on the table, NATO also had to consider the future of the three Baltic republics, whose incorporation into the Soviet Union pursuant to the 1939 Molotov–Ribbentrop Pact the United States had never recognised. Especially given their location and small size, those three countries shared a concern about possible Russian aggression, or at least political domination. They all joined PfP expecting that it would lead to NATO membership, which would buttress their internal political developments. Furthermore, several NATO allies near the Baltics, notably Denmark, wanted them in the Alliance. Moscow objected but still recognised that the Baltic states could be special cases even though they abutted Russia. None could pose much of a threat to Russian interests, though their membership did play into the narrative about being disrespected by NATO.

While senior officials in the George H.W. Bush and Clinton administrations appreciated the historical and geopolitical sensitivities in restructuring European security, the prevailing view in the George W. Bush administration was that, since the Soviet Union had lost the Cold War, the US and NATO could do as they pleased. Increasingly evident revanchist Russian impulses, backed by an emerging capacity to act on them, were ignored. Thus, in November 2002, NATO invited not just the three Baltic states but also Bulgaria and Romania to join, further encircling Russia from its perspective. To make matters worse, in June 2002 the United States withdrew from the 1972 Anti-Ballistic Missile (ABM) Treaty, which it no longer considered relevant in the absence of a US–Soviet nuclear confrontation. That was true enough, but the ABM Treaty had been one of the few indicators that Russia, as the principal legatee of the Soviet Union, was recognised by the United States as still being in the big leagues. Abandoning the treaty freed the US to deploy anti-ballistic missiles in Poland and the Czech Republic in 2007 to defend the US homeland (and in theory Western Europe) against possible missile attacks by North Korea or Iran. Although Washington noted correctly that these defences would be too limited to degrade the Russian nuclear deterrent, Russia was still insulted at being strategically dismissed and threatened to deploy new offensive missiles. In July 2007, Russia suspended its observance of the 1990 Treaty on Conventional Armed Forces in Europe, citing NATO's expansion and its plan for missile defences in Central Europe.

Substantially because of these developments, the Russian national perception of the post-Cold War era tends to be one of humiliation. Putin himself has hyped the point, stating that the collapse of the Soviet Union was the greatest geopolitical disaster of the twentieth century. At the annual Munich Security Conference in January 2007, his presentation was notable for its candour in a forum that historically has been placid and matter-of-fact. He singled out the United States for, among other things, the creation of a unipolar world: 'One single center of power. One single center of force. One single center of decision making. This is the world of one master, one sovereign.' Among many other purported sins, 'primarily the United States has overstepped its national borders, and in every area'. He put special emphasis on NATO expansion:

> I think it is obvious that NATO expansion does not have any relation with the modernisation of the Alliance itself or with ensuring security in Europe. On the contrary, it represents a serious provocation that reduces the level of mutual trust. And we have the right to ask: against whom is this expansion intended? And what happened to the assurances our western partners made after the dissolution of the Warsaw Pact? Where are those declarations today? No one even remembers them. But I will allow myself to remind this audience what was said. I would like to quote the speech of NATO General Secretary Mr Woerner in Brussels on 17 May 1990. He said at the time that: 'the fact that we are ready not to place a NATO army outside of German territory gives the Soviet Union a firm security guarantee.' Where are these guarantees?[11]

Putin did note some areas in which Russian and Western interests were compatible, including in energy, space, arms control, non-proliferation and economic security. But US leaders and journalists focused on his negative comments.[12] In November 2009, Russia proposed a new security treaty for Europe. Its main purpose was clearly to weaken the role of NATO, which was just as clearly unacceptable to the US and NATO. They did not take the proposal seriously, and it is questionable whether Putin ever meant it to be regarded as such. He may have intended merely to send a strong signal of Russia's presence and dissatisfaction. In any case, the West's dismissiveness only reinforced Putin's point that it was refusing to treat Russia as a major power.

The 2008 Bucharest Summit saw a major breakpoint in the evolution of NATO and the West's relations with Russia. It came about almost accidentally. The Bush administration sought NATO endorsement for a step towards membership for Ukraine and Georgia. Membership Action Plans for these countries gained virtually no support from other allies. Some were concerned about stoking Moscow's fear of encirclement. Moreover, the allies were not prepared to make security commitments to Ukraine or Georgia, particularly the robust mutual and collective ones contained in Article 5 of the North Atlantic Treaty, even though it contains no automatic requirement that any ally go to war or use military force to repulse aggression. But Bush was politically exposed, and the allies judged that he could not be sent home empty-handed. So, instead of ratifying Membership Action Plans for the two countries, they stated generally that 'we agreed today that these countries will become members of NATO'.[13]

Despite the statement's literal meaning, it was in fact intended to defer Ukraine's and Georgia's NATO membership indefinitely – that is, forever. But Mikheil Saakashvili, Georgia's president, read it as a formal commitment to make Ukraine and Georgia allies. He soon tested the proposition by taking military action to try to regain disputed Georgian territories in South Ossetia from the Russian Federation, ignoring a last-minute telephone plea by a senior US State Department official to desist. Russia crushed the Georgian effort in five days. While the US provided some military support to Georgia, not a single NATO ally was prepared to come to its defence. The Bucharest formulation, basically a drafting accident, was proven empty. NATO would have been wise to jettison it permanently. Unfortunately, it has been repeated in subsequent NATO summit communiqués and at the November 2021 NATO foreign-ministers meeting.[14] The allies have thus appeared to validate Putin's argument about NATO's seeking to surround Russia.

In the 1990s, NATO did indicate that any European country emerging from the wreckage of the Soviet Union, the Warsaw Pact and Yugoslavia could seek to join. But it also made clear that not all applicants would necessarily be accepted as NATO members.[15] Overall, this NATO position is more than a little disingenuous, since the chances of membership for most formally eligible countries remain remote. There is one overarching requirement for NATO membership – unanimous approval of existing allies – and it is difficult to attain. NATO has established several subsidiary steps. Undertaking a Membership Action Plan is one, joining the PfP another. These are designed to help countries become Westernised, democratic nations to provide for their own security, even if they do not join NATO. From the beginning, it has been evident that NATO made the freedom-of-choice declaration without any intention of admitting aspirants as a matter of right, but has now been trapped by its own verbiage.

Another development leading to the current crisis derives in major part from internal developments in Ukraine, as it has struggled to fashion a viable political economy as well as a stable strategic position. The period surrounding the presidency of Viktor Yanukovych was crucial. In late 2013, he had been working on an agreement with the EU that would have provided benefits for Ukraine and would, in the process, have drawn it closer to the West. In November 2013, however, he abandoned the agreement, which led to massive street protests. Following bloody confrontation between opposing sides in Kyiv, he fled to Russia in February 2014.[16] The United States clearly supported the protesters, whom Victoria Nuland, the assistant secretary of state for European and Eurasia Affairs, actively encouraged on a visit to Kyiv. More significantly, she later made a phone call on an open line to Geoffrey Pyatt, the US ambassador in Kyiv, discussing how to facilitate new leadership in Ukraine favourable to the United States.[17] The term 'coup plotting' may be too strong, but Nuland and Pyatt – whether acting on their own or on instructions from top-level US officials – were clearly seeking to draw Ukraine firmly into the US orbit. In addition to being subject to Moscow's efforts to influence its politics, Ukraine was now indisputably contested between Russia and the West.

The Russians began the seizure of Crimea and intervention in Ukraine's Donbas region 16 days after the Nuland–Pyatt phone call was leaked. Given the magnitude and complexity of these military operations, planning for them must have been in the works for some time. Whether the Nuland–Pyatt phone call was a proximate cause of their activation, or just a convenient pretext for Putin, is not clear. It certainly didn't help. In response to Russian military intervention, NATO has increased its military and other capabilities, including in Central Europe.[18] While differences on how to deal with Russia remain in NATO, Putin's conduct has also fostered a high degree of unity in the West behind defying his efforts to sow division by posturing Russian forces for possible further military aggression against Ukraine. From Putin's standpoint, this is an unwelcome result – in a word, blowback.[19]

US–Russia relations

Within the US policy community, as part of the backdrop to the Ukraine crisis and US–Russia relations more broadly, there is a widespread conviction that the United States must be 'number one' and cannot tolerate challenges from a so-called near-peer competitor. US officials and experts also are uncomfortable with ambiguity and tend to divide other countries simplistically into friends and enemies. Towards countries falling into the latter category, suspicion becomes the default position.[20] Thus, in the last several years, strategic differences with Russia, exacerbated by its violation of the Budapest Memorandum and Helsinki Final Act regarding Ukraine, have led some American academics and think tanks to proclaim a new cold war.[21]

Certainly, what Russia did in February 2014 and afterwards in Ukraine – along with other hostile cyber activities, election interference, intrigue in the Baltic states and generally unfriendly language – made normal diplomatic interaction more difficult and bolstered the 'cold war' construct. There were even doubts about whether the United States and Russia would agree to extend the New Strategic Arms Reduction Treaty (START), though in fact at the beginning of the Biden administration it was extended with little fuss or bother. Much else in US–Russian relations was at best put on hold, as Russia gained military capabilities, became more assertive and clamoured to be treated as an equal.[22] Thus, aggressive Russian behaviour and the West's imposition of economic sanctions led to the severing of formal relations between Russia and NATO, which had been channelled through the NATO–Russia Council.[23]

A critical risk is that the invocation of a cold war premised on a high degree of hostility would structurally dim expectations, which would make engagement even on matters where cooperation is of mutual interest much harder. It would become difficult, if not impossible, to identify such issues. As a cold war, once declared, played out, bureaucratic and political structures and processes would work merely to perpetuate confrontation.[24]

Direct Russian interference in the 2016 US election has only made matters worse. The extent of that interference continues to be disputed, along with whether it could have been so significant as to guarantee Donald Trump's victory. The latter seems unlikely, given the social, economic and political character of the states whose electoral votes apparently made the difference in the Electoral College, the partisan divisions in American society, the political deficits of the Democratic candidate and the conduct of her election campaign. Although Hillary Clinton accepted the results of the election, the suspicions of her Democratic supporters and much of the mainstream media that Russia had made the difference persisted.

These suspicions had a major negative impact on US–Russia relations that has continued. In particular, it became hard to consider issues such as the Ukraine crisis and European geopolitics dispassionately. Trump himself intensified the problem at a press conference with Putin at their July 2018 summit in Helsinki.[25] Trump seemed to many observers to side with Putin and against US intelligence agencies on the issue of Russian interference in the 2016 election. The two leaders also mentioned areas of potential constructive dialogue, such as strategic stability, non-proliferation, the extension of New START, the Intermediate-Range Nuclear Forces Treaty, counter-terrorism, cyber security, regional crises, terrorism and transnational crime, environmental risks, Korea, Iran and the nuclear deal, Ukraine and Syria. But pre-existing perceptions of Russian interference, amplified by Trump's obtuseness, blinded much of the US audience to diplomatic opportunities.

In general, tension between a realist and a values-driven approach is endemic to American society and politics in dealing with other countries. Russian interference in US elections made realism a tougher sell and punishment an easier one, as many Democrats perceived Putin as complicit in Trump's victory. Russia also clearly tries to destabilise democracies in Europe. In addition, US congressional and public concerns about Putin's increasing centralisation of power and contempt for civil liberties and human rights have also complicated any American effort to seek more conciliatory means of easing tensions with Russia.

Putin's game and the West's response

Against this background, a key question is why Putin has chosen this time to intensify his hostility and pressure on Ukraine, NATO and the West in general. The most plausible explanation is that he has bided his time until Russia has recovered from its debilitated post-Soviet condition – though it remains a second-tier economic nation – and reached the point where he believes that Russia can demand that its role as a great power be acknowledged and has developed sufficient power to assert a sphere of influence in its near abroad.

In theory, the crisis might have been averted had the United States continued the policy begun under George H.W. Bush and Bill Clinton of treating Russia as a potential partner rather than a defeated nation, although it may be that Russia inevitably would have wanted to assert power no matter what the West had done; we can never know. Now, however, the military terms of power have shifted. The most significant development has been the well-advertised Russian deployment of well over 100,000 troops on the Ukrainian frontier, accompanied by Putin's verbal threats and challenges. Quite appropriately, the West has taken them seriously. But it is open to question whether Putin intends to undertake further direct military aggression in Ukraine or elsewhere in Europe. As he has threatened, he has other instruments at his command to press what he sees to be Russia's interests, without the overt act of invasion. These include cyber capabilities, energy leverage and democracy destabilisation.

Holding Russia at bay is not a matter of deterrence in the classical sense, involving threatened military or economic punishment.[26] Putin must know that any further military aggression would come up against not only a unified NATO military front but also a unified NATO political front, which has in fact coalesced. He would also have to recognise that Russia's place in the world would be compromised for a long time to come were he to engage in further open military aggression in Ukraine. In effect, he would find himself in a new cold war that would benefit Russia even less than it did the Soviet Union. He must also know that China provides no serious alternative other than that of a junior partnership, which Beijing would exploit.

The treaties are an invitation to talk

Russia has now floated two draft treaties, one for US–Russia relations and one for NATO–Russia relations.[27] These are only opening bids, and the US and its NATO partners were right to reject them. But the very fact that the Russians promulgated them is diplomatically and strategically significant. The fact that the treaties have been tabled is an invitation to talk, rather than just to prepare for conflict. Their maximalist nature should be read as a prompt to the West to counter with its own requirements. In this vein, the proposed treaties should serve as indicators of Russia's security concerns and points of reference for more considered negotiations. It is unrealistic to expect that negotiations would produce viable treaties, especially given that a formal treaty would require ratification by the US Senate and the parliaments of other NATO allies. The Russians surely know this. Thus, their demand for enforceable, legal guarantees are for bargaining and propaganda purposes, and do not constitute serious diplomatic proposals.

For his part, President Joe Biden has also signalled a desire to turn confrontation as much as possible into conversation. This effort has included treating Putin personally with measured respect and, more importantly, ruling out using US military force, at least in the near future, to defend

Ukraine against further Russian aggression, which would automatically produce a cold-war confrontation – or worse – and constrain diplomatic flexibility. Biden also understands that neither the American people nor the allies want war if it can be avoided. In part because Biden has foreclosed the use of US military force for now, he and his top advisers have been trying to deter Putin and reassure Europeans of US resolve with vigorous talk about imposing severe sanctions. They are doing so even though the record of sanctions elsewhere casts doubt on whether they would be effective if Putin genuinely believes that invading Ukraine is in Russia's security interests.

A least in the short term, the Biden administration has a more difficult negotiating task than does Russia, because it has to satisfy so many constituencies simultaneously. Domestically, they include Congress, Republican critics and hardliners in abundance who are willing to accept a new cold war.[28] Internationally, they include the United States' 29 NATO allies, each with particular interests, though the group is generally responsive to US leadership and more cohesive than it was during the Trump administration, as concerns that the US might default on Article 5 have eased. The US must also deal with Ukraine, Georgia and other countries with aspirations to join NATO. Thus, the requisite diplomacy involves three main channels: the US and Russia, NATO and the OSCE. Together these include all the players directly relevant to European security, and the United States has the primary responsibility in the West for coordinating them – admittedly, a prodigious political and diplomatic task.

Positive results are unlikely to emerge rapidly, except perhaps in the form of confidence-building measures. These should logically start with the withdrawal of Russian forces from the Ukrainian frontier as a demonstration of Putin's seriousness, in parallel with some comparable reductions of Western military capability in Ukraine. This could usefully include invoking practices from the Helsinki Final Act, as well as reissuing and updating the Treaty on Conventional Armed Forces in Europe.[29] A wide range of additional confidence-building measures is also possible, between both NATO and Russia and the US and Russia. These would be of more practical value than 'binding guarantees' that are in fact unenforceable in terms of reducing tensions and turning diplomacy in productive directions.

Putin is clearly seeking to establish Russia as a key player in European security and to create a Russian sphere of influence in Russia's near abroad. However the crisis plays out, the most important requirement of successful US-led negotiations with Russia is that Moscow demonstrate that it is prepared to be a responsible international actor. From the West's perspective, that means, among other things, that Russia must stop meddling in internal Western politics and society, both episodically in elections and generically in the democratic process, whether directly or through proxies. Russia, for its part, has been demanding guarantees from the West. But the West should also press for guarantees from Russia. In neither case, however, can guarantees be literally binding. What matters is what is done in practice, in terms of transparency, direct observation and defined criteria – tried-and-true tools of arms-control processes developed during the Cold War. Provided both Russia and the West see agreement as preferable to confrontation, these can be taken off the shelf, dusted off and used again to salutary effect.

*   *   *

The United States and its NATO partners face a knotty problem of their own making: the putative right of each European country to join NATO and thereby not only increase its security but also improve its economic opportunities and outlook. No such right exists, given that to join, a country must gain a consensus of current members. For non-member European countries, except perhaps one or two small ones left in the Balkans – and perhaps Finland and Sweden, should they ever wish to apply – that possibility is practically zero. That applies to both Ukraine and Georgia, whose leadership the United States and others have misled.[30] In terms of overall security in Europe and NATO's effective functioning as an alliance, the organisation has already taken in more countries than it requires and can easily manage. This is not to say, of course, that a country is barred from choosing a Western political orientation, which the PfP and parallel EU agencies, along with non-governmental organisations and the private sector, can facilitate.

Nor does it mean that Ukraine or Georgia must be consigned to a Russian sphere of influence. But it does mean that, in practice, they will be geopolitically

neutral as between Russia and NATO save for NATO's and the EU's cooperative arrangements, which are already in place.[31] Given the nature of global
and European economics and democratic aspirations, over time these two
countries' Western orientation will be assured, absent military intervention
from outside. Putin undoubtedly understands this. The fact remains that
Russia's military intervention in Ukraine carries enormous risks for Moscow.

At the same time, Ukraine has responsibilities, which include not just
developing a more functional political system and massively reducing corruption but also structurally devolving limited powers to different parts
of the country.[32] It will never regain Crimea and has no need for it. In the
Donbas region, both ethnicity and language argue for some form of autonomy. Ukrainian leaders should recognise that Ukraine will have a greater
chance of success if it recognises divergent interests within the country as
opposed to denying that they exist or just blaming them on Russia.

War cannot be ruled out entirely, and would generate its own momentum
and unforeseeable consequences. However, provided the Biden administration can ground its diplomacy on sound strategic calculations, and Putin
understands that he has already reached the limit of Russia's territorial
ambitions in Europe, failed to move Russia much beyond a rentier economy
and would risk a decline in political influence with further military adven-
turism, there are possibilities for a reduction of tensions over Ukraine and
potentially more broadly. It's Putin's choice whether to gain recognition of
Russia's legitimate interests or to pursue a sphere of interest or even reconstruction of the Soviet Union. If the former, Russia can be accommodated;
if the latter, the US and its European allies and partners will oppose Russia
with whatever means and to the degree necessary.

In the longer term, there is still George H.W. Bush's goal of a 'Europe
whole and free' and at peace in the wake of the twentieth century's two hot
wars and one cold one. If Putin will set Russia on a course to be a good-
faith participant in European security and politics rather than a spoiler, an
arrangement that meets everyone's legitimate security needs may in time be
possible. He has made all aware that Russia has risen from the ashes of the
Soviet Union. Now he must show that he will play a constructive role and
not a destructive one that would eventually profit Russia little or nothing.

As is often the case with statecraft, in adjusting power relations between countries with differing interests, the key is to arrive at a viable process for shaping diplomacy. For Russia and the West, it cannot be limited to the three sets of negotiations beginning January 2022 but needs to carry on indefinitely, as the evolving realities of power and politics require. That process has now begun.

Notes

1   Of course, Russian ambitions are not limited to Europe but extend far wider. This can be seen in its involvements in the Middle East, the Transcaucasus, the Arctic and Central Asia, most recently Kazakhstan, as well as in its cyber activities and efforts to destabilise Western democracies. This article focuses on the Ukraine crisis due to its immediate practical and symbolic importance.

2   See 'How Nikita Khrushchev Gave Crimea to Ukraine', Russian Culture, 7 March 2014, https://allrus.me/nikita-khrushchev-gave-crimea-ukraine/#:~:text=How%20Nikita%20Khrushchev%20gave%20Crimea%20to%20Ukraine.%20February,was%2C%20in%20fact%2C%20presented%20to%20Ukraine%20by%20Khrushchev.

3   'Treaty on the Final Settlement with Respect to Germany, September 12, 1990', available at US Diplomatic Mission to Germany, https://usa.usembassy.de/etexts/2plusfour8994e.htm.

4   See, for instance, M.E. Sarotte, *Not One Inch: America, Russia, and the Making of Post-Cold War Stalemate* (New Haven, CT: Yale University Press, 2021).

5   The key administrative arrangement, devised by General George Joulwan, who was both the NATO and the US commander in Europe, was to have Russian troops report to him only in his latter capacity, thus allowing Russia to claim that it was not under NATO command but rather under the command of the 'equal' power.

6   Similarly, providing US security guarantees to reinforce confidence within Western European countries had been a major factor in the formulation of the 1949 North Atlantic Treaty and the creation of NATO following the Marshall Plan.

7   NATO, 'Declaration of the Heads of State and Government Participating in the Meeting of the North Atlantic Council Held at NATO Headquarters, Brussels, on 10–11 January 1994', https://www.nato.int/docu/pr/1994/p94-003.htm.

8   See NATO, 'Founding Act on Mutual Relations, Cooperation and Security between NATO and the Russian Federation', 27 May 1997, https://www.nato.int/cps/en/natohq/official_texts_25468.htm. The Founding Act was essentially drafted in Washington and agreed by the other allies prior to negotiations with Moscow.

9   'Memorandum on Security Assurances in Connection with

Ukraine's Accession to the Treaty on the Non-Proliferation of Nuclear Weapons', Budapest, 5 December 1994, available at PIR Center, http://www.pircenter.org/media/content/files/12/13943175580.pdf.

10   See NATO, 'Charter on a Distinctive Partnership between the North Atlantic Treaty Organization and Ukraine', 9 July 1997, https://www.nato.int/cps/en/natohq/official_texts_25457.htm. The author conducted the final negotiation of this charter, on behalf of both the United States and NATO, with the Ukrainian representative to PfP/EAPC, Ambassador Boris Tarasyuk.

11   President of Russia, 'Speech and the Following Discussion at the Munich Conference on Security Policy', 10 February 2007, http://en.kremlin.ru/events/president/transcripts/24034. On rereading Putin's speech and remarks, I wonder how many other major leaders would be as capable of that level of strategic analysis – of course largely but not entirely self-serving – as Putin was on this occasion. From the inception of the Munich Security Conference in the mid-1960s until the end of the Cold War, it served as the main opportunity for US officials – almost always the secretary of defense along with a congressional delegation – to lay out US preferences, or 'marching orders', for NATO and other aspects of European security for the following year. Allies paid close attention. Since the end of the Cold War, the conference has become more wide-ranging, extending to issues far beyond Europe. I have participated in about 20 such conferences, and they have almost always been civil. Indeed, Putin also remarked, in counterpoint to his criticisms, that 'in spite of all our disagreements I consider the President of the United States my friend. He is a decent person and I know that today the wolves can blame the United States for everything that is being done on the international arena and internally. But I know that he is a decent person and it is possible to talk and reach agreements with him. And when I talked to him he said: "I proceed from the fact that Russia and the USA will never be opponents and enemies again." I agree with him. But I repeat once again that there are symmetries and asymmetries here, there is nothing personal. It is simply a calculation.'

12· See, for instance, Thom Shanker and Mark Landler, 'Putin Says U.S. Is Undermining Global Stability', New York Times, 11 February 2007, https://www.nytimes.com/2007/02/11/world/europe/11munich.html; and Rob Watson, 'Putin's Speech: Back to Cold War?', BBC News, 10 February 2007, http://news.bbc.co.uk/1/hi/world/europe/6350847.stm.

13   NATO, 'Bucharest Summit Declaration Issued by the Heads of State and Government Participating in the Meeting of the North Atlantic Council in Bucharest on 3 April 2008', https://www.nato.int/cps/en/natolive/official_texts_8443.htm.

14   Most recently, NATO Secretary General Jens Stoltenberg said: 'We stand by the decisions we have made, also on Ukraine and membership. I was present at the NATO Summit in Bucharest where we first made the

decision. And we support Ukraine on this path towards membership, Euro-Atlantic integration, by supporting reforms, fighting corruption and modernizing the security and defence institutions of Ukraine. To become a member of NATO, you have to meet NATO standards, and there has to be a decision by 30 Allies. We need consensus in the Alliance to enlarge and to invite a new country to join our Alliance. The political message is that Russia does have no right whatsoever to interfere in that process. Ukraine is a sovereign, independent nation. And every sovereign, independent nation has the right to choose its own path, including what kind of security arrangements it wants to be part of. So it is up to Ukraine and 30 Allies to decide when Ukraine is ready to join the Alliance. [Russia] has no veto, no right to interfere in that process.' NATO, 'Press Conference by NATO Secretary General Jens Stoltenberg at the Meeting of NATO Ministers of Foreign Affairs, Riga', 20 November 2021, https://www.nato.int/cps/en/natohq/opinions_189146.htm. But Stoltenberg was careful to distinguish between countries that belong to NATO and those that don't: 'I think it is important to distinguish between NATO Allies and partner Ukraine. NATO Allies, there we provide [Article 5] guarantees, collective defence guarantees, and we will defend and protect all Allies. Ukraine is a partner, a highly valued partner. We provide support, political, practical support. Allies provide training, capacity building, equipment and I am absolutely certain that Allies will recommit and reconfirm their strong support to Ukraine also during the meeting today. But as I said there's a difference between a partner Ukraine and an Ally like for instance Latvia.' NATO, 'Doorstep Statement by NATO Secretary General Jens Stoltenberg at the Meeting of NATO Ministers of Foreign Affairs, Riga', 30 November 2021, https://www.nato.int/cps/en/natohq/opinions_188767.htm.

15 See, for example, NATO, 'Doorstep Statement by NATO Secretary General Jens Stoltenberg'.

16 See 'Profile: Ukraine's Ousted President Viktor Yanukovych', BBC News, 28 February 2014, https://www.bbc.com/news/world-europe-25182830. The Russian role in Yanukovych's decisions regarding the agreement with the EU is unclear, but the fact of his fleeing to Russia is material to the continuing crisis. There is also the argument – which I made in the late 1990s – that, viewed objectively from Putin's perspective of seeking to dominate Russia's near abroad and intensify his political control in Russia, he should be more concerned with the European Union than with NATO enlargement due to the appeal to the Russian population of greater EU prosperity. The salient historical analogue is Mikhail Gorbachev's experiment with glasnost and perestroika in the 1980s.

17 A recording of the intercepted phone call was published on the internet, presumably by Russia, on 4 February. For a BBC annotation of the phone-call transcript, see Jonathan Marcus, 'Ukraine Crisis: Transcript of Leaked Nuland–Pyatt Call', BBC News, 7

February 2014, https://www.bbc.com/ news/world-europe-26079957?piano-modal. Reaction in the West to the leaked phone call focused on an epithet used by Nuland to describe the EU. Notably, she cited Biden, then vice president, who had major responsibilities for Ukraine in the Obama administration, as the person who would give final approval – an 'attaboy'. 'So Biden's willing', she told Pyatt.

18 See, for example, NATO, 'Wales Summit Declaration Issued by the Heads of State and Government Participating in the Meeting of the North Atlantic Council in Wales', 5 September 2014, https://www. nato.int/cps/en/natohq/official_ texts_112964.htm.

19 Ukraine's and Georgia's circum-stances are different. Georgia's geographical location is far less strate-gically significant than Ukraine's.

20 Even with allies there can be difficul-ties. The United States has frequently been at odds with France on foreign-policy issues, as when Charles de Gaulle withdrew France from NATO's integrated military command struc-ture in 1966 and France opposed the US-led 2003 invasion of Iraq.

21 One definition of a cold war is a situ-ation in which it is not possible to discriminate between issues on which agreement is possible and impossible, with confrontation becoming the rule. That is clearly not the case now – at least not yet – with respect to US and NATO relations with Russia.

22 One notable exception, excluded from the general US government policy of limiting agreements and cooperation with Russia, has been the Arctic Council, where common interests between the two countries, along with the other members of the council, allowed considerable cooperation, even though some US military commentators began warning of confrontation in that region. I was a member of the State Department's International Security Advisory Board, which in September 2016 adopted a report on the Arctic endors-ing continued cooperation, though with a weather eye out for possible changes in Russian behaviour. The US Coast Guard, among other agen-cies, supported this approach. See US Department of State, 'International Security Advisory Board: Report on Arctic Policy', 21 September 2016, https://2009-2017.state.gov/t/avc/ isab/262342.htm.

23 It has long been understood that the most valuable aspect of US–Soviet strategic-arms-control talks during the Cold War was to promote positive change, over time, in political relations. Similarly, the concept of 'parity' in nuclear systems had mainly political, as opposed to operational, significance.

24 The most important military require-ment for ending the Cold War, mutual assured destruction, was achieved by the mid-1960s and effectively ratified by the 1972 ABM Treaty, but it still took until 1989 for the Cold War to come to an end.

25 See 'Transcript: Trump and Putin's Joint Press Conference', NPR, 16 July 2018, https://www. npr.org/2018/07/16/629462401/ transcript-president-trump-and-russian-president-putins-joint-press-conference.

26 Economic sanctions, to be effective, must be agreed by virtually all countries that provide goods and services to the affected country, impervious to any internal offsetting measures or seen by the target country's leadership and populace as deleterious to national security. Sanctions probably played a role in the end of apartheid in South Africa and in Iran's seriously negotiating the Joint Comprehensive Plan of Action (JCPOA), but there are few other obvious examples. Indeed, US maximum economic pressure on Iran following the United States' 2018 withdrawal from the JCPOA has had little visible effect on Iran's negotiating posture.

27 See Ministry of Foreign Affairs of the Russian Federation, 'Treaty Between the United States of America and the Russian Federation on Security Guarantees', 17 December 2021, https://mid.ru/ru/foreign_policy/rso/nato/1790818/?lang=en; and Ministry of Foreign Affairs of the Russian Federation, 'Agreement on Measures to Ensure the Security of the Russian Federation and Member States of the North Atlantic Treaty Organization', 17 December 2021, https://mid.ru/ru/foreign_policy/rso/nato/1790803/?lang=en.

28 The old saw that 'politics should stop at the water's edge' may never have been true in US foreign policy; it is certainly not true today. One of the remarkable achievements in the last half-century or so is that NATO has always been a bipartisan matter, even when there has been political nibbling at the edges, beginning with the original deal cut between Harry Truman and Arthur Vandenberg, the chairman of the Senate Committee on Foreign Relations, at NATO's founding.

29 The Intermediate-Range Nuclear Forces Treaty should also be resuscitated. The United States understandably wants China to be involved, but Washington should not wait until that becomes possible to renew the bilateral commitment with Russia if it is amenable. It may well be receptive, given that a renewed agreement would tend to bolster Russia's status as a great power.

30 The European Communities/European Union acted similarly towards Turkey, making pledges of membership that were never to be honoured. In response, Turkey has developed a non-European orientation that has had negative consequences for the West.

31 On optimising these, see Nicolò Fasola and Alyssa J. Wood, 'Reforming Ukraine's Security Sector', *Survival*, vol. 63, no. 2, April–May 2021, pp. 41–54.

32 See Valentyna Romanova and Andreas Umland, 'Decentralising Ukraine: Geopolitical Implications', *Survival*, vol. 61, no. 5, October–November 2019, pp. 99–112.

Hope Deferred: Russia from 1991 to 2021

Rodric Braithwaite

Halfway through our traditional Christmas dinner on 25 December 1991, my wife Jill and I stepped onto the balcony of the British Embassy to look across the river at the Kremlin as the Soviet flag fluttered down for the very last time and the Russian flag rose in its place. Mikhail Gorbachev had handed over power to the Russian president Boris Yeltsin formally and peacefully. Nothing like it had ever happened before in Russian history. Then the United Kingdom's ambassador to Moscow, I went down to the office to cable London a report, titled 'Gorbachev Goes: The End of an Era', whose draft I had long been carrying in my head. It concluded that, as winter closed in, and public order became more fragile, Yeltsin would be tempted to make Gorbachev the scapegoat for the difficulties that were piling up around him. 'We shall see', I said, 'how Yeltsin's liberal principles weather the strain.'[1] Alas, by the time Christmas came round 30 years later, those principles had been eroded almost to nothing. The current Ukraine crisis is one of many consequences.

Experts argue about whether the Cold War ended in 1989 with the fall of the Berlin Wall and the collapse of the Soviet empire in Eastern Europe, or with the disintegration of the Soviet Union itself at the end of 1991. Either way, by Christmas 1991 the whole world could heave a sigh of relief. The nuclear confrontation was over. Gorbachev called it a victory for the whole

Rodric Braithwaite was the British ambassador in Moscow from 1988–92 and chairman of the Joint Intelligence Committee from 1992–93.

Survival | vol. 64 no. 1 | February–March 2022 | pp. 29–44   https://doi.org/10.1080/00396338.2022.2032954

of humanity. But for the West the immediate future looked very different than it did to Russia.

The Americans and their allies failed to avoid triumphalism. George H.W. Bush said in his State of the Union message in January 1992: 'By the grace of God, America won the cold war … A world once divided into two armed camps now recognizes one sole and preeminent power, the United States of America. And they regard this with no dread. For the world trusts us with power, and the world is right.'[2] It was an injudicious statement for a man known for his sober caution. The belief that it was the world's sole superpower led America into one diplomatic misjudgement after another over the next three decades. By Christmas 2021, there was even doubt about America's most fundamental strength: the stability of its democratic system, which had been a beacon for so many for so long.

In winter 1991, Russians shared the world's relief at the end of the nuclear confrontation. Many still hoped that Yeltsin would lead them towards the prosperous democracy that Gorbachev had promised but failed to deliver. But the immediate reality was very grim. The economy was spiralling out of control. The brilliant young economist Yegor Gaidar, appointed by Yeltsin to carry through radical economic reform, feared that the country could face actual famine. Even basic commodities failed to reach the shops. Ordinary people lost their jobs, their pensions and their social benefits. Factory workers were paid, if at all, in kind not cash. The health service collapsed. Old ladies sold their last possessions on the streets of Moscow in order to survive. Officers were sacked, tanks rusted at their bases, the strategic nuclear forces were unable to maintain their equipment.

Meanwhile, the Americans acted as if Russia's foreign and domestic policy was theirs to shape. Yeltsin's first foreign minister, Andrei Kozyrev, later vilified by his countrymen for conceding too much to the West, protested to president Bill Clinton's adviser Strobe Talbott that 'it's bad enough having you people tell us what you're going to do whether we like it or not. Don't add insult to injury by also telling us that it's in our interests to obey your orders.' Talbott commented that 'Russia is either coming our way, or it's not, in which case it's going to founder, as the USSR did'.[3]

All this seeped into the Russian public consciousness and aroused an overwhelming sense of humiliation and resentment. It coloured Russian attitudes and the making of Russian policy for decades, and was persistently underestimated by Western policymakers and commentators.

Was the Soviet collapse inevitable?

It is not possible to predict the future in detail. But the idea that the collapse was unforeseeable and unforeseen is wrong. The trend was visible for decades, even if individual events often caught even well-informed observers by surprise.

The process can be dated from the death of Josef Stalin in March 1953. By the application of the most brutal methods, and the death of millions of people, Stalin assembled a heavy industry that successfully produced the weapons needed to beat the Germans in war. But without the dictator, his dysfunctional system and the accompanying terror could not work. The regime's own heavily doctored statistics showed that the economy was growing ever more slowly. Some of the regime's own economists preferred the figures put out by the CIA, but these too failed to give an accurate picture.

For most of its existence the Soviet Union was largely closed to foreign observation. But the regime could not prevent diplomats, journalists, students and other foreigners living in Moscow from seeing for themselves how very poor the country was: the villages on the outskirts of the capital still had no running water, the sidewalks were still paved in wood. Some of those advising Western governments on the Soviet Union, many with Russian backgrounds, knew this well enough. But others had no direct knowledge of the country and did not speak the language. Many based their analysis on a literal reading of the writings of Karl Marx, Vladimir Lenin and Stalin, and the public pronouncements of Soviet politicians. In the decades that followed they nurtured a picture of Soviet strength and menace that was not entirely false but was often misleading.

Western governments and their peoples were mesmerised by the Soviet Union's prowess in space, its growing military power, its successes in the developing world. They overestimated Soviet strength and determination, and feared – without solid evidence – that the Russians might attack them unprovoked. Few appreciated that the Russians were at least as afraid of us as we were of them. Western misjudgements were exacerbated by an almost complete lack of reliable intelligence about the hopes, fears and intentions of the Soviet leaders.

The exaggerations were not entirely innocent. In America they helped generate public support for an immensely expensive policy of overmatching the Russians in every sphere – military, political and economic. When it was all over, Caspar Weinberger, who had served as US secretary of defense during the Reagan administration, justified the multiplication of weapons thus: 'You can't afford to be wrong. If we won by too much, if it was overkill, so be it.'[4] The distortions and misunderstandings were fully matched on the Russian side.

At the height of the Cuban Missile Crisis, John F. Kennedy tried to see events through Nikita Khrushchev's eyes. But he admitted to a confidant: 'It isn't wise politically to understand Khrushchev's problem in quite this way.'[5] Raymond Garthoff, then a State Department official, believed that 'the inability to empathize with the other side and visualize its interests in other than adversarial terms' was one reason American analysts often got the Soviet Union wrong. Garthoff warned that an American official who departed from 'the implicit stereotypical cold war consensus' risked damage to his career and influence.[6] Garthoff was of course right. Empathy is too often confused with sympathy even today. You risk being called a *Putinversteher* if you try too hard to understand what the Russian president is up to.[7]

Tinkering with a failing system

Khrushchev replaced Stalin after a vicious struggle with his colleagues. He knew very well what a mess the country was in, and in the early 1960s he tried to put it right. He permitted a genuine public debate between those who thought that only market mechanisms could save the economy and those who insisted that computers could make state planning work. These 'men of the Sixties' provided much of the intellectual underpinning for Gorbachev's subsequent reforms. But neither then nor later could they agree on practical conclusions. Khrushchev shied away from fundamental changes that would have transformed the system. The measures that he introduced were half-baked and wholly inadequate.

The nuclear confrontation

Stalin feared that the Americans would use their nuclear monopoly after 1945 to blackmail him. He was determined to match them. His nuclear project was ruinously expensive. His people, who had hoped for relief after the war, were plunged back into near famine. But the programme was successful. He had his bomb by 1949, a mere four years after the Americans got theirs. The success was due primarily to the excellence of Soviet scientists and engineers rather than the formidable skills of Soviet spies.

The nuclear confrontation that followed defined the Cold War and set the tone of its diplomacy. The American side developed elaborate and implausible theories about 'graduated escalation', 'extended deterrence', and 'limited nuclear war' in Europe and elsewhere to deter or repel a local Soviet attack. The Russians were sceptical: even some of their generals believed that once the first rocket was launched things could spiral fatally out of control. Similar doubts existed in London and Washington too. All nevertheless continued to develop the most elaborate, expensive and sometimes pointless weapons of which they were capable.

The Russians demonstrated their scientific and engineering prowess when they launched the world's first artificial satellite, *Sputnik*, in 1957. They put the first man into space, Yuri Gagarin, in 1961. These were spectacular achievements, of which Russians remain justly proud. But the Americans soon forged ahead. By the early 1960s they had more than 1,500 nuclear bombers and a ring of bases surrounding the Soviet Union from which they could hit Moscow. The Russians only had 150 long-range bombers, a few clumsy long-range missiles and nothing that could reliably hit Washington.

To right the balance, Khrushchev hit on a dangerously ingenious scheme. In summer 1962, he agreed with the Cuban leader, Fidel Castro, to deploy in Cuba nuclear missiles that could threaten much of America and deter the Americans from invading the Caribbean island. In October, US intelligence detected the arrival of the missiles, but not the presence of tens of thousands of Soviet troops armed with battlefield nuclear weapons. American generals and admirals pressed Kennedy to launch a pre-emptive strike on Cuba. The crisis could have ended in a nuclear exchange that would have devastated the Soviet Union and cost America several cities. The prospect appalled Kennedy as much as Khrushchev. A fraught negotiation led to a peaceful outcome.

But Khrushchev's credibility in Moscow was fatally undermined. His colleagues were increasingly unimpressed with his futile attempts at reform. In October 1964, the Communist Party, the army and the KGB removed him from power.

Stagnation

Under Khrushchev's successor, Leonid Brezhnev, an exhausting effort enabled the Soviet Union to match the United States in space and at cutting-edge military technology. But the weaknesses ran deep. In 1976, Soviet per capita consumption was said to be one-third that of the United States – probably an exaggerated figure.[8] In 1989, the Soviet health minister said that 24% of Soviet hospitals had no drains and 15% had no running water, not least because the Soviet Union spent less on healthcare than any other developed country.[9] Russians scornfully called Brezhnev's rule the 'period of stagnation'. There was a modest improvement in living standards, but consumer goods, even foodstuffs, remained in short and erratic supply. To catch them, housewives had to queue for hours.

Brave people had occasionally spoken out even under Stalin. Most came to a bad end. Under his successors people spoke more freely. But it still required courage, and you could easily find yourself packed off to a labour camp. Andrei Sakharov, the physicist who had helped to devise the Soviet hydrogen bomb, told Brezhnev in 1970 that the Soviet Union would become a second-rate provincial power unless its bureaucratic style were replaced by measures of democratisation. The powers banished him to the provinces and cut his contact with the outside world.

Unease was not confined to such brave dissidents. Government and party officials, military officers, industrial managers, scientists, economists, even the head of the State Planning Committee, were increasingly convinced that things were going badly wrong. In 1983, Marshal Nikolai Ogarkov, the Soviet chief of staff, lamented to Leslie Gelb, then a *New York Times* journalist and earlier a senior US Defense and State Department official, 'We will never be able to catch up with you in modern arms until we have an economic revolution. And the question is whether we have an economic revolution without a political revolution.'[10] Though dissidents and an increasingly angry intelligentsia played an important role, insiders were the main driving force for change that was to come.

The arrival of Gorbachev

The men in the Politburo were elderly, conservative and unimaginative. But they were not stupid, and they could not ignore the crisis. Gorbachev came from a poor peasant family in Southern Russia: the Moscow intelligentsia sneered at his provincial accent. Brilliant at school, he got a scholarship and studied law at Moscow University. He then worked back home until the Communist Party brought him back to the centre and into the Politburo. In March 1985, they chose Gorbachev – young, energetic, effective, apparently orthodox – to put things right. The man they hoped would save the Soviet Union accelerated its collapse.

He believed that bureaucratic central planning was strangling the economy, and that the crippling burden of defence spending could only be reduced by bringing the Cold War under control. The country was stagnating because the initiative of ordinary people had been stifled. They needed to be brought into the business of running it.

Russians now forget how popular Gorbachev was at first. They flocked to listen as he spoke with a lively frankness unmatched by his predecessors. They believed he might give them what they called a 'normal country': open to the world, prosperous, at peace with its neighbours, where their rulers at last listened to their views and acted accordingly. Gorbachev hoped to save the Soviet Union from itself. His first tentative steps were intended to preserve the 'socialist' essence of the system. Looking for his support, he brought Yeltsin, the first party secretary of the Sverdlovsk region, likewise the son of a peasant, into the Politburo. Immensely ambitious and a brilliant instinctive politician, Yeltsin preferred to make himself popular by publicly attacking Gorbachev's policies as fraudulently inadequate. In Stalin's day he would not have escaped with his life. In Khrushchev's he would have been exiled. Gorbachev threw him out of the Politburo but allowed him to continue in politics. It was a measure of how far things had already changed.

In April 1986 the nuclear reactor at Chernobyl in Ukraine exploded after a mismanaged test. The government immediately undertook remedial measures. The people on the ground acted heroically to limit the damage. But the fallout and the news leaked to the West. Gorbachev mismanaged the publicity. Some Russians trace their final disillusion with the Soviet system to this catastrophe.[11]

A kind of democracy comes to the Soviet Union

As his initial measures stumbled and the economy continued to decline, Gorbachev set out to revolutionise Soviet politics. He encouraged glasnost, 'openness', about the conduct of public business. The press attacked official abuse relentlessly. Sakharov, whom Gorbachev allowed to return to Moscow, demanded that the Communist Party be stripped of its constitutional monopoly of power. He and others set up Memorial, an organisation to celebrate the memories of the individuals – men, women, even children – who has disappeared into unmarked graves during Stalin's Great Terror. History became a national obsession. People joked that the Soviet Union was a country with an unpredictable past. One liberal author confided that the victory in the war against Adolf Hitler was the only thing that Russians could still be proud of.

In summer 1988, Gorbachev allowed the Russian Orthodox Church to celebrate the millennium of Russian Christianity. Churches and monasteries were rebuilt from the ruins into which the communists had allowed them to decay. Young people flocked to become priests and nuns. The leaders of the church grew closer to the politicians, the sources of prosperity and influence.

Next Gorbachev announced new elections. Previous Soviet elections had been empty rituals in which citizens voted in droves for the only available candidate. Now they would be able to choose freely among candidates. March 1989 saw the first real vote in Russia since 1917, complete with the trappings of democracy: vicious intrigue over the selection of candidates, noisy meetings on the streets, vitriol from an unshackled press. The vote swept senior communists from seats they had held for years as of right. Yeltsin was elected to the new 'Congress of People's Deputies' by four-fifths of Moscow's voters. A firestorm of criticism directed at the party, the government and the KGB broke out when this new congress opened in May. It was all shown on television. Glued to their TV sets, people abandoned their everyday work.

Our Russian friends feared it could end in bloodshed and civil war; they knew what had happened at Tiananmen Square. But in March 1991, under pressure from the streets, the congress abolished the party's constitutional monopoly of power. Political pluralism was no longer illegal. A kind of fragile democracy had arrived.

Ending the Cold War

Gorbachev passionately believed that the nuclear confrontation was absurdly dangerous. He was determined to dismantle it. He was fortunate in his interlocutor. Ronald Reagan called the Soviet Union an 'evil empire', expanded his predecessor Jimmy Carter's rearmament programme and allowed the US military to mount provocative probes against the Soviet frontier. But he too was profoundly concerned about the confrontation. He reached out to Gorbachev. When the two met in Reykjavik in 1986, they made an unsuccessful attempt to abolish nuclear weapons altogether. Cold warriors in Washington and London were appalled. When Gorbachev announced in December 1988 that he was withdrawing significant forces from Eastern Europe, advisers to the incoming president, George H.W. Bush, called it another communist trick.[12]

But the international scene was now changing beyond recognition. Between 1954 and 1968, the Russians had put down dissent in East Germany, Hungary and Czechoslovakia. They got the Poles to do it for them in Poland in 1980. The Eastern Europeans were unconvinced when Gorbachev told them in June 1988 that they could find their own way. But once the Soviet elections demonstrated how much Russia itself was changing, the Poles immediately held their own elections and the Polish communists were thrashed. In November 1989, the Berlin Wall came down. Other Eastern Europeans followed the Poles to freedom. The demand for independence, or at least autonomy, was growing inside the Soviet Union itself, in the Baltic states and the Caucasus. Ukraine was ominously quiet. If it too began to move, the consequences could be dramatic indeed. We were, I thought, even before the wall came down, witnessing the break-up of the last great European empire.[13]

German reunification had now become an urgent possibility. Moscow and Washington realised that the only alternative to chaos was negotiation. The United States and its allies were determined that Germany should be reunited inside NATO. Gorbachev attempted to resist from a very weak negotiating position. Western negotiators gave him ambiguous assurances that NATO did not intend to expand any further.[14] He did not request, nor was he offered, anything in writing.

Over time, Western intentions changed. The Baltics and Russia's former Eastern European satellites eventually joined the Alliance. Many Russians believed they had been double-crossed. They were also shocked by NATO's bombing of Serbia in 1999, fearing that it was a foretaste of what Russia itself could expect. They came to believe that Western talk of democracy was a smokescreen hiding a determination to destroy Russia.

The coup of August 1991

By 1991, Russia's middle-class liberals had concluded that Yeltsin was the more authentic democrat and switched their support to him. Ordinary people were tired of Gorbachev's failure to improve their lives. His closest allies deserted him. He recruited replacements from among the reactionaries. When Soviet special-operations forces killed 13 people in Vilnius in January 1991, he could not escape responsibility. On 29 March, the government deployed troops in Moscow to counter a massive demonstration in support of Yeltsin. Bloodshed seemed quite possible. But Gorbachev blinked, and the troops were withdrawn. As his authority waned, it seemed only a question of time before he was ousted by the hard men or, through some unforeseeable chain of events, by Yeltsin. That night I roughed out the first draft of the telegram reporting his departure.

Rumours of a coup had abounded for years. But almost nobody – not Western leaders nor their intelligence agencies, nor I, nor Gorbachev himself – foresaw the actual event. On 18 August, conspirators from the party, the army and the KGB – the same combination that defenestrated Khrushchev – arrested Gorbachev in his Crimean holiday home, moved tanks into Moscow and formed an emergency administration. But they bungled their plans to arrest Yeltsin. He was besieged and defiant inside his office, the 'Russian White House'. Thousands of people flocked to support him. That evening the plotters tried to explain themselves on TV. Some were drunk. Three young men were killed the following night in a scuffle with soldiers. But the conspirators lacked the resolve to settle matters by storming the White House. They withdrew the tanks. Yeltsin had them arrested and banned the Communist Party.

Gorbachev returned to Moscow, but Yeltsin had won the game. That autumn he whittled away at Gorbachev's authority, using the collapsing economy and the prospect of Ukrainian independence as levers. On 8 December 1991, he secretly met his colleagues from Ukraine and Belarus to declare that the Soviet Union had ceased to exist. It was a breathless piece of opportunism for a man who, like most Russians, believed that Ukraine was an integral part of his country. For the Soviet Union, it was the death blow.

Back to the past?

There was much sympathy for ordinary Russians in the West. But Western governments' efforts to help Russia repair its economy, build a healthy politics and take part in the management of international affairs as a cooperative equal were half-hearted. Western businesses ruthlessly exploited opportunities for profit. Overpaid Western consultants peddled solutions that ignored Russian reality. Russia slid into economic misery, political dysfunction, deeply rooted corruption and a jungle capitalism in which rivals murdered one another for profit. As Yeltsin declined into alcoholism and ill health, his regime became increasingly incoherent. He groomed Vladimir Putin, a former KGB officer, as his successor.

Putin did not grow up under Stalin. Like Gorbachev and Yeltsin, he was a product of the Soviet system, but his emotional attachment to it was shallow, and he has denounced its excesses. He started to emerge from the obscurity of a mediocre career in the KGB while working for the liberal mayor of Leningrad after the 1991 coup. Most foreigners underestimated him, if they noticed him at all. Yeltsin's talent scouts recruited him to work backstage in the Kremlin. He impressed Yeltsin with his administrative competence, his intelligence, his political cunning, his ruthless determination and his loyalty. When he succeeded Yeltsin in January 2000, a new era of Russian politics began.

It was never likely that one man or one generation could move Russia from age-old autocracy and a stultified economy to political and economic liberalism. When I left Moscow in May 1992, my view was that democracy could take firm hold in Russia. But its culture would have to change radically. That would take three or more generations – a hundred years – and there would be plenty of setbacks on the way.[15]

Putin has turned out to be a very serious setback indeed, as illustrated by his recent decision to mass troops on the Ukrainian border. He is said to have told George W. Bush at a NATO meeting in Bucharest in April 2008: 'You don't understand, George, that Ukraine is not even a state.' Putin subsequently set forth his beliefs in an article in July 2021.[16] His ideas are not new, and many Russians agree with him wholeheartedly. They believe that today's Russia is the direct descendant of the mediaeval state of Kievan Rus, and that Ukraine and its language are merely a subset of a greater Russian story. The history is tangled. But a strong sense of Ukrainian national identity was developing from at least the end of the eighteenth century; many Ukrainians would place the date very much earlier. Outbursts of Ukrainian nationalism were brutally repressed by the tsars and the communists alike. Ironically, it was Stalin who gave Ukraine the skeleton institutions of government and a founding place in the United Nations, which the Ukrainians turned to account after independence in 1991.

The related dispute about whether the Ukrainians have a 'right' to their own country is futile. Of course they do, just as much right as any other country in the hodgepodge we call Europe. How long a country has existed as an independent state is equally irrelevant. Rather few of the states in today's Europe existed before the First World War. When Christopher

Columbus discovered America, Germany, Italy and Russia, even Britain and France, were still fragmented, and the Polish–Lithuanian Union was on the way to becoming the largest state in Europe. But Ukraine's history and geography, like those of many other European countries such as Poland and Ireland, greatly complicate the diplomacy and politics that surrounds it.

Since 1991, Western diplomacy in Eastern Europe has been by turns arrogant and incompetent. The initial enlargement of NATO to include the Baltic states, the Czech Republic, Hungary and Poland was probably unavoidable, both politically and morally: the West could not afford to betray Eastern Europeans with false promises yet again, as they had in 1938, 1956 and 1968. But the Americans and their allies continue to mutter pieties about the Ukrainians' right to choose their own alliances, while simultaneously announcing that they have no intention of sending combat troops to defend Ukraine should it need them. That is an unserious position, and risks setting up the wretched Ukrainians for yet another betrayal.

Putin's military posturing is irresponsible

Putin's military posturing around Ukraine is several degrees more irresponsible. It may be intended to generate enough anxiety among the Americans to force them into a negotiation that would correct Gorbachev's failure to get written assurance about NATO enlargement. But America can hardly accept the ultimatum Putin has issued. The chances of getting his proposed treaty on Ukraine through the US Senate are zero. His experts in the Russian Foreign Ministry know that perfectly well. No doubt, like other leaders, he prefers to rely on his unaided intuition. If so, he is taking a page out of the playbook Khrushchev used when he placed missiles in Cuba. Perhaps both sides can repeat the success of 1962 and negotiate an arrangement whereby each can claim 'victory' without the Ukrainians being betrayed. That would require ingenuity and goodwill, both currently in short supply.

At first Putin was a domestic success. The economy boomed, Russians prospered as never before and many welcomed the skilful way he stood up to foreigners, not least by his decisive use of the military in Georgia. They saw his increasingly brutal methods of government as an acceptable trade-off. That honeymoon has been fading for a decade or more. Putin has been in office so long that his judgement has coarsened. He may believe he can help his faltering domestic position by playing the 'Crimean card' again. But the evidence from the polls seems to be that a majority of Russians dread a Ukrainian quagmire.[17]

On 28 December 2021, the Russian Supreme Court used the law on 'foreign agents', directed against non-governmental organisations critical of Putin or his government, to close the most prestigious of them all, the Memorial, which had persisted in turning up inconvenient facts about Stalin's Terror. Ordinary Russians will doubtless regard the closure of Memorial as the least of their woes. But it is a terrible measure of how sour the heady liberalism of the early Gorbachev days has turned.

*   *   *

Can Russia escape the cycle of bungled reform and brutal repression that has marked so much of its history?

Russia was a very different country from what the Soviet Union had been, its huge size diminished by jet aircraft, modern communications and the internet; its people urban, educated, open to the world, comparatively well informed and prosperous by the standards of the past. But the questions remained. Would the Russians ever put together the 'normal country' for which so many of them have hoped? Where they could choose and sack their political leaders as they saw fit? Where it would no longer be true, as a tsarist secret policeman once said, that the law was for underlings only, not for their bosses?[18]

Japan reinvented itself in the nineteenth century and again after 1945. The Germans, the Italians and the Spaniards experimented with brutal dictatorship and abandoned it. French, German, Spanish and Swedish armies terrorised Europe for centuries, then decided they preferred peace after all. The Europeans gave up their empires and turned instead to liberal democracy. Only the most obstinate historical determinist would insist that Russians are congenitally unable to make similar changes. Nothing is predictable, but one thing is sure. Russia's future will be shaped by the

Russian people themselves, regardless of the hopes, fears and wishful thinking of foreigners.

There's another thing. Despite Putin's success in reinserting Russia onto the world scene, the Soviet Union's role as the second superpower is no longer available. That place has been taken by China, with ten times Russia's population, ten times its national wealth and three times its expenditure on defence. And China makes things that everyone wants to buy. The Soviet Union was never able to do that, and Russia seems unable to do it either. So the temptation to see the rivalry between China and America as a replay of the Cold War needs to be avoided. It is only too easy to draw the wrong lessons from the past.

Notes

1   The telegram was included in a collection of the British embassy's 1991 reports from Moscow published by the British Foreign Office in December 2021. See Foreign, Commonwealth & Development Office, 'The Last Days of the Soviet Union: Reporting from the British Embassy, Moscow', History Note: No. 24, December 2021, https://issuu.com/fcohistorians/docs/last_days_of_the_soviet_union_fcdo_hn_24.

2   George Bush, 'Address Before a Joint Session of Congress on the State of the Union', 28 January 1992, American Presidency Project, University of California at Santa Barbara, https://www.presidency.ucsb.edu/documents/address-before-joint-session-the-congress-the-state-the-union-0.

3   Strobe Talbott, *The Russia Hand: A Memoir of Presidential Diplomacy* (New York: Random House, 2003), pp. 74–6.

4   Quoted in, for example, Anne H. Cahn, *Killing Detente: The Right*

Attacks the CIA (University Park, PA: Pennsylvania State University Press, 1998), pp. 1–2.

5   Quoted in Richard E. Neustadt and Ernest R. May, *Thinking in Time: The Uses of History for Decision Makers* (New York: Free Press, 1986), p. 12.

6   Raymond L. Garthoff, *Assessing the Adversary: Estimates by the Eisenhower Administration of Soviet Intentions and Capabilities* (Washington DC: Brookings Institution, 1991), p. 9.

7   The German term means 'Putin understander', and is often used as a term of abuse.

8   See Joint Economic Committee, US Congress, 'Consumption in the USSR: An International Comparison', 1981, https://www.jec.senate.gov/reports/97th%20Congress/Consumption%20in%20the%20USSR%20-%20An%20International%20Comparison%20(1058).pdf.

9   *Izvestia*, 11 July 1989.

10 Leslie H. Gelb, 'Who Won the

Cold War?', *New York Times*, 20 August 1992, https://www.nytimes.com/1992/08/20/opinion/foreign-affairs-who-won-the-cold-war.html. See also Vladislav M. Zubok, *A Failed Empire: The Soviet Union in the Cold War from Stalin to Gorbachev* (Chapel Hill, NC: University of North Carolina Press, 2007), pp. 277, 307.

11 See Rodric Braithwaite, 'Chernobyl: A "Normal" Accident?', *Survival*, vol. 61, no. 5, October–November 2019, pp. 149–58.

12 See Rodric Braithwaite, *Armageddon and Paranoia: The Nuclear Confrontation* (London: Profile Books, 2017), p. 360 and sources cited therein.

13 Personal diary entry, 10 September 1989.

14 The record is clear, despite doubts cast by some in the West. See Rodric Braithwaite, 'NATO Enlargement: Assurances and Misunderstandings', European Council on Foreign Relations, 7 July 2016, https://ecfr.eu/article/commentary_nato_enlargement_assurances_and_misunderstandings/; and M.E. Sarotte, *Not One Inch: America, Russia, and the Making of Post-Cold War Stalemate* (New Haven, CT: Yale University Press, 2022).

15 I set out this view in my Moscow despatch to the Foreign and Commonwealth Office of 17 May 1992, titled 'The Obsession with Russia'. The text is available in Matthew Parris and Andrew Bryson, *Parting Shots* (London: Penguin, 2011).

16 See President of Russia, 'Article by Vladimir Putin "On the Historical Unity of Russians and Ukrainians"', 12 July 2021, http://en.kremlin.ru/events/president/news/66181.

17 See 'Ukraine and Donbas', Yuri-Levada Analytical Center, 16 April 2021, https://www.levada.ru/en/2021/04/16/ukraine-and-donbas/.

18 See Rodric Braithwaite, *Across the Moscow River: The World Turned Upside Down* (New Haven, CT: Yale University Press, 2002), pp. 22–3 and sources cited therein.

Connecting Intelligence and Policy

Gregory F. Treverton

Linking intelligence and policy is crucial for advancing national strategic interests. An effective effort to improve the connection might prompt three questions. Firstly, what is the most important trend in national security that policymakers are not paying enough attention to? One strong candidate is the extent to which private entities are geopolitical actors in their own right. The Gates Foundation spends more on health in Africa than the World Health Organization. Google is a more important international actor than, say, Spain.

Secondly, what is the single data point that the president of the United States (or other world leader) should see every day to better understand the future of national security? The question itself illustrates a fallacy: there is no single data point which, if monitored daily, would help the president better understand future national security. Indeed, most daily numbers, like global temperatures for climate change, are more noise than signal. Ditto for, say, numbers related to China's technological advance, which on their own say nothing about the future social and political context in China and the world.

Gregory F. Treverton was Chair of the US National Intelligence Council from 2014 to 2017 and Vice-chair from 1993 to 1995. He is now Professor of the Practice at Dornsife College at the University of Southern California, Chair of the Global TechnoPolitics Forum and Executive Advisor to SMA Corporation. This article was drafted for the 2021 Global Order Colloquium at Perry World House, the University of Pennsylvania's global-affairs hub. The workshop was made possible in part by the generous support of Carnegie Corporation of New York.

Survival | vol. 64 no. 1 | February–March 2022 | pp. 45–50   https://doi.org/10.1080/00396338.2022.2032957

Thirdly, what are the odds that a major military confrontation will arise between the United States and China over the next five years? A plausible ballpark estimate would be 80%, but much turns on how 'major military confrontation' is defined. For a genuine shooting war, the odds might drop to about 30%, which is still way too high. At the lower end of 'major', the increased Chinese presence in the disputed areas of the South China Sea coupled with increasing US interest in contesting that presence with freedom-of-navigation operations make likely some repeat of the 2001 Hainan Island incident, in which an American signals-reconnaissance plane collided with a Chinese fighter near the Chinese island. At the highest end of 'major' would be serious Chinese pressure or even a direct attack on Taiwan, which has a 10% chance of occurring over the next five years. Chinese President Xi Jinping appears to be in a hurry, realising that time is not entirely on his side, so a rash move, perhaps partly out of miscalculation, is all too possible.

Probability and confidence

I was first struck by the difficulty of communicating about low-probability/high-consequence eventualities like a Chinese attack on Taiwan when I was writing a case on the possible swine-flu epidemic (that ultimately wasn't) in 1976. Policy officials kept pressing doctors for the likelihood of a major pandemic, but the doctors, professionally cautious to a fault, kept refusing to give one. One even said something like, 'I don't know, somewhere between zero and a hundred'. Worse, his policy interlocutor interpreted that to mean 50-50, which was far higher than any of the doctors privately assessed.

Efforts to be more precise about what language means for probability reach back at least half a century, to 'Words of Estimative Probability', the now-declassified paper written in 1964 by Sherman Kent, long-serving chief of the CIA's Office of National Estimates.[1] Now, many intelligence analyses include a chart connecting language such as 'extremely likely' to a probability range. In my experience chairing the National Intelligence Council (NIC), no policy official ever noticed the chart, much less used it, but it was good discipline for the analysts.

Confidence and probability are related insofar as, logically, a very high or very low judgement of probability implies relatively high confidence.

Yet the two are not the same, as we know from myriad studies indicating that experts typically are far too confident of their judgements. In intelligence, most treatments of confidence are little more than hand-waves: at one point, NIC products came with a footnote saying something to the effect that, unless otherwise noted, all the judgements in the document were of medium confidence. Had that been a comment in a student paper, I would have marked it NSS (for 'No S*** Sherlock') in large letters in the margin.

The furthest I got in refining the concept of confidence was a checklist of questions: (1) How reliable is the available evidence? (2) What is the range of opinion on the issue? (3) What would it take for me to change my view? The challenge of the first question is that interesting issues for intelligence often begin where the evidence ends, especially those that are strategic as opposed to forensic or tactical. The second implies that the narrower the range of opinion, the more confident the judgement, though 'groupthink' always lurks in the background. My favourite is the third, which seems wise counsel about life as well as intelligence. If it is hard to think of anything that would make me change my mind, high confidence seems warranted.

I suggest an additional, related question: why does this assessment appeal to me? This question may be especially useful for analysts closely linked to operators, who may be tempted by assessments that are simply convenient. I was struck by this point when the Polish government declared martial law in 1981 to crack down on the Solidarity movement. While that dispensation was probably less bad for Poland than if Soviet and other Warsaw Pact troops had poured across the border, it was also something of a surprise because the latter option was more familiar in the Western playbook.

Crowdsourcing

While chairing the NIC, I had the opportunity to provide a home for the prediction market that had grown out of the Good Judgment Project, an initiative of the US Office of the Director of National Intelligence's Intelligence Advanced Research Projects Activity associated closely with the work of political scientist Philip Tetlock, who also participated in the project. The idea was to ask two groups, one composed of outsiders and the other of intelligence insiders, to 'bet' – or, more clinically, provide probability estimates – on interesting future events.[2] Tetlock and his colleagues made two happy discoveries.[3] The first was that, just as some people are better athletes than others, so too are some people better predictors. The second, happier still, was that a small amount of training enables people to predict better. Not surprisingly, that training seeks to help people keep an open mind just a shade longer.

For the short run, I thought of the prediction market as a kind of internal 'red cell'. I didn't care about the numbers, but if the line analysts thought the chance of a coup in some country was small while the prediction market called it likely, that was the basis for a conversation: why the difference? In one instance, it turned out that the gap in assessments of an upcoming election was not about the vote itself but, rather, about whether the results would be fairly counted. Thus, the process led to a question that is always crucial in thinking about the future: what is the right question?

My longer-term aim was to apply the prediction market to more strategic issues. That would have entailed decomposing those longer-term outcomes into short-term intermediate outcomes on which participants might bet. In the process, I hoped we could make progress in turning those way stations into what intelligence professionals call 'indicators'. In the warning trade, these are meant to be signals that events are moving one way or another, but they are usually not well formulated. My idea was that turning the prediction market towards more strategic issues would help us do better.

In any event, the intelligence profession has much to learn from the best of the private-sector open-source intelligence analysts, like those at Bellingcat, who operate and participate in what amount to crowdsourcing networks and have had notable impacts on policy.[4] Over a decade ago, I did two RAND papers looking at the use of social media by intelligence agencies, first for external exploitation, then for internal collaboration.[5] Early in the course of that work, I met with CIA analysts who had created 'Intellipedia', a classified internal wiki. Their cards labelled them 'Intellipedia evangelists', which prompted me to joke that I hoped they didn't suffer the same fate as the original evangelists. But I've since taken as my watchword what one of them said. He was in favour of the CIA being out there on social media, clearly identified as the CIA. He said that of course they'd get lots of disinformation, but they got that anyway, adding that 'there may be people out there who'd like to help us'.

Notes

1   Sherman Kent, 'Words of Estimative Probability', Central Intelligence Agency, Fall 1964, declassified 16 December 1993, National Archives Catalogue, https://catalog.archives. gov/id/7282770.

2   In 2003, due to understandably bad optics, the Pentagon's Defense Advanced Research Project Agency (DARPA) aborted a plan for an online 'Policy Analysis Market' that was to involve a far broader range of participants than the groups in the NIC's prediction market. Under the DARPA plan, those who accurately predicted terrorist attacks, assassinations and coups were to be rewarded. See, for example, Eric Schmitt, 'Poindexter Will Be Quitting Over Terrorism Betting Plan', *New York Times*, 1 August 2003,
    https://www.nytimes.com/2003/08/01/ us/poindexter-will-be-quitting-over-terrorism-betting-plan.html.

3   See Philip E. Tetlock and Dan Gardner, *Superforecasting: The Art and Science of Prediction* (New York: Crown, 2015).

4   See Eliot Higgins, *We Are Bellingcat: Global Crime, Online Sleuths, and the Bold Future of News* (New York: Bloomsbury, 2021).

5   See Gregory F. Treverton, 'New Tools for Collaboration: The Experience of the U.S. Intelligence Community', Center for Strategic and International Studies, 29 January 2016, https:// csis-website-prod.s3.amazonaws. com/s3fs-public/legacy_files/files/ publication/160111_Treverton_ NewTools_Web.pdf.

Geopolitical Forecasting and Actionable Intelligence

Ian S. Lustick

Eighty years ago, Japan launched a devastating surprise attack on Pearl Harbor. Sixty years later, al-Qaeda killed even more Americans in attacks on New York and Washington. US government reactions to both events included major expansion and reorganisation of intelligence capacities. On both occasions, Washington made major investments in its ability to forecast threats to vital interests and then to mitigate or prevent them. In the 1940s, this meant creating specialised agencies dedicated to espionage and analysis focused mainly on military threats from rival great powers. In the 2000s, it meant harnessing computerised collection of masses of political, social, economic and cultural data from all countries to forecast threats to American interests from the 'universal adversary' – that is, those liable to arise from any direction at any time.

While technologies and targets have changed, however, there has never been strong confidence in geopolitical forecasting as a scientifically grounded and reliable basis for foreign-policy and national-security decision-making. It is widely understood that what drives most American policies are the personalities, prejudices, shrewdness and bureaucratic and political interests of officials ranging from the president down to supervisors of intelligence analysts. But since real progress has been made in the relevant social sciences,

Ian S. Lustick is emeritus professor of political science at the University of Pennsylvania and holds the Bess W. Heyman Chair in the Department of Political Science there.
This article was drafted for the 2021 Global Order Colloquium at Perry World House, the University of Pennsylvania's global-affairs hub. The workshop was made possible in part by the generous support of Carnegie Corporation of New York.

Survival | vol. 64 no. 1 | February–March 2022 | pp. 51–56   https://doi.org/10.1080/00396338.2022.2032959

and as the amount of data relevant to predicting what the future may hold has vastly increased, it has become far more important to distinguish forecasts and forecasting techniques that are creditable from those that are not.

The validation requirement

Ultimately, whether the validity of geopolitical forecasts matters depends on the purpose they are designed to serve. If the metric used to assess their value is the satisfaction of customers – be they on the seventh floor of the State Department or in corporate C-suites – how valid they are may not matter much at all. If forecasts merely support scenario-generating exercises designed to structure or enhance discussion or broaden thinking, correct predictions are unnecessary. Improvements in forecasting will then turn on what affords customers a sense of satisfaction at a low cost in terms of time, cognitive load or budgetary commitment. That may mean 'products' that call merely for technical virtuosity but not substantive knowledge, refrain from rocking political or institutional boats, do not disturb delicate and convenient presumptions, and prompt discussions that *feel* useful even if they are not.

But if forecasts are used as actual inputs into a policy- or decision-making process, they do need to be accurate, precise and reliable. If lives and treasure are to be wagered on those forecasts, it matters crucially whether the probabilities of events they lay out conform to the pattern of outcomes the world would produce if it could be rerun many times from the same starting point (thereby accounting for accidents and randomness), and whether confidence levels are specified in ways that enable those using the inputs to assess risk and calculate expected costs and benefits. Without denigrating the admirable efforts made within the US intelligence community and the Pentagon to measure the performance of different forecasting techniques developed under their auspices, the fact remains that, at policy- and decision-making levels, forecasts seldom change minds or reorient thinking. Instead, they tend to support or oppose contending positions with degrees of influence that have more to do with their confirmation of the premises of supervisors and policymakers, or the seductiveness of their presentation, than with the validity of their claims.[1]

Creating the expectation that forecasts will be validated and then actually validating the techniques that produce them are daunting challenges. Validation is particularly difficult when probability forecasts are made, since the non-occurrence of an event said to have, say, an 80% chance of happening does not disprove or invalidate the forecast. Neither does the occurrence of the event prove it was correct. Only streams of outcomes that exhibit the forecasted probability can corroborate the validity of the forecast and the techniques used to produce it. The standard statistical technique for accomplishing this is known as Brier scoring, based on the size of the errors a forecast would lead one to make over many attempts. Extrapolation, simulation, machine learning, super-forecasting and the like are now all subject to Brier-score assessments (or their equivalents) for judgements about their validity as techniques for making geopolitical forecasts.

The verification challenge

In addition to validation of whether a given model is accurate, reliable and precise, there is another, less understood or appreciated metric: verification. This concerns whether the model was built correctly, performs according to the rules prescribed to govern it and forecasts outcomes that can be traced to meaningful causal relationships. It is perfectly possible to predict the price of used cars in the United States by correlating that variable with the price of lemons in Mexico, but as valid as that model might be in terms of accurate prediction, it cannot be considered verified in terms of reflecting a causal relationship. Even if the data-collection procedures and statistical techniques used to generate the correlations are replicated, there is no basis for tracing the causal connections between the two variables.

Without verification, the utility of even empirically valid forecasts is strictly limited by two factors. Firstly, if the substantive reasons why a model produces a particular forecast are unavailable – that is, if outcomes cannot be traced to particular combinations of antecedent variables according to a body of corroborated knowledge – then decision-makers cannot know how to make use of the forecast to enhance the prospects of attractive outcomes or decrease the likelihood of undesirable ones. An analyst or model might forecast an insurrection in Iran within the next year as 75%

probable. But if even an accurate forecast is unaccompanied by any theory or explanation as to why or where the insurrection will arise and who will initiate it, it can provide little guidance to policymakers as to what levers to push, what actions to avoid or what measures to take to enhance or diminish the prospect of rebellion. Secondly, unless the substantive reasons why an analyst makes a prediction or why a model yields a particular forecast are understood, it is impossible to establish what conditions should prompt policymakers or supervisors to call upon the talents of that particular analyst or deploy that model.

This is not an easy problem to solve. But its difficulty is mainly a function of the state of knowledge in exceedingly complicated domains of interest. Aeronautics and nuclear physics have advanced so successfully that experts operating in those fields now have simulation tools that produce forecasts that are so well validated and verified that they can be considered equivalent to real-world experience. Pilots can be trained mostly on flight simulators. Nuclear weapons can be designed, built and deployed without ever having been tested in the physical world.

In the social sciences, sufficient progress has been made in the last 60 years that clusters of solid, well-corroborated theory are available, yielding models that specialists can understand and deploy. Advances in political science, sociology, anthropology and economics have produced an immense and largely untapped potential source for systematic simulations of complex social and political problems. But they need to incorporate massive amounts of deep idiographic knowledge and relevant data from specific geographic areas, cultures and societies of interest to be effectively utilised.[2] The task is to combine the finesse and judgement of social scientists with the computing power that enables flight simulation and nuclear-weapons design. Only in this way can forecasting models capture social and political realities that emerge from the phenomena studied in separate fields of inquiry.

*　　　*　　　*

It is widely recognised that computing is crucial to forecasting. But while machine learning, artificial intelligence and the natural language processing that those techniques often rely on can make crucial contributions, they cannot solve the verification problem without being programmed to apply substantive theories of how the world works. Only when political scientists and sociologists are as prominent in the design and assessment of forecasting tools as engineers, computer scientists and cognitive psychologists will geopolitical forecasting become an effective tool for policymakers.

Progress in this direction has been slow. The big money for research and development in the intelligence community is still mostly controlled by engineers. Their penchant is for investments in supercomputing and the brute-force empiricism associated with machine learning and artificial intelligence. But when it comes to what policymakers really need – actionable intelligence – only models capable of answering why and how questions, not just what, where and when questions, will fit the bill. Those models, though, require substantive knowledge about specific cultures, international affairs, political science, sociology and economics. Until expertise in those fields is tapped much more systematically than it is at present, geopolitical forecasting, however teched-up, will remain of limited practical utility.

Notes

[1] On the influence that an agency's analytic line has on how studies are framed, conducted and reported within the intelligence community, see Rob Johnston, *Analytic Culture in the U.S. Intelligence Community: An Ethnographic Study* (Washington DC: Center for the Study of Intelligence, 2005). See also David Halberstam, *The Best and the Brightest* (New York: Random House, 1972), his classic study of how analysts and policy advisers were systematically punished or rewarded for reports and recommendations in line with what their superiors believed or wanted. As an analyst in the State Department's Bureau of Intelligence and Research, I was repeatedly warned of the need to remove enough of the truth that contradicted the beliefs or preferences of superiors so that my memos and reports would actually be read.

[2] See Ian S. Lustick and Philip E. Tetlock, 'The Simulation Manifesto: The Limits of Brute-force Empiricism in Geopolitical Forecasting', *Futures & Foresight Science*, vol. 3, no. 2, February 2021; and Sean P. O'Brien, 'Crisis Early Warning and Decision Support: Contemporary Approaches and Thoughts on Future Research', *International Studies Review*, vol. 12, no. 1, March 2010, pp. 87–104.

War with China: Five Scenarios

Stacie L. Pettyjohn

Senior US military officers have asserted that the odds of China starting a war to forcibly unify with Taiwan are growing. Admiral John Aquilino, the head of US Indo-Pacific Command (INDOPACOM), announced in March 2021 that 'this problem is much closer to us than most think', while his predecessor said that China could invade Taiwan by 2027.[1] Yet the head of intelligence at INDOPACOM noted in July 2021 that Taiwan is 'one scenario and, frankly, it may not be the most likely'.[2] Assessing the odds of a major war between the United States and China over the next five years requires looking not just at a Taiwan invasion, but rather at a range of scenarios. Consideration of five of these suggests that none of the wars that China might intentionally start are very attractive from Beijing's perspective. This provides the United States and its allies with time to strengthen deterrence, thereby reducing the probability of war. Instead, the greatest risk of a Sino-American conflict in the near term is inadvertent or accidental escalation caused by misperception or miscalculation. The US Department of Defense should take steps to mitigate the risks of accidental escalation by creating communication mechanisms and establishing norms for US–China military competition.

Stacie L. Pettyjohn is a Senior Fellow and Director of the Defense Program at the Center for a New American Security. This article was drafted for the 2021 Global Order Colloquium at Perry World House, the University of Pennsylvania's global-affairs hub. The workshop was made possible in part by the generous support of Carnegie Corporation of New York.

Survival | vol. 64 no. 1 | February–March 2022 | pp. 57–66   https://doi.org/10.1080/00396338.2022.2032960

Five Sino-American war scenarios

American military planners rightly devote most of their attention to a Taiwan-invasion scenario because it is both the most consequential and the most challenging situation that the US military might face. This does not make it the most likely scenario, however, nor the only situation in which American and Chinese forces could find themselves engaged in conflict. At least five different scenarios could lead to a major Sino-American war.

Invasion of Taiwan

The Defense Department's 'pacing' – or touchstone – defence-planning scenario is a Chinese invasion of Taiwan to force unification with the mainland.[3] The Chinese Communist Party (CCP) insists that Taiwan is an integral and sacred part of the People's Republic of China, and that Taipei must eventually submit to Beijing's rule. Chinese President Xi Jinping appears to be losing patience with the country's 'peaceful reunification' strategy, as he has been ordering the increasingly modernised and capable People's Liberation Army (PLA) to undertake frequent, brazen military operations near Taiwan.[4] In light of these advances, Beijing might conclude that it could successfully invade Taiwan. Until recently, most believed that Taiwan could repel an amphibious assault, especially with US assistance.[5]

That outcome is currently less certain as the balance of power within the first and second island chains has shifted in China's favour.[6] China has notably improved its amphibious and airborne forces, which would be critical in an invasion. The country's navy is projected to have more than 400 battleships by 2025, while the US fleet is rapidly ageing and shrinking.[7] The PLA Air Force can increasingly project power far from China's shores with its expanding inventory of stealth fighters, improved bombers, missiles and mobility aircraft. The PLA has also enhanced its air and missile defences, improving the survivability of its forces, while its ballistic and cruise missiles hold at risk all US military bases in the region, including Guam. The PLA also plans to launch pre-emptive cyber, electromagnetic and kinetic attacks on key US military space assets, information systems, networks and headquarters.[8] A large, multifaceted air and missile attack against US forces, coupled with attacks against US communications and command and control, could cause significant destruction. Moreover, it may be sufficient to deter the United States from intervening on the side of Taiwan, or render American military assistance ineffective.[9]

Other Taiwan scenarios

Beijing may adopt less risky military approaches to try to compel a union with Taiwan. China could attack Taiwan with a limited coercive cyber, air and missile campaign; seize an outlying island such as Kinmen, Matsu or Pratas/Dongsha;[10] impose an air and naval blockade of Taiwan;[11] or extend its influence or control over Taiwan's semiconductor industry through grey-zone tactics.[12] China's theory of victory is that it could gradually subordinate Taiwan through a series of small gains or fait accomplis, and that Chinese punishment and intimidation would eventually inflict enough pain and psychological stress that Taiwan would capitulate to Beijing's rule. Strategies that rely on imposing costs and pain, however, can backfire and stiffen a target's resolve to fight. Historically, punishment strategies have rarely produced the desired results.

South China Sea escalation

Washington has contested China's assertion of sovereignty within the nine-dash line in the resource-rich South China Sea, but China could take a variety of actions to press its claims that could lead to war.[13] A likely path would involve the Philippines, a US treaty ally. Senior American officials have pledged to defend not only the main Philippine islands, but also Philippine military forces and civilian ships and aircraft operating in the South China Sea.[14]

There are two major roads to war in the South China Sea: an attempted fait accompli by China against a feature controlled by another country;[15] and inadvertent or accidental escalation during a crisis.[16] In the former scenario, Chinese military or paramilitary forces successfully seize a contested feature while assuming that the United States will not intervene because of the low stakes. Yet China's attack inadvertently crosses an American red line, and the United States decides to roll back the land grab.[17] Alternatively, China could build on the Philippine-claimed Scarborough

Shoal[18] or attack Philippine forces, prompting Manila to invoke its treaty with the United States.[19]

In the latter scenario, a relatively limited skirmish between China's maritime militia or navy and a US ally or partner could escalate into a large-scale conflict between the two great powers if the US decided to militarily intervene against China. Alternatively, or within the same crisis, an American ship on a routine patrol or freedom-of-navigation operation could collide with a Chinese ship engaging in a game of brinkmanship. Or, an American military aircraft patrolling the skies and collecting valuable intelligence could be shot down by a Chinese fighter or surface-to-air missile.[20] Chinese or American leaders may not intend for their forces to undertake the actions that cause the accident. Alternatively, Chinese leaders might intentionally risk escalation under the assumption that the United States would seek to avert a full-blown war. If tensions are high, however, each side might feel that it needs to appear strong for domestic or international audiences, turning the crisis into a conflict.

East China Sea

Similarly, an East China Sea war might begin due to deliberate Chinese aggression, or an accident or miscalculation. Japan and China both lay claim to the Japanese-administered Senkaku or Diaoyu islands, around which the countries' militaries have been jockeying with each other.[21] Clashes between Japanese and Chinese forces operating in the East China Sea could prove to be a flashpoint that escalates into a full-blown war between China and Japan. The United States would be drawn into the war because of the US–Japan defence treaty, which covers the Senkaku/Diaoyu islands.[22]

North Korean collapse

The United States and China could also find themselves engaged in a large-scale war on the Korean Peninsula. In this scenario, North Korea could collapse after the unexpected death of Kim Jong-un or the fractionalisation of the country's elites due to dire domestic circumstances.[23] China views North Korea as a buffer against the United States and has a deep interest in ensuring that instability on the peninsula does not bleed into its territory.[24]

The United States might intervene to secure North Korea's nuclear arsenal and other weapons of mass destruction in the belief that Beijing would welcome these actions. China would likely view American troops near its border with North Korea as a serious threat, leading to direct conflict.[25]

Assessing the paths to war

In these scenarios, war begins through three primary mechanisms: China deliberately chooses to start a war; China or the United States inadvertently crosses its opponent's escalation thresholds; or Chinese or American forces undertake risky operations that result in accidents.[26]

An invasion of Taiwan would be a case of intentional escalation in which Chinese leaders recognise that the operation will not be easy, but determine that the costs could be tolerable, especially given Taiwan's growing support for independence.[27] Several factors reduce the likelihood of an invasion. Firstly, large-scale amphibious assaults are among the most challenging military operations, and Beijing would have to gamble on its largely unproven forces at a time when the stakes would be incredibly high.[28] Chinese forces would need to coordinate all-domain attacks on hundreds of targets across the Indo-Pacific, secure air and maritime superiority around Taiwan, rapidly establish a lodgement on Taiwan, quickly transport hundreds of thousands to millions of troops ashore and supply these forces. Under any circumstances, this would stress the PLA and require a massive mobilisation, including of civilian assets.[29] If others intervene in support of Taiwan, which appears increasingly likely, the operation would be even more taxing.[30] Moreover, the PLA might face urban warfare and potentially a long counter-insurgency operation.[31] Finally, Beijing risks international isolation and incurring significant economic losses.

Other scenarios involving Taiwan rely on less proven methods of winning and thus are premised on minimising the costs by keeping US forces out, so a war with the United States would be inadvertent. The same is true if Beijing seized a feature in the South or East China Sea. Inadvertent paths appear unlikely given that the benefits to China are lower while the risks of escalation remain significant. Similarly, limited-war scenarios against Taiwan or in the East or South China Sea should appear unappealing to Beijing because the United States would have the capability to roll back this aggression. As noted, punishment strategies have a poor track record;[32] blockades take significant time to work and have rarely succeeded in isolation.[33] A blockade of Taiwan would be costly to the PLA forces vulnerable to Taiwanese anti-ship missiles and US air, maritime and undersea attacks.

The PLA risks expending its stockpiles of ballistic and cruise missiles during a coercive strike campaign that would cause pain, but not necessarily capitulation. Missile strikes could provoke a rally-round-the-flag effect, strengthening support for Taiwanese independence and rousing a stronger multinational countervailing coalition. Moreover, this option cedes the initiative and leaves the PLA less able to launch a surprise knockout attack against Taiwan, while also leaving US aircraft, ships and submarines intact.

China has long had the ability to terrorise or seize its neighbours' islands, but has usually chosen not to do so for strategic reasons. China could emerge looking weaker rather than stronger, even if it obtains its limited objective. Small-scale operations could expose weaknesses in the PLA, much as the American interventions in Grenada and Panama did for US forces. Moreover, American officials have clarified that US commitments to defend Japan and the Philippines include disputed territories, reducing the risks of inadvertent escalation. In North Korea, the Kim regime appears to have a strong grip on power. Should it collapse, however, there is a chance that American misunderstanding of China's perceptions and stakes could lead to war. Accidental escalation is the most worrying near-term path to war because American and Chinese forces frequently operate in close proximity, thus increasing the opportunities for miscalculations and errors.

Strengthening deterrence

These five scenarios should concern American defence officials, but they also provide a glimmer of hope. If the United States acts quickly, it can strengthen deterrence and reduce the risk that China makes the deliberate choice to invade Taiwan.[34] A challenge is that the United States needs to demonstrate that it has the capability and willingness to stop Chinese aggression without accidentally precipitating a conflict. Many of the actions that the Defense Department can take to bolster deterrence increase the risk of accidental confrontation. The US must, therefore, simultaneously put in place crisis-management mechanisms to prevent accidents from spiralling into a conflict.

Ultimately, the perceptions of China's leadership about the relative balance of power and the likelihood that the United States will come to Taipei's defence are paramount. These factors will influence Beijing's decision-making as to whether attempting an invasion is worth the enormous risk of losing, which would deliver a blow to China's military power, produce significant economic losses and place the legitimacy of CCP rule in jeopardy. It is not just the odds of a conflict that matter, but also the odds of losing.

Notes

1   Brad Lendon, 'China Threat to Taiwan: "Closer to Us than Most of Us Think", Top Admiral Says', CNN, 24 March 2021, https://www.cnn.com/2021/03/24/asia/indo-pacific-commander-aquilino-hearing-taiwan-intl-hnk-ml/index.html; and Mallory Shelbourne, 'Davidson: China Could Try to Take Control of Taiwan in "Next Six Years"', USNI News, 9 March 2021, https://news.usni.org/2021/03/09/davidson-china-could-try-to-take-control-of-taiwan-in-next-six-years.

2   Bill Gertz, 'U.S. Pacific Intel Chief: Coming Chinese Attack on Taiwan Could Target Other Nations', Washington Times, 8 July 2021, https://www.washingtontimes.com/news/2021/jul/8/us-pacific-intel-chief-coming-chinese-attack-taiwa/.

3   'Statement by Dr. Ely Ratner Assistant Secretary of Defense for Indo-Pacific Affairs, Office of the Secretary of Defense, Before the 117th Congress Committee on Foreign Relations, United States Senate', 8 December 2021, https://www.foreign.senate.gov/imo/media/doc/120821_Ratner_Testimony1.pdf.

4   See Oriana Skyler Mastro, 'The Taiwan Temptation: Why Beijing Might Resort to Force', Foreign Affairs, July/August 2021, https://www.foreignaffairs.com/articles/china/2021-06-03/china-taiwan-war-temptation.

5   See David A. Shlapak, David T. Orletsky and Barry Wilson, Dire Strait? Military Aspects of the China–Taiwan Confrontation and Options for U.S. Policy (Santa Monica, CA: RAND Corporation, 2000), https://www.rand.org/pubs/monograph_reports/MR1217.html.

6   See Eric Heginbotham et al., The U.S.–China Military Scorecard: Force, Geography, and the Evolving Balance of Power, 1996–2017 (Santa Monica, CA: RAND Corporation, 2015), https://www.rand.org/content/dam/rand/pubs/research_reports/RR300/RR392/RAND_RR392.pdf; and US

Department of Defense, Office of the Secretary of Defense, 'Military and Security Developments Involving the People's Republic of China 2021', https://media.defense.gov/2021/Nov/03/2002885874/-1/-1/0/2021-CMPR-FINAL.PDF.

7   See Ronald O'Rourke, *China's Naval Modernization: Implications for U.S. Navy Capabilities – Background and Issues for Congress* (Washington DC: Congressional Research Service, 2021), https://sgp.fas.org/crs/row/RL33153.pdf; and Ronald O'Rourke, *Navy Force Structure and Shipbuilding Plans: Background and Issues for Congress* (Washington DC: Congressional Research Service, 2021), https://sgp.fas.org/crs/weapons/RL32665.pdf.

8   See Chris Dougherty, *More than Half the Battle: Information and Command in a New American Way of War* (Washington DC: Center for a New American Security, 2021), https://s3.amazonaws.com/files.cnas.org/CNAS+Report-Command+and+Info-2021.pdf.

9   See Alan J. Vick, *Air Base Attacks and Defensive Counters: Historical Lessons and Future Challenges* (Santa Monica, CA: RAND Corporation, 2015), pp. 19–39, https://www.rand.org/pubs/research_reports/RR968.html; and Christopher Dougherty, *Why America Needs a New Way of War* (Washington DC: Center for a New American Security, 2019), https://s3.amazonaws.com/files.cnas.org/ CNAS+Report+-+ANAWOW+-+FINAL2.pdf.

10   See David Lague and Maryanne Murray, 'T-Day: The Battle for Taiwan', Reuters, 5 November 2021, https://www.reuters.com/investigates/special-report/taiwan-china-

wargames/; and Chris Dougherty, Jennie Matuschak and Ripley Hunter, *The Poison Frog Strategy: Preventing a Chinese Fait Accompli Against Taiwanese Islands* (Washington DC: Center for a New American Security, 2021), https://www.cnas.org/publications/reports/the-poison-frog-strategy.

11   See Benjamin Brimelow, 'An Invasion Isn't the Only Threat from China that Taiwan and the US Have to Worry About', *Insider*, 16 June 2021, https://www.businessinsider.com/taiwan-and-us-also-face-risk-of-china-blockading-taiwan-2021-6.

12   See Becca Wasser and Martijn Rasser, *When the Chips Are Down: Gaming the Global Semiconductor Competition* (Washington DC: Center for a New American Security, 2022).

13   See Oriana Skylar Mastro, 'Military Confrontation in the South China Sea', Center for Preventive Action, Contingency Planning Memorandum No. 36, 21 May 2020, https://www.cfr.org/report/military-confrontation-south-china-sea.

14   See Andreo Calonzo, 'Philippines Says U.S. Vowed to Help if There's a Maritime Attack', Bloomberg, 28 January 2021, https://www.bloomberg.com/news/articles/2021-01-29/philippines-says-u-s-vowed-to-help-if-there-s-a-maritime-attack.

15   See Lyle J. Morris et al., *Gaining Competition Advantage in the Gray Zone: Response Options for Coercive Aggression Below the Threshold of Major War* (Santa Monica, CA: RAND Corporation, 2019), pp. 8–10, https://www.rand.org/pubs/research_reports/RR2942.html.

16   See Kurt M. Campbell and Ali Wyne, 'The Growing Risk of Inadvertent

Escalation Between Washington and Beijing', Lawfare, 16 August 2020, https://www.lawfareblog.com/growing-risk-inadvertent-escalation-between-washington-and-beijing.

[17] Stacie Pettyjohn, Becca Wasser and Jennie Matuschak, *Risky Business: Future Strategy and Force Options for the Defense Department* (Washington DC: Center for a New American Security, 2021), pp. 18–19.

[18] A similar scenario could occur over Ita Ibu or Pratas islands claimed by Taiwan.

[19] See Gregory Winger, 'The Little-known Agreement that Could Lead the U.S. and China to War', *Washington Post*, 23 June 2021, https://www.washingtonpost.com/outlook/2021/06/23/little-known-agreement-that-could-lead-us-china-war/.

[20] See Karen Leigh, Peter Martin and Adrian Leung, 'Troubled Waters: Where the U.S. and China Could Clash in the South China Sea', Bloomberg, 17 December 2020, https://www.bloomberg.com/graphics/2020-south-china-sea-miscalculation/.

[21] See Todd Hall, 'More Significance than Value: Explaining Developments in the Sino-Japanese Contest over the Senkaku/Diaoyu Islands', *Texas National Security Review*, vol. 2, no. 4, September 2019, https://tnsr.org/2019/09/more-significance-than-value-explaining-developments-in-the-sino-japanese-contest-over-the-senkaku-diaoyu-islands/.

[22] See Richard Fontaine et al., *A Deadly Game: East China Sea Crisis 2030* (Washington DC: Center for a New American Security, 2020), https://www.cnas.org/publications/video/a-deadly-game-east-china-sea-crisis-2030.

[23] See Michael J. Mazarr et al., *The Korean Peninsula: Three Dangerous Scenarios* (Santa Monica, CA: RAND Corporation, 2018), pp. 14–19, https://www.rand.org/pubs/perspectives/PE262.html.

[24] See Richard C. Bush, 'China's Response to Collapse in North Korea', Brookings Institution, 23 January 2014, https://www.brookings.edu/on-the-record/chinas-response-to-collapse-in-north-korea/.

[25] See Andrew Scobell, 'China and North Korea: Bolster a Buffer or Hunkering Down in Northeast Asia', testimony presented before the U.S.–China Economic and Security Review Commission, 8 June 2017, https://www.rand.org/pubs/testimonies/CT477.html.

[26] See Forrest E. Morgan et al., *Dangerous Thresholds: Managing Escalation in the 21st Century* (Santa Monica, CA: RAND Corporation, 2008), p. 20, https://www.rand.org/pubs/monographs/MG614.html.

[27] See Oriana Skyler Mastro, 'The Taiwan Temptation: Why Beijing Might Resort to Force', *Foreign Affairs*, July/August 2021, https://www.foreignaffairs.com/articles/china/2021-06-03/china-taiwan-war-temptation.

[28] See Timothy R. Heath, 'China's Untested Military Could Be a Force – or a Flop', *Foreign Policy*, 27 November 2018, https://foreignpolicy.com/2018/11/27/chinas-untested-military-could-be-a-force-or-a-flop/.

[29] See Thomas Shugart, 'Mind the Gap: How China's Civilian Shipping Could Enable a Taiwan Invasion', *War on*

the Rocks, 16 August 2021, https://warontherocks.com/2021/08/mind-the-gap-how-chinas-civilian-shipping-could-enable-a-taiwan-invasion/.

30 See Anthony Kuhn, 'After Being Silent for Decades Japan Now Speaks Up About Taiwan – and Angers China', NPR, 2 August 2021, https://www.npr.org/2021/07/26/1020866539/japans-position-on-defending-taiwan-has-taken-a-remarkable-shift; and Zack Cooper and Sheena Greitens, 'What to Expect from Japan and Korea in a Taiwan Contingency', in Henry D. Sokolski (ed.), *New Frontiers for Security Cooperation with Seoul and Tokyo* (Arlington, VA: Nonproliferation Policy Education Center, 2021), pp. 16–19, https://npolicy.org/article_file/2101_New_Frontiers_Occasional_Paper.pdf.

31 See Ian Easton, 'Why a Taiwan Invasion Would Look Nothing Like D-Day', *Diplomat*, 26 May 2021, https://thediplomat.com/2021/05/why-a-taiwan-invasion-would-look-nothing-like-d-day/; and Wang Mouzhou, 'What Happens After China Invades Taiwan', *Diplomat*, 24 March 2017, https://thediplomat.com/2017/03/what-happens-after-china-invades-taiwan/.

32 See Robert A. Pape, *Bombing to Win:*

Air Power and Coercion in War (Ithaca, NY: Cornell University Press, 1996); and Michael Horowitz and Dan Reiter, 'When Does Aerial Bombing Work? Quantitative Empirical Tests, 1917–1999', *Journal of Conflict Resolution*, vol. 45, no. 2, April 2001, https://journals.sagepub.com/doi/abs/10.1177/0022002701045002001.

33 See James Holmes, 'Could China Successfully Blockade Taiwan?', *National Interest*, 29 August 2020, https://nationalinterest.org/feature/could-china-successfully-blockade-taiwan-168035?page=0%2C1; Gabriel Collins, 'A Maritime Oil Blockade Against China: Tactically Tempting but Strategically Flawed', *Naval War College Review*, vol. 71, no. 2, Spring 2018, pp. 49–78; Erik Sand, 'Desperate Measures: The Effects of Economic Isolation on Warring Powers', *Texas National Security Review*, vol. 3, no. 2, Spring 2020, pp. 12–37, https://tnsr.org/2020/04/desperate-measures-the-effects-of-economic-isolation-on-warring-powers/#_ftn3; and Gabriel B. Collins and William S. Murray, 'No Oil for the Lamps of China?', *Naval War College Review*, vol. 61, no. 2, Spring 2008, pp. 79–95.

34 See Pettyjohn, Wasser and Matuschak, *Risky Business*, p. 24.

National Security and Climate Change: The Attention It Deserves?

Erin Sikorsky

While international initiative and collaboration are important in inspiring and coordinating efforts to mitigate the effects of climate change, the national commitment and competence of states in doing so remain indispensable.[1] Furthermore, the strategic and security effects of climate change are among the most important factors in any nation's security. Policymakers are not paying enough attention to them.

At first blush, this charge may appear unfair. In many ways, the nexus of climate change and national security finally reached centre stage in 2021. On the first day of his presidency, Joe Biden brought the United States back into the Paris climate agreement and a week later he issued an executive order designating climate change an 'essential element' of US foreign and security policy. The order prescribed concrete actions for security agencies, tasking the director of national intelligence with preparing a National Intelligence Estimate on climate change and the Pentagon with composing its Defense Climate Risk Analysis and reinstating the 2016 Presidential Memorandum on Climate Change and National Security.[2] A few months later, the administration held the Leaders Summit on Climate, which included a panel discussion led by Secretary of Defense Lloyd J. Austin III, US Ambassador to the United Nations Linda Thomas-Greenfield and Director of National

Erin Sikorsky is a Visiting Fellow at Perry World House and Director of the Center for Climate and Security, and served as Deputy Director of the Strategic Futures Group on the National Intelligence Council. This article was drafted for the 2021 Global Order Colloquium at Perry World House, the University of Pennsylvania's global-affairs hub. The workshop was made possible in part by the generous support of Carnegie Corporation of New York.

Survival | vol. 64 no. 1 | February–March 2022 | pp. 67–73   https://doi.org/10.1080/00396338.2022.2032961

Intelligence Avril Haines. Climate change was mentioned 27 times in the Interim National Security Strategic Guidance, and is repeatedly invoked as one of the 'three Cs' that the Pentagon is focused on: China, climate and COVID-19.[3] It is likely that the forthcoming National Security Strategy and National Defense Strategy, slated for publication in January 2022, will discuss the risks posed by climate change as well.

The United States is not alone in its elevation of climate-change risks. In February, the United Kingdom led a United Nations Security Council meeting on climate security, and in June, NATO adopted its Climate Change and Security Action Plan.[4] From Eastern Europe to East Asia to East Africa, high-level security discussions have featured climate change. This year, for the first time, Japan included climate security in its Defense White Paper.[5] Russia mentions climate change in its latest national security strategy.[6]

Insufficient strategic attention

Despite these high-level proclamations, in practice, climate change still occupies relatively narrow, siloed slices of the United States' and others' day-to-day national-security agendas. When the Biden administration says climate change is central to its foreign policy, what that has meant thus far is that, at the US State Department, US Special Presidential Envoy for Climate John Kerry and his team have been pushing other countries to raise their ambitions to cut carbon emissions. Meanwhile, a large portion of the Pentagon's climate-security agenda remains focused on the direct effects of climate change on military infrastructure and equipment.

Both avenues of work are, of course, critically important. As the Center for Climate and Security's 2019 security-risk assessment of climate change found, without significant and rapid emissions cuts, climate security risks will be catastrophic in the second half of the century.[7] Increasing the resilience of military bases and installations could save the United States billions of dollars and help ensure future readiness. Yet neither line of effort can prepare the US for the systemic shocks and fundamental reshaping of national security that climate change will bring about in the next 10–20 years. Jeff Colgan projects an 'altered landscape' in which climate change is not merely a discrete issue but rather 'a pervasive background condition that is intrinsically connected to most other areas of interstate competition and cooperation'.[8] Through this lens, it is clear that climate-change-induced mass migration, diminished food and water security, and resource competition will shift power dynamics within and between states. Even more concerning – and less understood or acknowledged – are the discontinuities and shocks prompted by climate change that are coming our way. Climate scientists warn that as the world approaches two degrees Celsius of warming, it will enter a phase in which humans have no experience, and therefore a severely limited comprehension of how different extreme events will affect one another.[9]

It is clear that climate change will alter the behaviour of US competitors and adversaries and compel the United States and its allies and partners to adapt. An approach to strategic planning that does not take into account the effects of climate change across all areas of US national interest will leave policymakers flat-footed.

Effects on governance

The impact of climate change on the ability of states to govern effectively has not received enough attention. Many states are already struggling to meet their citizens' needs: there is a growing mismatch between what publics expect and what states are able or willing to deliver, according to the latest 'Global Trends' forecast of the US National Intelligence Council.[10] Climate change contributes to that mismatch, creating an additional layer of stress and interfering with governments' abilities to deliver goods and services to their populations.

A landmark 2019 study conducted by the US Agency for International Development (USAID) examined the 'double burden' of state fragility and climate exposure facing many states, and its implications for peace and security.[11] The researchers noted that states incurring such double burdens were ill-equipped to respond to climate shocks, and therefore more vulnerable to humanitarian crises and instability. They found that the highest combined fragility and climate risks were concentrated in sub-Saharan Africa, with other areas of high risk sprinkled across the Middle East and North Africa, South and Southeast Asia, and parts of South America.[12] For example, the

East Africa region began 2020 with 21 million people already food-insecure. As the year progressed, they experienced flooding related to climate change, one of the worst locust plagues in 70 years and the COVID-19 pandemic. As the head of the World Food Programme for the region noted, 'it's shock upon shock upon shock'.[13]

The double-burden phenomenon was on display across the Middle East as well. Iran, Iraq and Lebanon – all of which rank highly on the Fragile States Index[14] – faced violent street protests after record temperatures and drought caused water shortages. For these countries, it was not climate change alone that sparked the crises, but the combination of climate stress and long-standing government mismanagement. Meanwhile, Algeria and Turkey – which are considered less fragile but still at 'elevated warning' – tried to deflect responsibility for poor performance in fighting climate-change-induced fires by blaming their enemies – respectively, Israel- or Morocco-linked terrorist groups and Kurdish militants. Such behaviour clearly increases risks of violence and conflict.

While climate security risks to orderly governance are most acute in fragile states, stronger states are also vulnerable. This is due in part to the speed at which climate change is changing weather patterns and the unprecedented nature of the shocks. For example, in summer floods in Germany, China and the United States, people died because infrastructure or other governmental systems were not designed to withstand emerging extreme weather. In Germany it was the warning system, in China the subway network and in the US the regulatory apparatus.[15] The USAID researchers identified capacity and legitimacy as two key measures of state fragility with respect to climate exposure. The brutal reality is that without a significant shift in allocation of resources and attention to resilience measures, few if any states will have the capacity to satisfactorily manage the climate shocks the world will confront in the coming years. No country is safe from climate change.

*   *   *

What, then, would a foreign- and security-policy apparatus look like if national-security policymakers gave climate change the attention it deserved? Most critically, it would systematically integrate the considerable forecasting tools and capabilities that have been developed as to the physical risks of climate change to inform its analysis and policy choices. These include the new Intergovernmental Panel on Climate Change Interactive Atlas and the work of leading scientific organisations such as the Woodwell Climate Research Center.[16] It would be led by an interdisciplinary, inter-agency and regionally networked workforce with the scientific literacy required to understand such forecasting and the implications for their work. It would develop new frameworks for understanding and evaluating compounded risks. It would avoid a rigidly comparative approach to prioritising climate risks (for instance, climate change is a bigger or smaller threat than China) in favour of an integrated, systemic one focused on how climate change shapes the behaviour of other countries and geopolitical competition. Having at last recognised the magnitude of the threat of climate change, the United States and other countries should now move towards establishing such a framework to ensure national governmental competence in meeting that threat.

Notes

1   See Anatol Lieven, 'Climate Change and the State: The Case for Environmental Realism', *Survival*, vol. 62, no. 2, April–May 2020, pp. 7–26.

2   White House, 'Executive Order on Tackling the Climate Crisis at Home and Abroad', 27 January 2021, https://www.whitehouse.gov/briefing-room/presidential-actions/2021/01/27/executive-order-on-tackling-the-climate-crisis-at-home-and-abroad/.

3   White House, 'Interim National Security Strategic Guidance', 3 March 2021, https://www.whitehouse.gov/briefing-room/statements-releases/2021/03/03/interim-national-security-strategic-guidance/.

4   North Atlantic Treaty Organization,

'NATO Climate Change and Security Action Plan', 14 June 2021, https://www.nato.int/cps/en/natohq/official_texts_185174.htm.

5   Japanese Ministry of Defense, 'Defense of Japan 2021', https://www.mod.go.jp/en/publ/w_paper/wp2021/DOJ2021_EN_Full.pdf.

6   See Atle Staalesen, 'Climate Change Finds a Place in Russia's New National Security Strategy', *Barents Observer*, 6 July 2021, https://thebarentsobserver.com/en/security/2021/07/climate-change-finds-place-russias-new-national-security-strategy.

7   See National Security, Military and Intelligence Panel on Climate Change,

'A Security Threat Assessment of Global Climate Change', Center for Climate and Security, 2020, https:// climateandsecurity.org/wp-content/ uploads/2020/03/a-security-threat-assessment-of-climate-change.pdf.

8 Jeff D. Colgan, 'Climate Change, Grand Strategy, and International Order', Wilson Center, 23 July 2021, https://diplomacy21-adelphi.wilsoncenter.org/article/ climate-change-grand-strategy-and-international-order.

9 See Kate Mackenzie, 'What Smart People Get Wrong About Climate Change', Bloomberg Green, 10 September 2021, https://www.bloomberg.com/ news/articles/2021-09-10/ what-smart-people-get-wrong-about-climate-change-extremes.

10 See Office of the Director of National Intelligence, 'Global Trends 2040: A More Contested World', March 2021, https://www.dni.gov/index.php/ gt2040-home/emerging-dynamics/ state-dynamics/.

11 See Ashley Moran et al., 'Policy Summary: The Nexus of Fragility and Climate Risks', US Agency for International Development, March 2019, https://reliefweb.int/ sites/reliefweb.int/files/resources/ PA00TKRR.pdf.

12 See Ashley Moran, Joshua Busby and Clionadh Raleigh, 'Stretched Thin: When Fragile States Face Climate Hazards', *War on the Rocks*, 20 November 2018, https:// warontherocks.com/2018/11/ stretched-thin-when-fragile-states-face-climate-hazards/.

13 Quoted in Peter S. Goodman,

Abdi Latif Dahir and Karan Deep Singh, 'The Other Way Covid Will Kill: Hunger', *New York Times*, 11 September 2020, https://www.nytimes. com/2020/09/11/business/covid-hunger-food-insecurity.html.

14 Fragile States Index, 'Fragile States Index 2021 – Annual Report', May 2021, https://fragilestatesindex.org/ wp-content/uploads/2021/05/fsi2021-report.pdf.

15 See, respectively, Karl Mathiesen, Joshua Posaner and Laurenz Gehrke, 'Europe's Floods: How a Modern Warning System Was Overwhelmed', *Politico*, 23 July 2021, https://www.politico.eu/article/ unnatural-disaster-the-german-belgian-floods-climate-change/; Nectar Gan and Zixu Wang, 'Death Toll Rises as Passengers Recount Horror of China Subway Floods', CNN, 23 July 2021, https://edition. cnn.com/2021/07/22/china/zhengzhou-henan-china-flooding-update-intl-hnk/ index.html; and Christopher Flavelle, 'How Government Decisions Left Tennessee Exposed to Deadly Flooding', *New York Times*, 26 August 2021, https://www.nytimes. com/2021/08/26/climate/tennessee-flood-damage-impact.html.

16 Examples of these organisations' efforts to integrate predictive climate science with national-security analysis include Catherine Dill et al., 'Converging Crises in North Korea: Security, Stability and Climate Change', Woodwell Climate Research Center/Converging Risks Lab, July 2021, https://assets-woodwell. s3.us-east-2.amazonaws.com/wp-content/uploads/2021/07/27112357/

Global_Risk_and_Security_North_
Korea_Case_Study.pdf; Kate Guy et
al., 'Security and Climate Risk in the
Arctic: Temperatures and Tensions
Rise', Woodwell Climate Research
Center/Converging Risks Lab,
June 2021, https://assets-woodwell.

s3.us-east-2.amazonaws.com/wp-
content/uploads/2021/06/21162718/
Global_Risk_and_Security_
Arctic_Case_Study.pdf; and
Intergovernmental Panel on Climate
Change, 'IPCC WGI Interactive Atlas',
https://interactive-atlas.ipcc.ch/.

Noteworthy

Russia, Ukraine and the West

'**Article 1**

The Parties shall cooperate on the basis of principles of indivisible, equal and undiminished security and to these ends:

shall not undertake actions nor participate in or support activities that affect the security of the other Party;

shall not implement security measures adopted by each Party individually or in the framework of an international organization, military alliance or coalition that could undermine core security interests of the other Party.

Article 2

The Parties shall seek to ensure that all international organizations, military alliances and coalitions in which at least one of the Parties is taking part adhere to the principles contained in the Charter of the United Nations.

Article 3

The Parties shall not use the territories of other States with a view to preparing or carrying out an armed attack against the other Party or other actions affecting core security interests of the other Party.

Article 4

The United States of America shall undertake to prevent further eastward expansion of the North Atlantic Treaty Organization and deny accession to the Alliance to the States of the former Union of Soviet Socialist Republics.

The United States of America shall not establish military bases in the territory of the States of the former Union of Soviet Socialist Republics that are not members of the North Atlantic Treaty Organization, use their infrastructure for any military activities or develop bilateral military cooperation with them.

Article 5

The Parties shall refrain from deploying their armed forces and armaments, including in the framework of international organizations, military alliances or coalitions, in the areas where such deployment could be perceived by the other Party as a threat to its national security, with the exception of such deployment within the national territories of the Parties.

The Parties shall refrain from flying heavy bombers equipped for nuclear or non-nuclear armaments or deploying surface warships of any type, including in the framework of international organizations, military alliances or coalitions, in the areas outside national airspace and national territorial waters respectively, from where they can attack targets in the territory of the other Party.

The Parties shall maintain dialogue and cooperate to improve mechanisms to prevent dangerous military activities on and over the high seas, including agreeing on the maximum approach distance between warships and aircraft.

Article 6

The Parties shall undertake not to deploy ground-launched intermediate-range and shorter-range missiles outside their national territories, as well as in the areas of their national territories, from which such weapons can attack targets in the national territory of the other Party.

Article 7

The Parties shall refrain from deploying nuclear weapons outside their national territories and return such weapons already deployed outside their national territories at the time of the entry into force of the Treaty to their national territories. The Parties shall eliminate all existing infrastructure for deployment of nuclear weapons outside their national territories.

The Parties shall not train military and civilian personnel from non-nuclear countries to use nuclear weapons. The Parties shall not conduct exercises or training for general-purpose forces, that include scenarios involving the use of nuclear weapons.'

Excerpt from the draft 'Treaty Between the United States of America and the Russian Federation on Security Guarantees' released by Russia on 17 December 2021.[1]

'President Biden held a secure video call today with President Putin. The call covered a range of issues, but the main topic was Ukraine.

President Biden was direct and straightforward with President Putin, as he always is. He reiterated America's support for Ukraine's sovereignty and territorial integrity.

He told President Putin directly that if Russia further invades Ukraine, the United States and our European allies would respond with strong economic measures. We would provide additional defensive materiel to the Ukrainians above and beyond that which we are already providing. And we would fortify our NATO Allies on the eastern flank with additional capabilities in response to such an escalation.

He also told President Putin there's another option: de-escalation and diplomacy.

The United States and our European allies would engage in a discussion that covers larger strategic issues, including our strategic concerns with Russia and Russia's strategic concerns.

We managed to do this at the height of the Cold War, and we developed mechanisms to help reduce instability and increase transparency.

We've done this in the post-Cold War era through the NATO–Russia Council, the OSCE, and other mechanisms. There's no reason we can't do that … going forward, provided that we are operating in a context of de-escalation rather than escalation.

The United States, as we have been for some time, is also prepared to support efforts to advance the Minsk Agreement in support of the Normandy Format. This could include a ceasefire and confidence-building measures that help drive the process forward.

As I said before, the discussion between President Biden and President Putin was direct and straightforward. There was a lot of give-and-take. There was no finger-wagging. But the President was crystal clear about where the United States stands on all of these issues.'

US National Security Advisor Jake Sullivan briefs reporters following a video call between US President Joe Biden and Russian President Vladimir Putin on 7 December 2021.[2]

'You, Americans, are worried about our battalions, on Russian territory, thousands of kilometres from the United States. But we are truly concerned about our own security.'

Yuri V. Ushakov, an adviser to Putin, describes comments made by the Russian president during his call with Biden.[3]

'Nobody wants to be Putin's slave.'

Vitaly Barabash, mayor of the Ukrainian city of Avdiyivka, which is close to the Russian-controlled city of Donetsk.[4]

Sources

1 Ministry of Foreign Affairs of the Russian Federation, 'Treaty Between the United States of America and the Russian Federation on Security Guarantees', 17 December 2021, https://mid.ru/ru/foreign_policy/rso/nato/1790818/?lang=en.
2 White House, 'Press Briefing by Press Secretary Jen Psaki and National Security Advisor Jake Sullivan, December 7, 2021', https://www.whitehouse.gov/briefing-room/press-briefings/2021/12/07/press-briefing-by-press-secretary-jen-psaki-and-national-security-advisor-jake-sullivan-december-7-2021/.

3 Anton Troianovski, 'Russia Portrays Putin as Rebuffing Biden's Pressure on Ukraine', *New York Times*, 7 December 2021, https://www.nytimes.com/live/2021/12/07/world/biden-putin#russia-portrays-putin-as-rebuffing-bidens-pressure-on-ukraine.
4 Luke Harding, "Nobody Wants to Be Putin's Slave": On the Ukraine Frontline as Tensions Rise', *Guardian*, 10 December 2021, https://www.theguardian.com/world/2021/dec/10/nobody-wants-to-be-putins-slave-on-the-ukraine-frontline-as-tensions-rise.

Alliances and Nuclear Risk: Strengthening US Extended Deterrence

Stephan Frühling and Andrew O'Neil

At the 2021 Munich Security Conference, US President Joe Biden declared that 'America is back' and that 'the United States is determined to earn back our position of trusted leadership'.[1] Yet relations with allies are not the only area in which the new administration seeks to make a break from the recent past. In its 'Interim National Security Strategic Guidance', the administration returned to the Obama-era commitment to 'reduce the role of nuclear weapons in [US] national security strategy'.[2] Key players in the administration have expressed support for abolishing the low-yield warheads on US ballistic-missile submarines that had been introduced following the Trump administration's 2018 Nuclear Posture Review (NPR).[3] Biden himself is on the record as regarding the 'sole purpose' of US nuclear weapons to be deterring nuclear attack.[4] The liberal wing of the Democratic Party, led by Senator Elizabeth Warren, has strongly advocated a no-first-use commitment. The administration's first budget did preserve funding for nuclear modernisation, including low-yield warheads.[5] But influential members of the Democratic arms-control community still see an opportunity to curtail the recapitalisation, size and composition of US strategic nuclear forces.[6] US treaty allies in NATO and the Indo-Pacific regard those forces as crucial to their ultimate security.[7]

Stephan Frühling is a professor in the Strategic and Defence Studies Centre and Associate Dean (Partnerships and Engagement) in the College of Asia and the Pacific at the Australian National University. **Andrew O'Neil** is a professor of political science and Acting Dean of the Graduate Research School at Griffith University.

Survival | vol. 64 no. 1 | February–March 2022 | pp. 77–98   https://doi.org/10.1080/00396338.2022.2032969

Under the Trump administration, US nuclear policy, in notable contrast to other foreign-policy areas, was remarkable for how little controversy it attracted among US allies. The 2018 NPR stayed well within the NATO consensus on the need to adapt Alliance nuclear forces, and Japan publicly appreciated the fact that it 'clearly articulates the US resolve to ensure the effectiveness of its deterrence and its commitment to providing extended deterrence to its allies'.[8] However, the existential dependence of US allies on nuclear-policy and -posture decisions taken in Washington has long been a source of tension in US alliances, from US secretary of defense Robert McNamara's challenge to NATO's nuclear strategy of massive retaliation in the early 1960s to Barack Obama's first-term commitment to reduce the role of nuclear weapons in the face of rising nuclear threats in Northeast Asia.

Many in the Biden administration appear to regard the 2022 NPR as an occasion to reduce the role of nuclear weapons in US strategy, in declaratory as well as practical terms, to an even greater extent than in the Obama administration. The Washington arms-control establishment has echoed this approach, with two leading figures asserting that, with respect to a US sole-purpose declaration, 'allies cannot have a veto over US policy'.[9] This approach risks opening gaps with US allies that Biden seeks to re-engage. In Europe, while some governments and populations have always preferred a lesser role for nuclear weapons in NATO strategy, in practice they have consistently valued Alliance consensus on major questions of nuclear strategy.[10] In the Indo-Pacific, maintaining the credibility of US nuclear guarantees in Seoul and Tokyo has become increasingly difficult, as some South Korean security experts have called for the reintroduction of US tactical nuclear weapons and even for resurrecting the country's own nuclear-weapons development programme.[11] In Australia, Kevin Rudd, the former prime minister whose government in 2008 co-sponsored the Australian–Japanese International Commission on Nuclear Non-proliferation and Disarmament, has expressed support for an Asian Nuclear Planning Group in which Australia, Japan, South Korea and the United States would 'discuss specific policies associated with US nuclear forces and conduct war games and exercises, including those involving the highest political-level participation'.[12]

The credibility and purpose of US nuclear strategy

The stage now seems set for US nuclear policy to, once more, significantly challenge the political cohesion of US alliances. This is an inevitable consequence of the fundamentally dependent relationship that non-nuclear allies have with the United States. Domestic American debates on nuclear policy naturally emphasise strategic and operational considerations of the use or non-use of US capabilities in terms of the costs and risks of a given nuclear strategy to the United States. From a US perspective, questions of sufficiency primarily relate to nuclear capability in relation to likely scenarios for nuclear use and non-nuclear US options, with parenthetical consideration given to reassuring US allies. Reassurance amounts to either symbolic gestures or institutional attempts to convince allies of the sufficiency of US policy and capability for deterrence and damage limitation.

Due to their different geographic locations, the United States and its allies differ in their emphasis on generic, global nuclear risks and regional nuclear conflict, and in their assessment of the costs of escalating regionally confined conflict to nuclear use.[13] From the perspective of allies whose survival ultimately depends on extended US deterrence, US decisions about nuclear policy are primarily an indication of the United States' willingness to bear the costs and risks of its alliances. In this sense, a robust declaratory policy, in addition to an adequate force structure and posture, is necessary to maintain the credibility of US commitments.

Current US debates regarding no first use tend to underplay the broader alliance implications of any shift in US nuclear policy. In its overall enthusiasm for devaluing the role of nuclear weapons, the Biden administration may ask allies to dilute the nuclear dimension inherent in American extended-deterrence commitments. The timing of such an approach would be particularly poor in the case of America's Indo-Pacific allies, who are looking for confirmation of US resolve in the face of China's seeming inexorable rise to regional military dominance.[14] Ever-greater strain in articulating the strategic sufficiency or narrow distinction between different versions of no-first-use or sole-purpose declarations characterises current US debates.[15] These miss the point that the main challenge for current US nuclear policy, from an allied perspective, is ultimately political and that it needs to address risks that are specific to adversaries rather than globally generic.

At the same time, the United States and its allies need to think very deliberately and operationally about how and when nuclear weapons should be employed in the common defence. As crises involving nuclear powers in Europe and the Indo-Pacific escalate, nuclear weapons and beliefs about the likelihood and consequences of their use will inevitably be central to decisions on all sides. This is no mere academic discussion. Vince Manzo and John Warden have noted: 'If a conflict breaks out in Asia or Europe, an adversary of the United States and its allies may believe that it can conduct limited nuclear strikes and, rather than precipitate its own destruction, win the war – not in the sense of defeating the United States militarily, but by convincing Washington to refrain from bringing its full strategic-military power to bear on the conflict.'[16]

There are some indications that Chinese and Russian analysts suspect that Washington will force allies to back down during crises to avoid escalation to nuclear use and that US alliances, including NATO, lack the resolve to escalate and risk nuclear war even if their strategic interests are directly threatened.[17] Brad Roberts observes that 'the credibility of US promises to defend its allies from attack and to respond as necessary, perhaps even with nuclear weapons if the vital interests of those allies are put at risk, has eroded in recent years'.[18] Instances in which the US has pressured allies to de-escalate or failed to provide leadership in response to specific cases of aggression have reinforced this point. Motivated by a fear of entrapment, for example, the Obama administration in 2010 urged South Korea not to escalate its response to a North Korean artillery attack on South Korean territory.[19]

The United States and its European and Indo-Pacific allies therefore need to work much harder at making deterrence in the nuclear domain more relevant and credible in the face of the threats they now confront. This requires looking beyond the next round of arms-control talks and potential confidence-building measures to the nuts and bolts of nuclear strategy in a regional context, as great-power competition between the US and its rivals continues to intensify. Devising a more systematic and integrated approach to nuclear strategy and determining how this strategy interacts with crisis and escalation management are crucial. As a follow-on action from the next NPR, the Biden administration, together with US allies, should examine three key questions about the role of nuclear weapons in US extended deterrence: how does the balance in strategic nuclear forces relate to the security of US allies? How can US extended deterrence control risks of inadvertent escalation while also imposing them on adversaries? And should extended deterrence include the threat of limited nuclear use?

Allied security and the nuclear balance

During the 1950s, clear US nuclear superiority over the Soviet Union allowed the United States to threaten 'massive retaliation' against the Warsaw Pact for any major attack on US allies. As the US homeland became vulnerable to Soviet retaliation, however, that strategy lost credibility.

The emergence of parity, or strategic equivalence, between the superpowers led to arguments that questions of superiority and inferiority in the nuclear age were essentially redundant.[20] According to this perspective, mutual assured destruction was a reality in the sense that the sole purpose of nuclear weapons was deterring war between the major powers. Moreover, if the United States strove for superiority, this would have the effect of triggering strategic instability because Moscow would come to perceive that the US was preparing to strike first.[21] This worry did not stop US administrations from Richard Nixon's through to Ronald Reagan's from seeking operationally credible nuclear options in targeting and force planning.[22]

Yet, as Washington convinced itself that the loss of superiority was ultimately irrelevant, tensions in US nuclear policy merely shifted to the question of how the United States could maintain the credibility of extended nuclear deterrence under conditions of nuclear parity, a challenge that bedevilled allies until the end of the Cold War. While the NATO Alliance, with the notable exception of France, agreed on the new concept of 'flexible response' (or, more accurately, deliberate escalation) in 1967, the commonly used formulation that NATO would use nuclear weapons 'as late as possible, and as early as necessary' was a thinly disguised placeholder for underlying questions that were never fully resolved. During the latter part of the Cold War, the credibility of extended nuclear deterrence thus rested somewhat uneasily on what Josef Joffe called 'the First Commandment of Extended Deterrence Under Conditions of Parity – there shall be no sanctuaries'.[23]

'No sanctuaries' meant that the vulnerability of the US homeland – ensured by the size of Soviet nuclear forces and the limits placed on strategic defences by the 1972 Anti-Ballistic Missile Treaty – essentially offered up the US population as a hostage to allied security. In addition, allies sought the coupling of European security to the use of US strategic nuclear forces in a way that would make it difficult for the United States to address its own vulnerability by limiting a nuclear conflict to the territory of its allies. European interpretations of NATO's 1967 Strategic Concept as 'seamless' or 'gapless' deterrence required that any conflict in Europe entail unacceptable risks of escalation to the territory of both superpowers.[24]

Uncertainty about how committed the United States was to these conditions exacerbated European concerns about the Carter administration's approach to the SALT II negotiations in the late 1970s, and led NATO in its 'dual track' decision of 1979 to strengthen coupling by deploying new intermediate-range nuclear forces in Western Europe that could target the Soviet Union itself. For Europeans, however, the Reagan administration's pursuit of the Strategic Defense Initiative and its willingness to fully embrace the 'zero option' for the Intermediate-Range Nuclear Forces Treaty at the 1986 Reykjavik Summit demonstrated the shallowness of the US commitment to ensure the credibility of extended deterrence. NATO ended the Cold War with a significant disagreement on nuclear strategy that was simply cut short by the fall of the Soviet empire but never resolved.[25]

What strategic factors might make the threat of use of US strategic nuclear weapons on behalf of its allies today credible? In Europe, the contours of Cold War coupling remain embedded in NATO policy, force structure and US–Russian strategic relations. Numerical parity between US and Russian strategic nuclear forces has remained an important principle of the Strategic Arms Reduction Treaty (START) and its successors since the end of the Cold War, and US missile defences would not be a meaningful obstacle to a major Russian attack on the North American continent. Until 2014, the coupling role of remaining US forward-based nuclear forces in Europe was at best perfunctorily articulated, as political placation rather than genuine strategic posturing.[26] But as NATO now borders Russia itself, even relatively short-range dual-capable aircraft would allow NATO to conduct nuclear strikes against Russia's homeland, which would carry the risk of further escalation to the use of strategic nuclear forces. NATO summit communiqués since 2016 have resumed explicitly stating that British and French nuclear forces strengthen deterrence because having 'separate centres of decision-making' serves to 'complicate the calculations of potential adversaries'.[27] Nevertheless, the unspoken benefit for allied security is that they also potentially constrain Washington's ability to limit a nuclear conflict.

In the Indo-Pacific, however, the link between allied security and credible threats of the use of US strategic forces remains less clear and institutionalised than it is in Europe.[28] Since the withdrawal of US nuclear weapons from South Korea and their removal from US Navy attack submarines and surface ships in 1991, there have been no US nuclear forces that could perform a coupling role in the Indo-Pacific. China remains far from nuclear parity with the United States, but its increasing capacity to strike a wider target set across the US mainland with nuclear weapons, as well as North Korea's development of a long-range missile that can reach the continental United States with a nuclear warhead, has raised critical questions about whether Washington would accept the risk of escalation on behalf of regional allies.[29] In essence, continued US insistence that strategic nuclear forces based in North America can provide credible extended deterrence in Asia assumes that the coupling role of forward-based nuclear forces is only strategically necessary to address situations of nuclear parity, and not those in which an adversary has merely acquired a capacity for assured destruction.

China remains far from nuclear parity with the US

In this context, it is worth remembering that the major Cold War crisis of confidence in the credibility of US extended deterrence in NATO arose after the Soviets acquired an assured-destruction capability in the 1960s, not when they reached parity a decade later. Similar concerns now fuel anxiety in Seoul and Tokyo, manifested in their opposition to any shift in US policy towards no first use or acknowledgement of mutual vulnerability with

Beijing. Sugio Takahashi, a leading Japanese strategist, has argued that the latter would effectively undermine trust in the US–Japan alliance, even as the reality of US vulnerability has increased the importance of the conventional and nuclear in-theatre balance.[30] A sense of strategic uncertainty among US allies in Northeast Asia has emerged, reflected in military acquisition programmes and political rhetoric in South Korea and Japan that imply nuclear hedging.[31]

Controlling and creating risks of inadvertent escalation

Escalation risks are intrinsic to nuclear strategy and featured prominently in the calculations of policymakers during the Cold War. Indeed, the potential for deliberate or inadvertent escalation lies at the heart of nuclear deterrence. Kerry Kartchner and Michael Gerson observe: 'If nuclear weapons are a force for peace between nuclear-armed states, it is in large part because of the possibility of vertical escalation – from conventional to nuclear conflict, from limited to general war, from counterforce to countermilitary to countervalue targets.'[32] Along with accidental escalation resulting from miscalculation based on technical error, inadvertent escalation – that is, escalation that is deliberate but based on mistaken assumptions – is often seen as the most probable pathway to nuclear war.[33] Escalation can be inadvertent in two different ways. Firstly, a country could assume it is (or is about to be) under nuclear attack when that is not the case – for instance, by misidentifying incoming warheads.[34] Secondly, it could interpret conventional attacks on its forces or command-and-control systems as an attempt to disable its nuclear arsenal.[35]

China's nuclear posture reflects concerns about disarming US (and potentially Russian) strikes.[36] Co-mingling conventional and nuclear forces in operational deployments and broadening the range of nuclear-capable forces through dual conventional and nuclear capability help address such concerns. Recent scholarship has pointed to the escalatory risks associated with the dual-use attributes of China's mobile land-based missiles in particular, and DF-21 and D-26 medium- and intermediate-range ballistic missiles reportedly have actual or planned capability for conventional and nuclear missions.[37] The co-mingling of nuclear and conventional capabilities raises the questions of whether the US, in the fog of a crisis over Taiwan, would be capable of distinguishing a defensive dispersal of Chinese nuclear-capable missiles from preparation to launch a first strike against US or allied targets, and whether Washington's concerns about inadvertent escalation would lead it to restrict and constrain conventional operations against China's missile force.[38]

It is very likely that China and Russia have deliberately co-mingled their nuclear and conventional military systems on the assumption that the US would not risk nuclear escalation in the midst of a crisis. Unlike their US counterparts, 'Chinese leaders believe that nuclear weapons are "paper tigers", and because of the taboo against the use of nuclear weapons, they are unlikely to be used'.[39] In this respect, US views on inadvertent escalation and nuclear risk become relevant in assessing the credibility of US conventional deterrence as well. To offset doubts about US resolve among allies, the Biden administration needs to signal a willingness to hold adversary targets at risk as required to prevail in any regional conflict, including in cases where these targets are likely to be dual-use and whose destruction would carry risks of inadvertent escalation to nuclear war. This should not involve issuing threats of major escalation in response to minor or even moderate escalation from adversaries, but the United States must be able, as Kartchner and Gerson write, to 'threaten lower-level actions that, if executed, risk starting an uncertain process that could lead to further escalation'.[40]

Put another way, for the sake of its alliances, US policymakers need to focus more on how Washington can dominate or at least credibly implement escalation pathways, and less on how to avoid escalation. In the Indo-Pacific, these considerations reinforce the importance of the US national missile-defence system and general damage-limitation capabilities of US strategic forces against China.[41] In Europe, in response to the threat from Russia's mixture of conventional and nuclear forces, NATO members agreed in 2021 to 'strengthened integrated air and missile defence; advanced defensive and offensive conventional capabilities; steps to keep NATO's nuclear deterrent safe, secure, and effective; efforts to support and strengthen arms control, disarmament, and non-proliferation; intelligence; and exercises'.[42] They also reinforced the importance of Alliance integrated air and missile defence.[43]

If the US wishes to avoid a situation in which serious questions are raised about the credibility of its extended-deterrence guarantees – and by association the strength of its alliances worldwide – it must be willing to risk a nuclear exchange. Past NPRs have argued that improved conventional capabilities can help the United States reduce its reliance on nuclear weapons. But if the US is to fight a conventional war against nuclear-armed peer powers, it also has to address the vulnerability of conventional forces to nuclear attack and understand that the ability to manage nuclear escalation through nuclear deterrence influences the strategic credibility of the use of its conventional forces. The next NPR should therefore avoid stating or implying that escalation must be avoided if it runs the risk of inadvertently triggering a nuclear exchange, and articulate how the totality of US forces – not just nuclear systems – needs to evolve to manage and ultimately reduce the risk of nuclear conflict.

The NPR should also consider not just the risks but also the benefits of dual-capable systems insofar as the challenges they pose to the United States are also challenges for the adversary. Despite the dubious reputation of conventional–nuclear ambiguity in current strategic debates, the United States is not averse to exploiting it for its own purposes. Using B-2 and B-52 aircraft to fly reassurance missions in the Indo-Pacific and Europe certainly blurs the conventional–nuclear distinction. With such flights over the Korean Peninsula following provocations by North Korea, Washington deliberately used nuclear-capable platforms to amplify Pyongyang's historical fear of strategic bombing as well as to underscore its lack of high-quality air-defence and early-warning systems.[44]

Beyond signalling, the ability of dual-capable systems to complicate the risk calculus for adversaries' conventional counterforce campaigns will become increasingly important.[45] During the second half of the Cold War, NATO atomic demolition munitions and nuclear artillery were particularly useful in this regard, as they were deployed close to the front line and forced the Soviet Union to consider the risk of inadvertent nuclear escalation in contemplating a conventional offensive through NATO's Central Front.[46] In Europe, dispersal of NATO dual-capable aircraft in a crisis maintains some of this deterrent effect against widespread Russian attacks on NATO airfields. China, at present, does not have to contend with any such risks. Placing B-61 nuclear weapons on airfields in the Indo-Pacific, and nuclear cruise missiles on US attack submarines, would place the onus on Beijing, too, to manage risks of inadvertent escalation in contemplating any major attack on the United States and its allies.

Extended deterrence and the threat of limited nuclear use

A key element of the 2018 NPR was the argument that the United States needed new 'complementary' low-yield warheads 'to deny potential adversaries any mistaken confidence that limited nuclear employment can provide a useful advantage over the United States and its allies'.[47] Limited nuclear use raises both epistemological questions (would it be possible to keep nuclear escalation controlled and hence keep nuclear use limited?) and ontological ones (should deterrence be based on threats of limited use?), even though the distinction easily gets lost in practice. The answers to these questions are also not independent, insofar as a belief that escalation could not be controlled would make a policy of limited use redundant and, conversely, a policy based on unlimited use would itself make controlling escalation more difficult. Add to this the fact that a 'limited' nuclear war would be basically unlimited for front-line allies on whose territory a nuclear war was fought, and it is not surprising that the question of limited nuclear use has been one of the most vexing issues in the US and Alliance debates on nuclear deterrence since the 1950s.

In many respects, US nuclear strategy has been a search for means to keep even general nuclear war limited.[48] Most directly relevant for US alliances was the question of what role, if any, limited use of nuclear weapons would play on the escalation pathway from regional conflict in Europe to global nuclear war. By the mid-1960s, European NATO allies (except France) had followed Washington in moving beyond ideas of massive retaliation that rejected any limitations on the use of nuclear weapons. This did not mean, however, that they shared McNamara's conviction that nuclear war could not be limited, and therefore had to be avoided at almost any cost through a prolonged and robust conventional defence. Instead, the 1967 concept of flexible response assumed that there was scope for deliberate escalation below the level of general war, and hence the possibility of limited nuclear use, which therefore had some strategic utility.[49]

The guidelines on nuclear-weapons employment that allies endorsed in the NATO Nuclear Planning Group in the 1970s in fact reflected European preferences for early use, which emphasised its political rather than military effect and even included the possibility of a 'demonstration' event. By the 1980s, the Reagan administration had tilted towards military logic as the guiding principle, which implied employing nuclear weapons to dominate specific levels of escalation and even 'winning' the battle in Europe.[50]

After the Cold War, these questions quickly faded as the Soviet threat disappeared. Rather than look to limited nuclear use to 're-establish deterrence' and shape the escalation of a conflict, the United States and NATO simply considered any nuclear use to be 'extremely remote'.[51] Concerns about 'self-deterrence' due to the perceived lack of credibility of using relatively large-yield warheads against 'rogue states' led to proposals for new, low-yield warheads in the 2002 NPR, but this debate remained largely confined to the United States and ultimately foundered on congressional discord.[52]

Questions of limited nuclear use have returned

As the role of US nuclear weapons in managing conflict and competition with Russia, China and North Korea has returned to the foreground of Alliance relations, the ontological and epistemological questions of limited nuclear use have also returned, together with the fact that the costs of limited use could be very different for different allies. Russia's implicit nuclear coercion of NATO (as well as Sweden) suggests that nuclear use today is less remote than assumed in the 1990s and 2000s.[53] It raises the risk that Russia may be able to derive strategic gains from presenting credible threats that NATO cannot directly answer. Whether this means that Russia's threshold for nuclear use has been lowered, and that Moscow might conduct limited nuclear strikes to 'de-escalate' a conflict with NATO, remains a contested proposition.[54] But the 2021 NATO summit communiqué highlights the fact that allies are becoming more concerned about, and resolved to resist, Russian nuclear coercion, and to adapt the Alliance's deterrence posture in order to do so.[55] In this context, the Trump administration's decision in the 2018 NPR to introduce a low-yield version of the W76 warhead on US ballistic-missile submarines, and to develop a new low-yield warhead for submarine-launched cruise missiles, found general support among European allies.[56] In particular, the W76-2 embodies formidable operational characteristics – to wit, low yield, fast response time and penetration capability – that did not previously exist in the US nuclear arsenal.

Overall, the Trump administration's position was that the danger of adversaries contemplating nuclear use was not sufficiently remote to be discounted, and that the United States had to be prepared to use nuclear weapons to reinforce deterrence, even as it explicitly did not subscribe to the notion that nuclear war could or should remain limited.[57] This position leaves how the United States would react to limited nuclear use obscured behind the rhetorical veil, invoked by both the United States and NATO, that any adversary's use of nuclear weapons would 'fundamentally alter the nature of a conflict'.[58] From the standpoint of deterrence, ambiguity is often seen as an advantage, but here it may, on balance, be a weakness. Unsurprisingly, the few US analysts who have examined this question in detail remain, as during the Cold War, strongly concerned with keeping nuclear exchanges geographically confined to the territory of US allies and away from the US homeland – some to the point of hinting that perhaps even Russia itself should at first be considered a sanctuary even after it initiates nuclear warfare.[59] Likewise, concerns about the limited number (or 'magazine depth') of US low-yield warheads also speak to a US desire to keep nuclear use limited and avoid escalation to higher-yield warheads that might increase the risk of retaliation against the US homeland.[60] US nuclear policy continues to state that achieving US objectives should deterrence fail remains one of the fundamental tasks for US forces. But, at least in unclassified settings, US policymakers have remained silent on how to balance limiting damage to allies against limiting damage to the United States itself.[61]

During the Cold War, these questions caused divisive debate within NATO. Contemporary NATO has not reached that point. Russia is just one among several threats it faces, and allies have found it politically and intellectually easier to focus on political guidance for crisis management rather than actual operations. Alliance policymakers are also humbled by the realisation, in light of Warsaw Pact plans revealed after 1991 contemplating the widespread use of nuclear weapons, that NATO's endless Cold War debates regarding limited use were only tenuously connected to the likely shape that a conflict would have taken.[62] But if the Biden administration rolled back the current US position of preparing for limited war in order to not have to fight – either formally in declaratory policy or de facto by refraining from deploying the new W76-2 warheads – it is not obvious what alternative policy could replace it and still bridge the different concerns of Washington and its allies on how to deter an adversary's limited nuclear use.

Moreover, while the new complementary capabilities in the 2018 NPR were justified by developments in Russia's nuclear posture, their introduction also has strategic effects in the Indo-Pacific. Arguably, the reaction speed and low yield of the W76-2 provide a new capability at a limited level of escalation to meet the threat of North Korean nuclear use against US allies. Limited use of nuclear weapons by China, however, is a less immediate concern for US allies and Taiwan than the overall conventional balance, which increasingly calls into question the ability of the United States to prevail in a conflict in the Western Pacific. Recent war gaming indicates a range of scenarios in which the US and its allies could lose decisively against China.[63] In this light, as Vince Manzo and John Warden point out, 'nuclear weapons could improve US chances of efficiently destroying certain massed, fleeting, mobile or hardened targets, or compensate for the reduced effectiveness of US conventional forces'.[64] This possibility is particularly relevant given the maritime nature of the Indo-Pacific theatre, where nuclear strikes against Chinese surface fleets would avoid many of the disadvantages – such as massive collateral damage and the possibility of miscalculation as to US intentions – that strikes against the Chinese or Russian homelands would risk. Whereas a Chinese amphibious invasion across the Taiwan Strait might become feasible against modern conventional forces on the island, US use of nuclear weapons would surely consign such an attempt to failure.

Hard realities

In 2018, the US National Defense Strategy Commission noted that: 'Regional military balances in Eastern Europe, the Middle East, and the Western Pacific have shifted in decidedly adverse ways. These trends are undermining deterrence of US adversaries and the confidence of American allies … The U.S. military … might struggle to win, or perhaps lose, a war against China or Russia'.[65] A US defeat in a regional war would be a disaster for American allies directly involved in the conflict, but it would also have negative long-term implications for US allies worldwide. There is thus a clear and compelling need to articulate and strengthen the contribution of US nuclear weapons to deterring Chinese, Russian and potentially North Korean coercion and attack.

A prerequisite is to acknowledge that for the US to devalue nuclear weapons in its national strategy would be at odds with the range and scope of threats Washington and its allies now confront. Indeed, US debates on nuclear policy are driven more by rehashed arguments from arms-control advocates than by serious analysis of the challenges from China, North Korea and Russia.[66] Reducing the role of nuclear weapons is of course an important aspect of advancing nuclear disarmament. But just as Obama conditioned his vision of that goal with the acknowledgement that he did not expect it to be reached in his lifetime, allies – including the United States – have in recent years started to acknowledge the significant trade-offs involved, as when NATO governments stated their 'regret that the conditions for achieving disarmament are not favourable today', and that the Treaty on the Prohibition of Nuclear Weapons 'does not reflect the increasingly challenging international security environment'.[67]

At best, pursuing a lesser role for nuclear weapons in an environment in which hostile peer competitors are combining ambitious conventional- and nuclear-force modernisation programmes with increasingly aggressive strategic postures skirts the psychological reality that reassuring US allies in Europe and the Indo-Pacific will require greater, not lesser, emphasis on the potential for US nuclear escalation. At worst, it would signal that alliances and the security of allies are now simply of less concern to the United States, combining the worst aspects of Trump's isolationism and Obama's idealism.

*　　　*　　　*

Given the growing threat of nuclear-armed great powers against US allies, the Biden administration must explain more credibly and explicitly how US nuclear weapons can support allied security and strengthen US alliances in Europe and the Indo-Pacific. The bland and generic framing of 'reassurance' and 'extended deterrence' is not enough. A recent report by the Chicago Council on Global Affairs provides some sensible suggestions on possible new initiatives, including the establishment of an Asian Nuclear Planning Group.[68] Key to strengthening deterrence and US alliances is recognition that, ultimately, credible extended deterrence turns on the United States' willingness to assume risks of nuclear escalation on behalf of its allies. That is the fundamental challenge that an Asian Nuclear Planning Group – like its counterpart in NATO – would have to manage in addressing the role of nuclear weapons in Indo-Pacific alliances.

Forward-based nuclear forces are a central element in coupling allied and US security, creating risks of entanglement for the adversary and addressing adversary threats of limited use. NATO has such forces. In the NPR, the US should present for consideration the possibility of forward-basing nuclear weapons in the Indo-Pacific, as well as stationing dual-capable aircraft there, perhaps including some with South Korean and Japanese crews that are certified to carry out nuclear missions.[69] Given the relative lack of strategic buffer between South Korea and North Korea, and between China and the southern islands of Japan, even relatively short-range dual-capable aircraft systems could fulfil an important coupling role. As an operational expression of Washington's willingness to give allies some say in the avoidance of nuclear sanctuaries during a conflict, such forces would compel adversaries to take seriously the role of US nuclear capabilities in a major conflict. This dispensation would introduce escalation risks that China currently does not face into any counterforce campaign against the US and its allies.

Entrapment dynamics are an unavoidable feature of alliances. Critics may point to risks to the US of becoming trapped in regional conflicts if allies escalate unilaterally so as to pressure the US to resort to nuclear options sooner than Washington would prefer. But the flip side of the alliance security dilemma are fears of abandonment that might induce junior partners to take measures to mitigate perceived risks that a great-power ally might not defend their security at the moment of truth. Nuclear proliferation in the Indo-Pacific or bandwagoning with Beijing are hardly in Washington's interest. These challenges cannot be wished away, and today the case for increasing the prospects for nuclear escalation to enhance the credibility of US extended deterrence in the eyes of allies and adversaries alike is far stronger than it was a decade ago. For America's alliances to have strategic substance, its allies need to be convinced that US nuclear strategy is geared towards protecting their security in regional contingencies as well as protecting the American homeland.

Notes

1   White House, 'Remarks by President Biden at the 2021 Virtual Munich Security Conference, 19 February 2021', https://www.whitehouse.gov/briefing-room/speeches-remarks/2021/02/19/remarks-by-president-biden-at-the-2021-virtual-munich-security-conference/.

2   President Joseph R. Biden, Jr, 'Interim National Security Strategic Guidance', White House, March 2021, p. 13, https://www.whitehouse.gov/wp-content/uploads/2021/03/NSC-1v2.pdf.

3   See Bryan Bender, 'Biden's Arms Control Team Eyes Nuclear Policy Overhaul', *Politico*, 27 January 2021, https://www.politico.com/news/2021/01/27/biden-nuclear-weapons-policy-463335.

4   Joseph R. Biden, Jr, 'Why America Must Lead Again: Rescuing US Foreign Policy After Trump', *Foreign Affairs*, vol. 99, no. 2, March/April 2020, p. 75, https://www.foreignaffairs.com/articles/united-states/2020-01-23/why-america-must-lead-again.

5   See Lara Seligman, Bryan Bender and Connor O'Brien, 'Biden Goes "Full Steam Ahead" on Trump's Nuclear Expansion Despite Campaign Rhetoric', *Politico*, 2 June 2021, https://www.politico.com/news/2021/06/02/biden-trump-nuclear-weapons-491631.

6   See Joe Gould, 'Washington's Battle over Nuclear Weapons Budget Already Underway', *Defense News*, 22 March 2021, https://www.defensenews.com/congress/2021/03/22/battle-over-nuclear-weapons-budget-already-underway/.

7   The statement that 'the strategic forces of the Alliance, particularly those of the United States, are the supreme guarantee of the security of Allies' is standard in NATO summit communiqués, most recently in NATO, 'Brussels Summit Communiqué', 14 June 2021, para. 50,

https://www.nato.int/cps/en/natohq/
news_185000.htm.

8   Ministry of Foreign Affairs of Japan,
    'The Release of the US Nuclear
    Posture Review (NPR) (Statement by
    Foreign Minister Taro Kono)', press
    release, 3 February 2018, https://
    www.mofa.go.jp/press/release/
    press4e_001893.html.

9   'A New Nuclear Policy for the Biden
    Administration: Reducing the Risk
    of Accidental War and Maintaining
    Deterrence for Less', Statement of
    William Perry and Tom Collina Before
    the Senate Armed Services Committee
    Strategic Forces Subcommittee,
    Senate Armed Services Committee, 16
    June 2021, p. 3, https://www.armed-
    services.senate.gov/imo/media/doc/
    Perry-Collina%20statement%20to%20
    SASC%206-16.pdf.

10 See Amelia Morgan and Anna
    Peczeli (eds), 'Europe's Evolving
    Deterrence Discourse', Center for
    Global Security Research, Lawrence
    Livermore Laboratory, King's College
    London and Science Applications
    International Corporation, February
    2021, https://www.kcl.ac.uk/csss/
    assets/europes-evolving-deterrence-
    discourse.pdf. As Hans Binnendijk
    and David Gompert point out, despite
    the greater prominence of nuclear
    forces in recent NATO communiqués,
    NATO currently does not clearly state
    that adversary nuclear use would be
    met with a nuclear response. Hans
    Binnendijk and David Gompert,
    'Decisive Response: A New Nuclear
    Strategy for NATO', Survival, vol. 61,
    no. 5, October–November 2019, p. 118.

11 See, for example, Duyeon Kim,
    'How to Keep South Korea from

Going Nuclear', Bulletin of the Atomic
Scientists, vol. 76, no. 2, February 2020,
pp. 68–75.

12 Chicago Council on Global Affairs,
    'Task Force Report: Preventing
    Nuclear Proliferation and Reassuring
    America's Allies', Lester Crown
    Center on US Foreign Policy, February
    2021, https://www.thechicagocouncil.
    org/sites/default/files/2021-02/report_
    preventing-nuclear-proliferation-
    reassuring-americas-allies_0.pdf.

13 See Stephan Frühling, 'Managing
    Escalation: Missile Defence, Strategy
    and US Alliances', International Affairs,
    vol. 92, no. 1, January 2016, p. 84.

14 See Ashley Townshend, 'Biden's
    Defense Budget Will Worry
    America's Indo-Pacific Allies',
    Defense One, 22 June 2021, https://
    www.defenseone.com/ideas/2021/06/
    bidens-defense-budget-will-worry-
    americas-indo-pacific-allies/174870/.

15 See, for example, Ankit Panda and
    Vipin Narang, 'Sole Purpose Is Not
    No First Use', War on the Rocks, 22
    February 2021, https://warontherocks.
    com/2021/02/sole-purpose-is-not-
    no-first-use-nuclear-weapons-and-
    declaratory-policy/.

16 Vince A. Manzo and John K. Warden,
    'After Nuclear First Use, What?',
    Survival, vol. 60, no 3, June–July 2018,
    p. 133.

17 See Fiona Cunningham and M. Taylor
    Fravel, 'Dangerous Confidence?
    Chinese Views on Nuclear Escalation',
    International Security, vol. 44, no. 2,
    Fall 2019, p. 75; and Katarzyna Zysk,
    'Escalation and Nuclear Weapons
    in Russia's Military Strategy', RUSI
    Journal, vol. 163, no. 2, May 2018, p. 3.

18 Brad Roberts, 'Living with a Nuclear-

arming North Korea: Deterrence Decisions in a Deteriorating Threat Environment', 38 North, Special Report, 4 November 2020, https://www.38north.org/reports/2020/11/broberts110320/.

19 See Robert M. Gates, *Duty: Memoirs of a Secretary at War* (New York: Alfred A. Knopf, 2014), p. 497.

20 By 1974, Henry Kissinger, then secretary of state, observed during arms-control negotiations with the Soviet Union that 'one of the questions which we have to ask ourselves as a country is what in the name of God is strategic superiority? What is the significance of it, politically, militarily, operationally, at these levels of numbers? What do you do with it?' Quoted in Murrey Marder, 'Summit Clouded by Watergate', *Washington Post*, 4 July 1974, https://www.washingtonpost.com/wp-srv/inatl/longterm/summit/archive/july74.htm.

21 See Charles L. Glaser, *Analyzing Strategic Nuclear Policy* (Princeton, NJ: Princeton University Press, 1990), pp. 44–55.

22 See Desmond Ball and Robert C. Toth, 'Revising the SIOP: Taking War-fighting to Dangerous Extremes', *International Security*, vol. 14, no. 4, Spring 1990, pp. 65–92.

23 Josef Joffe, *The Limited Partnership: Europe, the United States and the Burdens of Alliance* (Cambridge, MA: Ballinger, 1987), p. 146.

24 See Ivo H. Daalder, *The Nature and Practice of Flexible Response: NATO Strategy and Theater Nuclear Forces Since 1967* (New York: Columbia University Press, 1991), pp. 40–69.

25 See Thomas E. Halverson, *The Last Great Nuclear Debate: NATO and Short-range Nuclear Weapons in the 1980s* (Houndsmills: Macmillan, 1995).

26 See Andrew Futter, 'NATO, Ballistic Missile Defense and the Future of US Tactical Nuclear Weapons in Europe', *European Security*, vol. 20, no. 4, December 2011, p. 557.

27 See NATO, 'Warsaw Summit Communiqué', 9 July 2016, para. 53, https://www.nato.int/cps/en/natohq/official_texts_133169.htm. The 'separate centres of decision making' theme can be traced back to NATO's Ottawa Summit in 1974.

28 See Michito Tsuruoka, 'Why the NATO Nuclear Debate Is Relevant to Japan and Vice Versa', Policy Brief, German Marshall Fund of the United States, 8 October 2010, https://www.gmfus.org/publications/why-nato-nuclear-debate-relevant-japan-and-vice-versa.

29 See, for example, Choi Jung Hoon, 'North Korea's Advanced Nuclear Weapons and US Extended Deterrence for Japan: An Assessment Based on Nuclear Deterrence Theory', *Journal of the Asia–Japan Research Institute of Ritsumeikan University*, vol. 3, 2021, pp. 109–34.

30 See Takahashi Sugio, 'Redefining Strategic Stability: A Japanese View', in James Schoff and Li Bin (eds), *A Precarious Triangle: US–China Strategic Stability and Japan* (Washington DC: Carnegie Endowment for International Peace, 7 November 2017), https://carnegieendowment.org/2017/11/07/redefining-strategic-stability-japanese-view-pub-74631.

31 See Eric Heginbotham and Richard Samuels, 'Vulnerable US Alliances

in Northeast Asia: The Nuclear Implications', *Washington Quarterly*, vol. 44, no. 1, Spring 2021, pp. 157–75.

32 Kerry M. Kartchner and Michael S. Gerson, 'Escalation to Limited Nuclear War in the 21st Century', in Jeffrey A. Larsen and Kerry M. Kartchner (eds), *On Limited Nuclear War in the 21st Century* (Stanford, CA: Stanford University Press, 2014), p. 152.

33 See International Commission on Nuclear Non-proliferation and Disarmament, 'Eliminating Nuclear Threats: A Practical Agenda for Global Policymakers', 2009, pp. 26–9, http://www.icnnd.org/reference/reports/ent/pdf/ICNND_Report-EliminatingNuclearThreats.pdf.

34 See James M. Acton, 'Is It a Nuke? Pre-launch Ambiguity and Inadvertent Escalation', Carnegie Endowment for International Peace, 2020, https://carnegieendowment.org/files/Acton_NukeorNot_final.pdf.

35 See James M. Acton, 'Cyber Warfare and Inadvertent Escalation', *Daedalus*, vol. 149, no. 2, Spring 2020, pp. 133–49.

36 See M. Taylor Fravel, *Active Defense: China's Military Strategy Since 1949* (Princeton, NJ: Princeton University Press, 2019), pp. 266–7.

37 See David C. Logan, 'Are They Reading Schelling in Beijing? The Dimensions, Drivers, and Risks of Nuclear–Conventional Entanglement in China', *Journal of Strategic Studies*, published online 12 November 2020, https://scholar.princeton.edu/sites/default/files/dlogan/files/logan_david_-_are_they_reading_schelling_in_beijing_-_jss_accepted.pdf; and Caitlin Talmadge, 'Would China Go Nuclear? Assessing the Risk of Chinese Nuclear Escalation in a Conventional War with the United States', *International Security*, vol. 41, no. 4, Spring 2017, pp. 74–5.

38 The judgement that inadvertent escalation is a serious risk is not uncontested. As with all matters relating to deterrence, however, it is how decision-makers' views influence their decisions that ultimately matter. See Matthew Kroenig and Mark J. Massa, 'Are Dual-capable Weapon Systems Destabilizing? Questioning Nuclear–Conventional Entanglement and Inadvertent Escalation', Issue Brief, Atlantic Council, Scowcroft Center for Policy and Security, June 2021, https://www.atlanticcouncil.org/wp-content/uploads/2021/06/Nuclear-Entanglement-IB-v7.pdf.

39 Wu Riqiang, 'Living with Uncertainty: Modelling China's Nuclear Survivability', *International Security*, vol. 44, no. 4, Spring 2020, p. 113.

40 Kartchner and Gerson, 'Escalation to Limited Nuclear War in the 21st Century', p. 149.

41 See Austin Long, 'US Nuclear Strategy Toward China: Damage Limitation and Extended Deterrence', in Caroline Dorminey and Eric Gomez (eds), *America's Nuclear Crossroads* (Washington DC: CATO Institute, 2019), pp. 47–56, https://www.cato.org/sites/cato.org/files/pdfs/americas-nuclear-crossroads-full.pdf.

42 See NATO, 'Brussels Summit Communiqué', 14 June 2021, para. 26, https://www.nato.int/cps/en/natohq/news_185000.htm.

43 See *ibid.*, paras 27–9.

44 See Vipin Narang and Ankit Panda, 'North Korea: Risks of Escalation',

Survival, vol. 62, no. 1, February–March 2020, p. 51.

45 See Kroenig and Massa, 'Are Dual-capable Weapon Systems Destabilizing?'

46 See Helmut Hammerich, 'Fighting for the Heart of Germany: German I Corps and NATO's Plans for the Defense of the North German Plain in the 1960s', in Jan Hoffenaar and Dieter Krüger (eds), *Blueprints for Battle: Planning for War in Central Europe, 1948–1968* (Lexington, KY: University Press of Kentucky, 2012), pp. 166–8.

47 US Department of Defense, 'Nuclear Posture Review 2018', February 2018, https://media.defense.gov/2018/Feb/02/2001872886/-1/-1/1/2018-NUCLEAR-POSTURE-REVIEW-FINAL-REPORT.PDF.

48 See Lawrence Freedman and Jeffrey Michaels, *The Evolution of Nuclear Strategy*, 4th ed. (London: Palgrave Macmillan, 2019), pp. 459–94.

49 See Daalder, *The Nature and Practice of Flexible Response*, especially chapter 2.

50 See Stephen J. Cimbala, 'Extended Deterrence and Nuclear Escalation Options in Europe', *Armed Forces & Society*, vol. 15, no. 1, Fall 1988, pp. 9–31.

51 See NATO, 'The Alliance's New Strategic Concept, Agreed by the Heads of State and Government Participating in the Meeting of the North Atlantic Council, 7–8 November 1991', last updated 26 August 2010, para. 56, https://www.nato.int/cps/en/natohq/official_texts_23847.htm.

52 See Robert S. Norris and Hans M. Kristensen, 'What's Behind Bush's Nuclear Cuts?', *Arms Control Today*, October 2004, https://www.armscontrol.org/act/2004-10/features/

whats-behind-bushs-nuclear-cuts.

53 See Karl-Heinz Kamp, 'Nuclear Reorientation of NATO', NDC Commentary 01/18, NATO Defense College, February 2018; and Michael Kofman and Anya Loukianova Fink, 'Escalation Management and Nuclear Employment in Russian Military Strategy', *War on the Rocks*, 23 June 2020, https://warontherocks.com/2020/06/escalation-management-and-nuclear-employment-in-russian-military-strategy/.

54 See Dave Johnson, 'Russia's Deceptive Nuclear Policy', *Survival*, vol. 63, no. 3, June–July 2021, pp. 123–42.

55 See NATO, 'Brussels Summit Communiqué', paras 21–9.

56 Authors' interviews with officials in Berlin, Brussels, London and Paris, 2019.

57 See Tiphaine de Champchesnel, 'The Role of Nuclear Weapons After the American Nuclear Posture Review', Research Paper No. 57, Institute de Recherche Stratégique de l'École Militaire, 28 June 2018, https://www.irsem.fr/data/files/irsem/documents/document/file/2969/RP_IRSEM_No_57_Translation.pdf.

58 US Department of Defense, 'Nuclear Posture Review 2018', p. 30; and NATO, 'Brussels Summit Communiqué', para. 41.

59 See John K. Warden, 'Limited Nuclear War: The 21st Century Challenge for the United States', Livermore Papers on Global Security No. 4, Lawrence Livermore National Laboratory, Center for Global Security Research, July 2018, pp. 49–52, https://cgsr.llnl.gov/content/assets/docs/CGSR_LP4-FINAL.pdf.

60 See Evan Braden Montgomery,

'Posturing for Great Power Competition: Identifying Coercion Problems in US Nuclear Policy', *Journal of Strategic Studies*, February 2021, https://www.tandfonline.com/doi/full/10.1080/01402390.2021.18869 32.

61   See US Department of Defense, 'Nuclear Posture Review 2018', sec. 4.

62   Authors' interviews with officials in Berlin, Brussels, London and Paris, 2019.

63   See Edward Geist, 'Defeat Is Possible', *War on the Rocks*, 17 June 2021, https://warontherocks.com/2021/06/defeat-is-possible/.

64   Manzo and Warden, 'After First Use, What?', p. 145.

65   United States Institute of Peace, 'Providing for the Common Defense: The Assessment and Recommendations of the National Defense Strategy Commission', 2018, https://www.usip.org/sites/default/files/2018-11/providing-for-the-common-defense.pdf.

66   See Brad Roberts, 'Debating Nuclear No-first-use, Again', *Survival*, vol. 61, no. 3, June–July 2019, pp. 39–56.

67   See, respectively, NATO, 'Warsaw Summit Communiqué', para. 65; and NATO, 'North Atlantic Council Statement as the Treaty on the Prohibition of Nuclear Weapons Enters into Force', 15 December 2020, para. 1, https://www.nato.int/cps/en/natohq/news_180087.htm.

68   See 'Preventing Nuclear Proliferation and Reassuring America's Allies'.

69   See Roberts, 'Living with a Nuclear-arming North Korea'.

Disruptive Technologies and Nuclear Risks: What's New and What Matters

Andrew Futter

Technological developments are changing the nature of nuclear risks.[1] This has been interchangeably labelled as the 'new', 'emerging' or 'disruptive' technology challenge, often a combination of all three, which has sometimes detracted from the coherence and clarity of debate. But it is safe to say that faster, more precise and often dual-use and dual-capable weapons; increasingly sophisticated sensing, tracking and processing capabilities; the potential for greater autonomy in these systems across all domains; and myriad possibilities presented by computer-network (or cyber) operations and non-nuclear counter-space capabilities are testing the axioms on which nuclear order, stability and risk reduction are based. These dynamics have reopened questions about counterforce strikes and deterrence by denial, imperilled mutual vulnerability as a central ordering mechanism in strategic affairs, presented more complex pathways towards escalation, blurred the nuclear–conventional distinction, and cultivated a more suspicious and fearful nuclear environment. They have also raised fundamental questions about the political and normative mechanisms required to maintain stability and peace.

We should be concerned about this emerging nuclear picture, and especially the risks of sleepwalking into a nuclear world substantially different from that of the Cold War, during which the central tenets of the nuclear order were conceived, and perhaps even from the 'second nuclear age' some have suggested succeeded it in the early 1990s.[2] But to suggest that

Andrew Futter is Professor of International Politics at the University of Leicester. His research for this article was funded by the European Research Council (grant number: 866155).

Survival | vol. 64 no. 1 | February–March 2022 | pp. 99–120   https://doi.org/10.1080/00396338.2022.2032979

these technological challenges are insurmountable is to fall into the trap of technological determinism, when in fact the problems that have arisen often – though not always – have political remedies. It is also important not to get too preoccupied with the 'new' aspect of the challenge: many of the dynamics that fall into the disruptive-technology category have been around for a while in one form or another. Moreover, perceived technological challenges to established nuclear thinking are hardly unprecedented.[3] All of this suggests that at least some of the developments of present concern are less alarming than feared, and that a somewhat less stable nuclear era can be politically managed.

Pre-emptive attack

Deploying nuclear weapons on silent submarines hidden in the ocean, or on land-based mobile platforms able to move along roads and rails and to hide, only to reappear when needed, has underpinned the nuclear order and particularly nuclear deterrence for decades. The idea is that if an opponent doesn't know where these delivery systems are, they cannot be reliably targeted in a surprise first strike. Thus, no rational actor would risk attempting such an attack owing to the risk of devastating retaliation. This is the basis of stability through mutual vulnerability and survivable second-strike forces.

While there is reason to believe that some submarines and mobile land-based missiles may not have been as invulnerable in the past as conventional wisdom suggests, the technical support infrastructure didn't exist to reliably track and destroy these systems with any great confidence, even with nuclear weapons.[4] Today, however, significant advances in remote-sensor technologies, more capable surveillance platforms across multiple domains, the ability to process and communicate enormous amounts of data quickly, and more precise non-nuclear and non-kinetic weapons systems could be closing the gap between 'the hiders and the seekers'.[5] Real-time imaging, ultra-sensitive acoustics and other data could be gathered by a variety of different, possibly stealthy sensor platforms (under the surface of the ocean or in space, and possibly uninhabited), sophisticated algorithms could be used to filter the data, and precision-guided weapons systems or computer-network operations[6] could be used to attack submarines or mobile missiles. This capability lies at the heart of what Keir Lieber and Daryl Press have termed as the 'new era of counterforce'.[7] If submarines and mobile missiles are becoming more vulnerable to attack, deterrence and stability would appear to be at risk.[8]

However, not all nuclear-armed submarines and mobile missiles are becoming vulnerable to the same degree.[9] It depends on whose missiles and submarines are being targeted, where they are located and who is doing the finding and attacking.[10] Nuclear-armed submarines operated by the United States and the United Kingdom, for example, are believed to be much quieter than the submarines deployed by other nations, and therefore more difficult to locate by purely acoustic means. American and British submarines are also probably harder to track than Russian or Chinese submarines when they leave port. While patrol areas may be limited by underwater mapping or missile ranges, these submarines can still hide in many millions of square miles of ocean, which would strain even state-of-the-art tracking systems.[11] That said, advances in anti-submarine-warfare capabilities would be particularly concerning for the UK given that it is the only nuclear-armed state that relies on just one form of nuclear delivery.

China and especially Russia have many mobile missiles as well as immense interior spaces in which to hide and move them (though this may be limited by the extent of road or rail networks). Tracking mobile missiles might be easier in a smaller country with less strategic depth, but it would still be difficult to attack with confidence before they could be launched. Given the high degree of accuracy required, even terminally guided precision conventional weapons would be hard-pressed to hit their targets. Moreover, knowing the exact location of a mobile missile at all times is difficult. In theory, satellites could provide constant surveillance of areas where mobile missiles are thought to be deployed, but comprehensive coverage would require numerous satellites in many different orbits.[12] Using uninhabited aerial vehicles (UAVs) might be an option, but they would probably have to be much closer to the target, flying through or even loitering in enemy airspace, and therefore would be more vulnerable than satellites.

The seekers also have to contend with countermeasures. Dummy mobile missiles can make it difficult to distinguish between real and false targets. Submarines may deploy a range of different countermeasures to confuse sensors. Any underwater sensing or weapons platform would presumably be vulnerable to attack. Securing the capability to find, track and strike mobile missiles and submarines requires significant investment and infrastructure. Furthermore, finding and tracking missiles or submarines is one thing, getting the required munitions close enough to attack them another. Submarines, for instance, could be moved into protected 'bastions' closer to shore that are beyond the reach of an adversary's underwater systems.[13]

Some targets could become more vulnerable to a non-nuclear strike. For example, the US could probably target North Korean mobile missiles (such as the recently unveiled *Hwasong*-15) and may have contemplated doing so during recent periods of high tension. But by the same token, if a new era of counterforce really is dawning, the United States will be its primary driver for the foreseeable future, and only certain countries' nuclear systems will become more vulnerable in some but not necessarily all scenarios.

The technical feasibility of a more transparent ocean or surgical attacks on land-based nuclear-delivery systems could drive modernisation and possibly arms races. But the fact that something is feasible doesn't mean it makes strategic sense. Perhaps the most important factor limiting the counterforce potential of new technologies will be the political reluctance to pursue such options.

But avoiding a steady descent towards an era of greater uncertainty about the security of second-strike nuclear forces will not come about automatically. Some type of strategic restraint, through either formal arms control or other types of agreement, will be necessary, and this in turn will require political effort from the major nuclear powers and a tacit acceptance of mutual vulnerability as a central ordering principle in global politics.

How destabilising are hypersonic missiles?

Perhaps no development better encapsulates the disruptive-technology thesis than hypersonic weaponry, dramatised by images of futuristic-looking projectiles or aircraft, glowing red due to the enormous heat produced by manoeuvring through the atmosphere at high speeds to strike targets with pinpoint accuracy. Such weapons will purportedly be able to travel very fast, evade missile defences, reduce warning times due to their trajectory and manoeuvre in flight to hit specific targets anywhere in the world. Hypersonic weapons are being developed by all major nuclear-armed states, and concerns about arms races have ensued.[14]

Hypersonic weapons are classified by the speed at which they travel – hypersonic, or Mach 5 and above, which is roughly one mile per second.[15] Current systems can be split into hypersonic glide vehicles (HGVs), which are launched from booster rockets before gliding unaided across the top of the atmosphere and falling to their targets, and hypersonic cruise missiles (HCMs), which are powered, air-breathing and stay inside the atmosphere.[16] HGVs potentially offer greater manoeuvrability and less predictable flight paths than current ballistic missiles, making them better at avoiding interception by mid-course ballistic-missile defences, while HCMs retain the accuracy and manoeuvrability of subsonic or supersonic cruise missiles but at much higher speeds and higher altitudes. HGVs and HCMs are therefore probably better thought of as variations of current ballistic and cruise missiles rather than something entirely new.

Hypersonic weapons armed with nuclear or non-nuclear payloads could be used for a variety of different strategic or tactical objectives: directly targeting nuclear weapons and command-and-control facilities, or destroying mobile missiles, anti-satellite weapons, radar installations, missile-defence assets, ships or other high-value targets. The US, Russia, China and India all have slightly different purposes for their respective programmes. The US appears to see HGVs and HCMs as part of a broader, conventional global prompt-strike mission and does not currently seem interested in developing nuclear-armed hypersonic weapons.[17] Russia's interest in hypersonic technology can be traced back to the 1980s.[18] It seems to be building hypersonic missiles, specifically the *Avangard* HGV, for the long-range delivery of nuclear weapons, and as a direct response to US ballistic-missile-defence plans. For China, hypersonic developments focus on regional anti-access/area-denial capabilities, and in particular on targeting an adversary's forces at sea (for instance, with the medium-range DF-17 missile). But growing fears of US surgical strikes against nuclear assets are driving China's interest in long-range HGVs, which includes the testing of a fractional orbital bombardment system with a hypersonic warhead in 2021.[19] It is not yet clear whether these systems will be nuclear or conventional. India appears to be developing HCMs, notably the *Brahmos*-II (in partnership with Russia), which may be nuclear-capable, to enhance regional deterrence against China and Pakistan.[20]

Hypersonic weapons pose a range of potentially heightened but not qualitatively new nuclear risks due to three ambiguities.[21] Firstly, the inability to know the intended destination of the warhead due to the unpredictable flight path means that it might be less clear which country is under attack than with ballistic missiles. Secondly, it could be difficult to know which targets are under attack – nuclear-weapons facilities, non-nuclear military installations or soft targets such as cities – and therefore to discern the intention of the attackers. In some cases, this problem is not very different from that posed by ballistic missiles. Thirdly, it is hard to ascertain whether the missile is armed with a nuclear or conventional warhead. While the same difficulty arises with both ballistic and cruise missiles, the possibility of using the same hypersonic delivery systems for nuclear and non-nuclear weapons could create confusion. These factors seem poised to exacerbate security dilemmas, increase chances of inadvertent escalation and make crisis management more difficult.

At the same time, there are important limitations to hypersonic weaponry that could prove consequential, particularly for arms control.[22] Perhaps the most significant is that HGVs do not offer many military advantages over current ballistic missiles. Most ballistic missiles already travel at hypersonic speeds, some are manoeuvrable and could be terminally guided to increase accuracy, and they can be flown at depressed trajectories to reduce warning time.[23] In addition, current ballistic missiles can probably penetrate or at least overwhelm most ballistic-missile defences now deployed or in development, especially if they are armed with countermeasures. HGVs are also likely to be travelling at much slower speeds than ballistic-missile warheads would be when they reach their targets (HGVs lose speed in flight depending on how much they have manoeuvred) and could be more susceptible to terminal missile defences.[24] Furthermore, HGVs and HCMs will produce enormous amounts of heat as they cut through the atmosphere, which could make them easier to track with space-based sensors than normal ballistic or cruise missiles. Perhaps above all, successful hypersonic flight is technologically difficult: mastering scramjet propulsion for HCMs, mitigating the effects of extreme heat, and finding a reliable and secure way to actively and perhaps even autonomously guide the warhead are all significant engineering challenges.

Under scrutiny, hypersonic weapons appear to offer relatively few military or strategic advantages over ballistic or cruise missiles, or other precision-strike capabilities, for tactical missions or strategic roles. As much as a genuine desire for a transformative weapon system, politics and a sense of technological wonder may be driving major powers' apparent fascination with such capabilities. Yet they are hardly innocuous. HGVs and HCMs are potentially more destabilising and escalation-prone than ballistic and cruise missiles, especially given the possibility of miscalculation and misperception when conventional and nuclear-capable hypersonic weapons and tactical and strategic missions become entangled.[25]

Managing these risks will involve balancing the demands of conventional warfare against the need for nuclear stability.[26] Limits could be imposed on deployment, for example, in US–Russian strategic relations by including long-range HGVs in New START and any follow-on treaty given that they would rely on similar if not identical launchers to those for ballistic missiles. But curtailing the spread of other types of hypersonic systems for other types of military missions might require a new set of agreements altogether. A clear geographical separation between the systems used to deliver nuclear and conventional weapons, and greater transparency about the types of weapons being deployed, would be sensible requirements of any arms-control regime applicable to hypersonic weapons.

Left-of-launch ballistic-missile defence

Shooting down a ballistic missile in flight is technologically demanding, but the difficulty depends upon the speed of the missile, how many missiles or warheads need to be intercepted, whether they are armed with countermeasures, and the type and sophistication of the interception method and supporting systems being used. Historically, the preferred method of interception was by a nuclear blast, as it did not require great accuracy to destroy incoming warheads; Russia still deploys nuclear-armed interceptors to defend Moscow. Over the past 20 years, however, advances in computing, sensor and processing power have focused attention on 'hit-to-kill' kinetic non-nuclear interception and the use of other technologies such as lasers and directed-energy weapons.[27] More broadly, interest in ballistic-missile defence (BMD) has spread beyond the United States and Russia, and BMD systems are currently being developed and deployed by all major nuclear-armed states.[28]

BMD is not new; the pursuit of such capabilities can be traced back to attempts in the 1940s to protect the United Kingdom against the German V-1 and V-2 rockets. Neither are concerns about BMD's potentially destabilising impact especially fresh. Since the 1960s, the deployment of active defences against ballistic missiles has been considered threatening to the nuclear order. But two developments have exacerbated the problem. The first, as mentioned, is the deployment and spread of increasingly capable active missile defences for kinetic, non-nuclear interception of nuclear and conventionally armed missiles after they have been fired – that is, right-of-launch capabilities. The second is a shift in thinking towards 'full-spectrum missile defence'

BMD is blurring the distinction between defence and offence

that combines capabilities for preventing missiles from being launched at all through computer-network operations or electronic warfare – that is, left-of-launch capabilities – with more traditional right-of-launch interception capabilities.[29] These developments may be making BMD more capable and credible against certain types of missile threats. But they are also blurring the distinction between defence and offence, and between protecting against nuclear and conventional threats, potentially enhancing the ability to launch pre-emptive strikes and creating new concerns about stability.

Right-of-launch BMD relies on sophisticated computers, processors, sensors and support systems to detect missile launches, track the missile in flight and launch and guide interceptor missiles or other weapons to the target, all in a matter of minutes. Sceptics often cite these technical challenges to cast doubt on the general efficacy of BMD, but some systems do appear to work better than others against certain targets.[30] The US

Aegis system, considered to be among the best, intercepted and destroyed an intercontinental ballistic missile in a November 2020 test.[31] And there is much hype about the potential capability of the Russian S-500 anti-air and anti-missile system.[32] Certainly, concerns that US right-of-launch BMD defences might well work have driven Russia's and China's nuclear modernisation, and in particular their development of hypersonic missiles and other 'exotic' but not necessarily new types of delivery systems.[33] Pakistan has similar concerns about Indian BMD plans. Of special concern is how BMD might be combined with other capabilities such as precision strike.[34] In one worrisome scenario, the US or another capable state might be able to conduct attacks that destroy nuclear weapons while relying on missile defence to neutralise any retaliation.

The idea behind left-of-launch capabilities is to increase the overall efficacy of missile defence by seeking to prevent missiles from being fired, or at least to interfere with the launch process so that they cannot hit their intended targets.[35] For example, malware might be inserted into a missile or delivery platform, preventing it from working. Electronic attacks could also be launched against guidance systems or other essential support apparatus so that the missile veers off course or explodes. It is possible that the US has already attempted to undermine North Korea's nuclear and missile programme in this way, although details, unsurprisingly, are scarce.[36] Left-of-launch operations could also be undertaken using kinetic precision-strike munitions, perhaps via hypersonic missiles.[37]

Such capabilities potentially decrease the stability of nuclear deterrence.[38] Right-of-launch BMD capabilities can be roughly ascertained in advance, incorporated into planning and plausibly countered. Left-of-launch capabilities cannot, at least not to the same degree or in the same way. Left-of-launch attacks, especially involving computer-network operations, would probably rely on breaking into systems before they are used. This not only effectively moves the BMD mission from defence to pre-emption or strategic coercion, but also raises the risk that the malware or intrusion could be discovered and lead to a crisis. Furthermore, attempting to infiltrate the computer systems used for nuclear and missile command and control could accidentally affect other systems unrelated to offensive capabilities but crucial to nuclear safety and security. More broadly, the stealthy nature of cyber attacks compared with the palpable operation of BMD radar and interceptors is likely to produce greater fear and uncertainty.

The fact remains that better and more diverse interception capabilities combined with pre-emptive left-of-launch operations could make BMD more credible against a broader range of missile threats. The US has already been quite explicit in stating that it sees the integration of these capabilities as key to future planning, and it is conceivable that others will follow suit. This is likely to be disruptive and highly destabilising.

Escalation pathways across different domains

Modern militaries, especially the United States', are increasingly reliant on outer space. While most military space-based assets are designed to support conventional military missions, some also play a role in nuclear operations with respect to missile-launch detection and early warning, tracking incoming missiles or aircraft, guiding precision munitions (including nuclear-armed cruise or hypersonic missiles), and providing broader situational awareness and military communications. An increasing dependence on such assets has created two interlinked concerns. Firstly, satellites might be targeted early in a crisis by an adversary; this makes targeting and destroying anti-satellite capabilities a priority, which could trigger escalation. Secondly, attacks on space assets may be misinterpreted because some satellites have dual functions.[39]

Anti-satellite weapons are not new.[40] Nuclear-armed blasts were contemplated in the 1950s and 1960s, and kinetic kill can be traced back to the 1980s. But the ability to conduct non-nuclear counter-space operations, through direct ascent and co-orbital weapons or by other means such as directed-energy weapons, has returned to the forefront of strategic thinking and planning.[41] All major nuclear-armed states are engaged in the development of anti-satellite weapons – which are technically similar to anti-ballistic missiles – and some already have demonstrated capabilities.[42] In 2007, a Chinese weapon destroyed a weather satellite at an altitude of 850 kilometres. The US destroyed a reconnaissance satellite at an altitude of 250 km in 2008.[43] In 2019, India destroyed a satellite at an altitude of 282 km.[44] And most recently, in November 2021, Russia destroyed a satellite at an altitude of 480 km.[45] It is unlikely that a state could orchestrate a 'perfect storm' and destroy all space assets in one go, but their vulnerability is clear.

Space capabilities are part of a broader quest for information superiority and dominance in an increasingly complex world. On account of real-time information flows facilitated by information technology, social-media platforms and global networks, it is becoming more difficult to discern what is and isn't true in a nuclear environment abundant with raw data.[46] This new environment complicates nuclear signalling and presents new challenges for crisis communications and crisis management. Different sources may use unorthodox means, such as Twitter.[47] Ambiguous communications could be interpreted incorrectly.[48] US Strategic Command's ill-conceived New Year's Eve tweet about 'dropping a bomb' appeared to be an example of this.[49] In addition, international events and actions that might preclude or exacerbate a nuclear crisis will be reported in real time and publicly available. This may make it difficult for leaders to take the time required to think through actions and increase the potential for an adversary to shape public opinion in dangerous ways. Imagine how the Cuban Missile Crisis would have played out if it had arisen today,[50] or what impact the 2018 false missile alert in Hawaii might have had during a real nuclear crisis.[51] There is also greater potential for 'weaponised social media', disinformation and misinformation, particularly from third-party actions that might lead to what Rebecca Hersman has described as 'wormhole escalation'.[52] Deep fakes or other types of fake news could be used deliberately to deepen a crisis. A bogus news story about how Israel might respond to Pakistani military assistance to Syria prompted Pakistan to issue a public warning to Israel in 2016.[53] It should be assumed that sophisticated information operations will be part of any future nuclear crisis or conflict.[54]

The possible pathways to inadvertent and deliberate escalation that could result in nuclear use are changing. This is due to both growing competition over the control of outer space and, less directly, changes in the global information ecosystem within which nuclear decisions and operations take place. Given the centrality of space and cyberspace to almost all aspects of nuclear operations, these developments will inevitably affect other military domains, missions and weapons systems.

Understanding the AI–automation–nuclear nexus

Artificial intelligence (AI) and automation already have a number of different applications across nuclear systems, and at least in primordial form have been around for decades.[55] But as these technologies become more sophisticated, they have the potential to increase instability and nuclear risks. The extent of their disruptiveness will depend on how such capabilities are deployed and what tasks they are assigned, which will turn on the risk–reward calculations of military planners.

AI essentially comprises coding, computer systems and software capable of performing tasks that require discretionary intelligence if carried out by humans. It is not one discrete system, but rather something than can be applied in different ways depending on the particular task. It is useful to distinguish between narrow AI, which has specific goals and is limited by its programming and the 'problem' to be solved, and general AI, which involves writing software that allows systems to 'learn' through analysing datasets.[56] Most of what we term AI, and especially with respect to the systems currently used in nuclear operations, involves narrow, rules-based 'if–then' protocols, though new computer and information technologies have generated the processing power and expertise required for wider applications.[57]

Autonomy or automation is the application of AI to particular tasks, some of which might involve robotics and, therefore, automated or autonomous weapons systems. They exist along a continuum of function and sophistication from discrete automated systems to more capable and goal-orientated autonomous systems.[58] Automation has been used for decades in nuclear early-warning, targeting and delivery systems, though mostly in ways that involve human control.[59] But improvements in AI potentially allow robotic systems to operate without human intervention, based on their interaction with their environment.

Applications of AI, robotics and machine learning are theoretically endless and could operate across the nuclear enterprise. At the moment, however, they are limited by the huge datasets and security protocols required for training, the problem of control and unpredictability, finite computational power and a prevalent desire to keep humans in the loop.

AI and autonomy are likely to play an important role in the software, computer and associated systems that support decision-making and nuclear command, control and communications.[60] Here too there is some precedent: both the US and Russia built nuclear early-warning systems during the Cold War that incorporated a degree of automation, the Soviet Union's so-called Dead Hand – a semi-automatic nuclear-response system that could be activated if the country came under nuclear attack – being a good example.[61] But AI and autonomy could well become increasingly important in data collection, data cleaning and complex data analysis, and for enhanced warning systems, targeting plans and situational awareness. This could, on balance, be a good thing, enhancing reliability and providing more headspace for decision-makers to deliberate in a nuclear crisis.[62]

Another area of nuclear operations likely to become more efficient from AI and greater autonomy is that of locating, tracking and targeting concealed and mobile nuclear systems. The combination of enhanced sensor capabilities across all domains (potentially deployed on semi-autonomous or autonomous platforms or in 'swarms'), the ability to transfer enormous caches of data quickly and analyse them in real time, and the ability to deploy uninhabited systems to attack targets may be changing the game of nuclear hide-and-seek.

AI and automation could improve the guidance and accuracy of nuclear and conventional weapons systems by making missiles and bombs 'smarter', so that they are able to respond to their environment and change flight paths after being launched.[63] A basic version of this type of AI is used in some cruise missiles and could be used in hypersonic missiles or other types of strategic delivery systems. Weapons that are thereby more accurate would render feasible surgical long-range counterforce strikes with conventional rather than nuclear weapons.

AI and automation could facilitate the deployment of increasingly autonomous nuclear and non-nuclear delivery platforms. The best example is the Russian *Status*-6 nuclear-armed torpedo, but it is possible that other future nuclear-delivery platforms could have a degree of autonomy (or at least be uninhabited).[64] In the future, nuclear-delivery platforms could be able to loiter stealthily near targets waiting to strike, like the autonomous *Harpy* UAV fielded by Israel.[65] This would, however, pose significant problems for command and control. It is unclear at the time of writing whether the United States' B-21 *Raider* next-generation strategic bomber will be capable of uninhabited nuclear operations. But others may be considering such a capability.[66]

Other applications could include intelligent computer software able to defend nuclear networks or facilitate left-of-launch attacks on command-and-control systems.[67] AI might also be used to generate deep fakes for disinformation campaigns that could precipitate or deepen a nuclear crisis.[68]

Such prospective uses are worrying insofar as they might undermine the security of second-strike forces, complicate civilian command and control or create unforeseen pathways towards escalation. Advanced sensing and processing capabilities, perhaps deployed on autonomous platforms and combined with more accurate kinetic and digital weapons, could be seen as a major threat to deterrence and stability, and drive arms races. In the worst case, military planners might become so concerned about the vulnerability of their nuclear forces that they assess that waiting to strike second may no longer be an option.

Yet the software and programming that makes AI-enabled weapons systems so capable may also prove to be their Achilles heel. Any type of AI would be vulnerable to hacking, spoofing and data poisoning, and the risk could increase the more sophisticated the capability became. The automated or autonomous platforms used for sensing, communications and weapons delivery would also remain vulnerable to air defences, jammers and cyber attacks.[69]

AI and automation are not going away, and are likely to play major roles in nuclear operations. However, so far nuclear-armed states have appeared reluctant to delegate the most safety-critical nuclear operations to machines due to wariness about exactly how these systems might perform in real-world circumstances and uncertainty about how more sophisticated systems would reach decisions. This suggests that while arms control for some applications of AI will be difficult to achieve, an agreement not to deploy fully autonomous nuclear weapons without human control is politically feasible.[70] Nevertheless, as the technical ability to deploy them increases, and if nuclear stability continues to erode, some states may see advantages in making nuclear weapons and support systems increasingly autonomous.

*   *   *

There is a growing sense that technological innovation is driving us, wittingly or not, into a more dangerous nuclear order, under which the risks of nuclear use increase.[71] Taken together, these developments appear to blur the delineation between nuclear and non-nuclear weapons systems, create new pathways for inadvertent escalation through entanglement and indistinguishability, alter the perception of possible non-nuclear first-strike capabilities, increase the speed of operations and reduce decision-making time, generate greater uncertainty, and perhaps shift the balance between humans and machines.

Compounding these worries is a sense that national political leaders do not fully appreciate the considerable implications of technological change for the global nuclear order combined with a return to great-power strategic competition. But the situation is less desperate than it may appear. There are reasons to be cautiously optimistic about the capacity of the existing nuclear order to absorb, or at least adapt to, the impact of disruptive technology. The advent of game-changing technology is not new in the nuclear realm, and periods of unsettling and rapid technological change have been managed in the past, with new mechanisms and frameworks developed accordingly. And while technology is clearly important in shaping the nuclear order, it has always been subject to political, budgetary, strategic and normative constraints. In this light, even if we are entering a new phase in the evolution of nuclear weapons, we should be able to alter the frameworks of global nuclear governance so as to sustain nuclear stability.[72]

Political engagement will be required to manage a more complex global nuclear environment. The escalation risks created by the deployment of new hard-weapons systems and softer technological dynamics need to be understood and factored into planning. Secure lines of communication, clear signalling and an understanding of an adversary's different systems and processes remain essential to preventing unwanted crises. While non-nuclear weapons are unlikely to supersede nuclear weapons soon – nothing else would have a comparable deterrent effect – increasingly capable non-nuclear and intangible weapons will probably play a more important role in nuclear politics, potentially creating different risks. Technological drivers are clearly important in shaping the nuclear order, but they are not insusceptible to political means of reducing risks and maintaining stability.

Notes

1   See Christopher Chyba, 'New
     Technologies and Strategic Stability',
     Daedulus, vol. 149, no. 2, Spring 2020,
     pp. 150–70; and Todd S. Sechser,
     Neil Narang and Caitlin Talmadge,
     'Emerging Technologies and Strategic
     Stability in Peacetime, Crisis, and
     War', *Journal of Strategic Studies*, vol.
     42, no. 6, September 2019, pp. 727–35.

2   On the Cold War dispensation, see,
     for instance, Bernard Brodie, *Strategy
     in the Missile Age* (Princeton, NJ:
     Princeton University Press, 1959);
     and Robert Jervis, *The Meaning of the
     Nuclear Revolution: Statecraft and the
     Prospect of Armageddon* (Ithaca, NY:
     Cornell University Press, 1989). On the
     second nuclear age, see, for example,
     Paul Bracken, *Fire in the East: The
     Rise of Asian Military Power and the
     Second Nuclear Age* (New York: Harper
     Collins, 1999); Colin Gray, *The Second
     Nuclear Age* (London: Lynne Rienner,
     1999); Vipin Narang, *Nuclear Strategy
     in the Modern Era: Regional Powers and
     International Conflict* (Princeton, NJ:
     Princeton University Press, 2014);
     and Keith B. Payne, *Deterrence in the
     Second Nuclear Age* (Lexington, KY:
     University Press of Kentucky, 1996).

3   See, for example, Carl Builder,
     *Strategic Conflict Without Nuclear
     Weapons* (Santa Monica, CA: RAND
     Corporation, 1983); Bernard T. Feld et
     al. (eds), *Impact of New Technologies on
     the Arms Race* (Cambridge, MA: MIT
     Press, 1971); and J.J. Gertler, *Emerging
     Technologies in the Strategic Arena: A
     Primer* (Santa Monica, CA: RAND
     Corporation, 1987).

4   Austin Long and Brendan Rittenhouse
     Green, 'Stalking the Secure Second
     Strike: Intelligence, Counterforce and
     Nuclear Strategy', *Journal of Strategic
     Studies*, vol. 38, nos 1–2, January 2015,
     pp. 38–73.

5   As Bryan Clark explains: 'Since the
     Cold War, submarines – particularly
     quiet American ones – have been
     assumed to be largely immune to
     anti-access threats. Yet the ability of
     submarines to hide through quieting
     alone will decrease as each successive
     decibel of noise reduction becomes
     exponentially more expensive and
     new detection techniques mature that
     rely on phenomena other than the
     sounds emanating from a submarine.'
     Bryan Clark, 'The Emerging Era
     in Undersea Warfare', Center for
     Strategic and Budgetary Assessments,
     2015, p. 8, https://csbaonline.org/
     uploads/documents/CSBA6292_
     (Undersea_Warfare_Reprint)_web.
     pdf. Similarly, Paul Bracken has
     argued that 'the hunt for mobile
     missiles is getting faster, cheaper, and
     better. Long recognized problems
     with mobile systems have combined
     with cyber technology breakthroughs
     to make these missiles vulnerable.'
     Paul Bracken, 'Nuclear Stability
     and the Hunt for Mobile Missiles',
     Foreign Policy Research Institute,
     8 April 2016, https://www.fpri.org/
     article/2016/04/nuclear-stability-
     hunt-mobile-missiles/. See also Paul
     Bracken, *The Hunt for Mobile Missiles:
     Nuclear Weapons, AI, and the New Arms
     Race* (Philadelphia, PA: Foreign Policy
     Research Institute, 2020).

6   'Computer-network operations' is

a better descriptor than the more nebulous 'cyber'. See Andrew Futter, 'Cyber Semantics: Why We Should Retire the Latest Buzzword in Security Studies', *Journal of Cyber Policy*, vol. 3, no. 2, August 2018, pp. 201–16.

7 Keir Lieber and Daryl Press, 'The New Era of Counterforce: Technological Change and the Future of Nuclear Deterrence', *International Security*, vol. 41, no. 4, Spring 2017, pp. 9–49. See also Ryan Snyder et al., 'Correspondence: New Era or New Error? Technology and the Future of Deterrence', *International Security*, vol. 43, no. 3, Winter 2018/19, pp. 190–3.

8 See James R. Holmes, 'Sea Changes: The Future of Nuclear Deterrence', *Bulletin of the Atomic Scientists*, vol. 72, no. 4, July 2016, pp. 228–33.

9 Ballistic missiles deployed in silos are probably also becoming more vulnerable due to increases in accuracy, but this isn't a new dynamic.

10 See, for example, Owen R. Cote, 'Invisible Nuclear-armed Submarines, or Transparent Oceans? Are Ballistic Missile Submarines Still the Best Deterrent for the United States?', *Bulletin of the Atomic Scientists*, vol. 75, no. 1, January 2019, pp. 30–5.

11 See Jonathan Gates, 'Is the SSBN Deterrent Vulnerable to Autonomous Drones?', *RUSI Journal*, vol. 161, no. 6, December 2016, pp. 28–35; and John Gower, 'Concerning SSBN Vulnerability – Recent Papers', *BASIC*, 10 June 2016, https://basicint.org/blogs/rear-admiral-john-gower-cb-obe/06/2016/concerning-ssbn-vulnerability-%C2%AD-recent-papers.

12 See Li Bin, 'Tracking Chinese Strategic Mobile Missiles', *Science & Global Security*, vol. 15, no. 1, January 2007, pp. 1–30.

13 See James Lacey, 'Battle of the Bastions', *War on the Rocks*, 9 January 2020, https://warontherocks.com/2020/01/battle-of-the-bastions/.

14 See R. Jeffrey Smith, 'Hypersonic Missiles Are Unstoppable. And They're Starting a New Global Arms Race', *New York Times Magazine*, 29 June 2019, https://www.nytimes.com/2019/06/19/magazine/hypersonic-missiles.html.

15 For an overview, see Kelley M. Sayler, 'Hypersonic Weapons: Background and Issues for Congress', Congressional Research Service, updated 25 August 2021, https://crsreports.congress.gov/product/pdf/R/R45811/21; and Richard H. Speier et al., *Hypersonic Missile Nonproliferation: Hindering the Spread of a New Class of Weapons* (Santa Monica, CA: RAND Corporation, 2017).

16 Other systems include hypersonic gun-launched weapons.

17 See Sayler, 'Hypersonic Weapons: Background and Issues for Congress', pp. 4–9.

18 *Ibid.*, p. 9.

19 See Bleddyn Bowen and Cameron Hunter, 'Chinese Fractional Orbital Bombardment', Policy Brief no. 78, Asia-Pacific Leadership Network, 2021, https://cms.apln.network/wp-content/uploads/2021/11/APLN-Policy-Brief-No.78-Bowen-and-Hunter.pdf; and Tong Zhao, 'Conventional Challenges to Strategic Stability: Chinese Perceptions of Hypersonic Technology and the Security Dilemma', Carnegie-Tsinghua

Center for Global Policy, 23 July 2018, https://carnegieendowment.org/files/Conventional_Challenges_to_Strategic_Stability.pdf.

20 See Kelsey Davenport, 'India Tests Hypersonic Missile', *Arms Control Today*, October 2020, https://www.armscontrol.org/act/2020-10/news/india-tests-hypersonic-missile.

21 See James M. Acton, 'Hypersonic Boost-glide Weapons', *Science & Global Security*, vol. 23, no. 3, September 2015, pp. 191–219; and Dean Wilkening, 'Hypersonic Weapons and Strategic Stability', *Survival*, vol. 61, no. 5, October–November 2019, pp. 129–48.

22 For a strong counter-argument, see Ivan Oelrich, 'Cool Your Jets: Some Perspective on the Hyping of Hypersonic Weapons', *Bulletin of the Atomic Scientists*, vol. 76, no. 1, January 2020, pp. 37–45.

23 A missile outfitted with a manoeuvrable re-entry vehicle (MARV) might have better terminal-phase manoeuvrability than a hypersonic missile. See Cameron L. Tracy and David Wright, 'Modeling the Performance of Hypersonic Boost-glide Missiles', *Science & Global Security*, vol. 28, no. 3, September 2020, p. 24. For an excellent primer on re-entry-vehicle technology, see Matthew Bunn, 'Technology of Ballistic Missile Reentry Vehicles', in Kosta Tsipis and Penny Janeway (eds), *Review of US Military Research and Development, 1984* (Washington DC: Pergamon, 1984).

24 Hypersonic glide vehicles could also be vulnerable to airborne directed-energy weapons during their gliding phase. See Aaron Kennedy et al., 'Hypersonic Missile Defence, Stopping the Unstoppable', UK Project on Nuclear Issues Papers, Royal United Services Institute, 2020.

25 See Andrew W. Reddie, 'Hypersonic Missiles: Why the New "Arms Race" Is Going Nowhere Fast', *Bulletin of the Atomic Scientists*, 23 January 2020, https://thebulletin.org/2020/01/hypersonic-missiles-new-arms-race-going-nowhere-fast/. Historically, there has been a fairly clear distinction between delivery vehicles for nuclear and non-nuclear payloads.

26 See Wilkening, 'Hypersonic Weapons and Strategic Stability', pp. 145–6.

27 See Henry 'Trey' Obering III, 'Directed Energy Weapons are Real … and Disruptive', *PRISM*, vol. 8, no. 3, January 2020, pp. 36–47.

28 See Keir Giles, *Russian Ballistic Missile Defense: Rhetoric and Reality* (Carlisle, PA: US Army War College, Strategic Studies Institute, 2015); Zafar Khan, 'India's Ballistic Missile Defense: Implications for South Asian Deterrence Stability', *Washington Quarterly*, vol. 40, no. 3, Fall 2017, pp. 187–202; and Bruce W. MacDonald and Charles D. Ferguson, 'Chinese Strategic Missile Defense: Will It Happen, and What Would It Mean?', *Arms Control Today*, November 2015, https://www.armscontrol.org/act/2015-11/features/chinese-strategic-missile-defense-happen-what-mean.

29 See Office of the Secretary of Defense, '2019 Missile Defense Review', US Department of Defense, 2019, p. viii, https://www.defense.gov/Portals/1/Interactive/2018/11-2019-Missile-Defense-Review/The%202019%20MDR_Executive%20Summary.pdf.

30 See Matt Korda and Hans Kristensen,

'US Ballistic Missile Defenses, 2019', *Bulletin of the Atomic Scientists,* vol. 75, no. 6, November 2019, pp. 295–306.

31 US Department of Defense, 'US Successfully Conducts SM-3 Block IIA Intercept Test Against an Intercontinental Ballistic Missile Target', press release, 17 November 2020, https://www.defense.gov/ Newsroom/Releases/Release/ Article/2417334/us-successfully- conducts-sm-3-block-iia-intercept-test- against-an-intercontinen/.

32 See Samuel Cranny-Evans and Mark Cazalet, 'S-500 Enters Service in Moscow Region', *Janes Defence News,* 14 October 2021, https://www.janes. com/defence-news/news-detail/s- 500-enters-service-in-moscow-region.

33 Current US systems are optimised for shooting down objects in low earth orbit (such as ballistic missiles) rather than in the upper atmosphere (hypersonics). Missile defence against hypersonic missiles is doable, but intercepting missiles from different platforms and different directions could be difficult. See Kyle Mizokami, 'How Do You Stop a Hypersonic Weapon? DARPA Is Looking for the Answer', *Popular Mechanics,* 28 January 2020, https:// www.popularmechanics.com/ military/weapons/a30679336/ darpa-hypersonic-missile/; and Leah Walker, 'Nuclear-powered Cruise Missiles: Burevestnik and Its Implications', *Journal of Science Policy & Governance,* vol. 16, no. 1, April 2020, https:// www.sciencepolicyjournal.org/ uploads/5/4/3/4/5434385/walker_ jspg_v16.pdf.

34 See, for example, M. Taylor Fravel and Evan S. Medeiros, 'China's Search for Assured Retaliation: The Evolution of Chinese Nuclear Strategy and Force Structure', *International Security,* vol. 35, no. 2, Fall 2010, pp. 48–87.

35 As Brian McKeon, then US prin- cipal deputy under secretary for defense, explained in 2016, 'we need to develop a wider range of tools and that includes the efforts underway to address such threats before they are launched, or "left of launch." The development of left-of- launch capabilities will provide U.S. decision-makers additional tools and opportunities to defeat missiles. This will in turn reduce the burden on our "right-of-launch" ballistic missile defense capabilities. Taken together, left-of-launch and right-of-launch will lead to more effective and resilient capabilities to defeat adversary ballis- tic missile threats.' Brian P. McKeon, statement before the Senate Armed Services Subcommittee on Strategic Forces, 13 April 2016, http://www. armed-services.senate.gov/imo/media/ doc/McKeon_04-13-16.pdf.

36 See, for example, David E. Sanger and William J. Broad, 'Trump Inherits Secret Cyber War Against North Korean Missiles', *New York Times,* 4 March 2017, https://www.nytimes. com/2017/03/04/world/asia/north- korea-missile-program-sabotage.html.

37 See Thomas Karako, 'Missile Defense and the Nuclear Posture Review', *Strategic Studies Quarterly,* vol. 11, no. 3, Fall 2017, pp. 48–64.

38 See Andrew Futter, 'The Dangers of Using Cyberattacks to Counter Nuclear Threats', *Arms Control Today,*

July/August 2016, https://www.
armscontrol.org/act/2016-07/features/
dangers-using-cyberattacks-counter-
nuclear-threats.

39 See James M. Acton, 'Escalation
Through Entanglement: How the
Vulnerability of Command-and-
Control Systems Raises the Risks
of an Inadvertent Nuclear War',
International Security, vol. 43, no. 1,
Summer 2018, pp. 56–99.

40 See Laura Grego, 'A History of
Anti-satellite Programs', Union of
Concerned Scientists, January 2012,
https://www.ucsusa.org/sites/default/
files/2019-09/a-history-of-ASAT-
programs_lo-res.pdf.

41 See Todd Harrison, Kaitlyn Johnson
and Thomas Roberts, 'Space Threat
Assessment 2018', CSIS Aerospace
Security Project, April 2018, https://
csis-website-prod.s3.amazonaws.
com/s3fs-public/publication/180823_
Harrison_SpaceThreatAssessment_
FULL_WEB.pdf.

42 See Brian Weeden and Victoria
Samson (eds), 'Global Counterspace
Capabilities: An Open Source
Assessment', Secure World
Foundation, April 2020, https://
swfound.org/media/206957/swf_
global_counterspace_april2020_es.pdf.

43 Gregory Kulacki and Jeffrey G.
Lewis, 'Understanding China's
Antisatellite Test', *Nonproliferation
Review*, vol. 15, no. 2, June 2008,
pp. 335–47.

44 Ashley Tellis, 'India's ASAT Test:
An Incomplete Success', Carnegie
Endowment for International
Peace, 15 April 2019, https://
carnegieendowment.org/2019/04/15/
india-s-asat-test-incomplete-success-

pub-78884.

45 See Ankit Panda, 'The Dangerous
Fallout of Russia's Anti-
satellite Missile Test', Carnegie
Endowment for International
Peace, 17 November 2021, https://
carnegieendowment.org/2021/11/17/
dangerous-fallout-of-russia-s-anti-
satellite-missile-test-pub-85804.

46 See Harold A. Trinkunas, Herbert Lin
and Benjamin Loehrke (eds), *Three
Tweets to Midnight: Effects of the Global
Information Ecosystem on the Risk of
Nuclear Conflict* (Stanford, CA: Hoover
Institution Press, 2020).

47 See Heather Williams and Alexi Drew,
'Escalation by Tweet: Managing the
New Nuclear Diplomacy', King's
College London Centre for Science
& Security Studies, July 2020,
https://www.kcl.ac.uk/csss/assets/
escalation-by-tweet-managing-the-
new-nuclear-diplomacy-2020.pdf.

48 See Jeffrey Lewis, *The 2020 Commission
Report on the North Korean Nuclear Attacks
Against the United States: A Speculative
Novel* (London: W.H. Allen, 2018).

49 See Matt Stevens and Thomas
Gibbons-Neff, 'Military Deletes New
Year's Eve Tweet Saying It's "Ready
to Drop Something"', *New York Times*,
31 December 2019, https://www.
nytimes.com/2018/12/31/us/strategic-
command-bomb-video.html.

50 See Danielle Jablanski, Herbert S. Lin
and Harold A. Trinkunas, 'Retweets
to Midnight: Assessing the Effects
of the Information Ecosystem on
Crisis Decision Making Between
Nuclear Weapons States', in Harold A.
Trinkunas, Herbert Lin and Benjamin
Loehrke, *Three Tweets to Midnight:
Effects of the Global Information*

Ecosystem on the Risk of Nuclear Conflict (Stanford, CA: Hoover Institution Press, 2020).

51 See Kristyn Karl and Ashley Lytle, 'This Is Not a Drill: Lessons from the False Hawaiian Missile Alert', *Bulletin of the Atomic Scientists*, 10 January 2019, https://thebulletin.org/2019/01/this-is-not-a-drill-lessons-from-the-false-hawaiian-missile-alert/.

52 See Rebecca Hersman, 'Wormhole Escalation in the New Nuclear Age', *Texas National Security Review*, vol. 3, no. 3, Summer 2020, https://tnsr.org/2020/07/wormhole-escalation-in-the-new-nuclear-age/.

53 See Emma Graham-Harrison, 'Fake News Story Prompts Pakistan to Issue Nuclear Warning to Israel', *Guardian*, 25 December 2016, https://www.theguardian.com/world/2016/dec/26/fake-news-story-prompts-pakistan-to-issue-nuclear-warning-to-israel.

54 Nautilus Institute, 'Social Media Storms and Nuclear Early Warning Systems: A Deep Dive and Speed Scenarios Workshop', Preventive Defense Project, Stanford University, 8 January 2019, http://nautilus.org/wp-content/uploads/2019/01/Social-Media-Nuclear-War-Synthesis-Report-Final-Jan8-2019.pdf.

55 This section draws on Andrew Futter, 'Artificial Intelligence, Autonomy and Nuclear Stability: Towards a More Complex Nuclear Future', Valdai Discussion Club, 15 October 2020, https://valdaiclub.com/a/highlights/artificial-intelligence-autonomy-and-nuclear-stability/.

56 See Vincent Boulanin, 'Artificial Intelligence: A Primer', in Vincent Boulanin (ed.), *The Impact of Artificial Intelligence on Strategic Stability and Nuclear Risk, Volume I, Euro-Atlantic Perspectives* (Stockholm: Stockholm International Peace Research Institute, May 2019), pp. 13–14, https://www.sipri.org/sites/default/files/2019-05/sipri1905-ai-strategic-stability-nuclear-risk.pdf.

57 See Edward Geist and Andrew Lohn, 'How Might Artificial Intelligence Affect the Risk of Nuclear War?', Document No. PE-296-RC, RAND Corporation, 2018, https://www.rand.org/pubs/perspectives/PE296.html.

58 See Paul Scharre, *Army of None: Autonomous Weapons and the Future of War* (New York: W. W. Norton & Co., 2018), pp. 27–34.

59 See Michael C. Horowitz, Paul Scharre and Alexander Velez-Green, 'A Stable Nuclear Future? The Impact of Autonomous Systems and Artificial Intelligence', Cornell University, December 2019, p. 7, https://arxiv.org/ftp/arxiv/papers/1912/1912.05291.pdf.

60 An interesting example of this is VYRAN – a computer program that was designed to warn Soviet leaders if the US achieved the potential for a nuclear strike. See Matt Field, 'As the US, China and Russia Build New Nuclear Weapons Systems, How Will AI Be Built In?', *Bulletin of the Atomic Scientists*, 20 December 2019, https://thebulletin.org/2019/12/as-the-us-china-and-russia-build-new-nuclear-weapons-systems-how-will-ai-be-built-in/.

61 See David E. Hoffman, *The Dead Hand: The Untold Story of the Cold War Arms Race and Its Dangerous Legacy* (New York: Doubleday, 2009); and Nicholas Thompson, 'Inside the Apocalyptic Soviet Doomsday Machine', *Wired*, 21

September 2009, https://www.wired.com/2009/09/mf-deadhand/.

62 See Horowitz, Scharre and Velez-Green, 'A Stable Nuclear Future?', p. 1.

63 See Jonathan Roberts et al., 'Human vs Machine: The Role of Artificial Intelligence in Nuclear Weapons Systems', in Luba Zatsepina-McCreadie and Tom Plant (eds), *The 2020 UK PONI Papers* (London: Royal United Services Institute, October 2020), https://static.rusi.org/202011_poni_papers_2020_web.pdf.

64 See David Hambling, 'The Truth Behind Russia's Apocalypse Torpedo', *Popular Mechanics*, 18 January 2019, https://www.popularmechanics.com/military/weapons/a25953089/russia-apocalypse-torpedo-poseidon/.

65 See Charlie Gao, 'The Ultimate Weapon of War No One Is Talking About', *National Interest*, 25 January 2019, https://nationalinterest.org/blog/buzz/ultimate-weapon-war-no-one-talking-about-42497.

66 See Kris Osborn, 'Stealth Time: The Air Force Has Big Plans for Its B-21 Raiders', *National Interest*, 7 July 2021, https://nationalinterest.org/blog/buzz/stealth-time-air-force-has-big-plans-its-b-21-raiders-189321; and Alexander Velez-Green, 'The Nuclear Mission Must Stay Manned', *Bulletin of the Atomic Scientists*, 9 August 2016, https://thebulletin.org/2016/08/the-nuclear-mission-must-stay-manned/.

67 See James Johnson and Eleanor Krabill, 'AI, Cyberspace, and Nuclear Weapons', *War on the Rocks*, 31 January 2020, https://warontherocks.com/2020/01/ai-cyberspace-and-nuclear-weapons/.

68 See Jon Christian, 'Experts Fear Face Swapping Tech Could Start an International Showdown', *Outline*, 1 February 2018, https://theoutline.com/post/3179/deepfake-videos-are-freaking-experts-out?zd=3&zi=54fxjizh.

69 For a view on why the UK's missile submarines will remain protected, see Gower, 'Concerning SSBN Vulnerability'.

70 See Matthijs M. Maas, 'How Viable Is International Arms Control for Military Artificial Intelligence? Three Lessons from Nuclear Weapons', *Contemporary Security Policy*, vol. 30, no. 3, February 2019, pp. 285–311.

71 See, for example, Andrew Futter and Benjamin Zala, 'Strategic Non-nuclear Weapons and the Onset of a Third Nuclear Age', *European Journal of International Security*, vol. 6, no. 3, February 2021, pp. 257–77.

72 See Michael T. Klare, 'A Strategy for Reducing the Escalatory Dangers of Emerging Technologies', *Arms Control Today*, December 2020, https://www.armscontrol.org/act/2020-12/features/strategy-reducing-escalatory-dangers-emerging-technologies.

Geography Lessons: American Decline and the Challenge of Asia

Barnett R. Rubin

'Foremost among the countless blessings of war', wrote an editor of the *New York Times* on 11 May 1884, 'is its power of teaching geography'. The anonymous scribe claimed that the 'Egyptian conflict and the Soudan rebellion' had 'brought out a great many maps and familiarized the world with East Africa'. At the time, British General Charles Gordon was besieged in Khartoum by 50,000 armed mujahideen commanded by Muhammad Ahmad, a Sufi leader called by his followers the Mahdi, or messiah. Gordon's Sudanese venture ended along with the transatlantic public's geography lessons the following January, when the Mahdi's army breached Khartoum's defences and slaughtered the garrison, including Gordon, to the last man. Gordon, whose reform efforts were blocked by massive corruption in the Anglo-Egyptian administration he served, failed to win the hearts and minds of the 'native tribes'. They apparently remained unpersuaded that, as the *Times* put it, 'all white men are not like the cut-throats and kidnappers whom they have hitherto known'.[1]

New geography lessons

Some belated if incomplete geography lessons could also be counted among the blessings of the United States' recently terminated war in Afghanistan,

Barnett R. Rubin is a non-resident senior fellow at the Center on International Cooperation, New York University; the Quincy Institute for Responsible Statecraft; the Center for Conflict and Humanitarian Studies; the Doha Institute; the Heart of Asia Society (Kabul); and the Tillotoma Foundation (Kolkata). He served as Special Advisor to the UN Secretary-General's Special Representative for Afghanistan and Senior Advisor to the US Special Representative for Afghanistan and Pakistan.

Survival | vol. 64 no. 1 | February–March 2022 | pp. 121–130   https://doi.org/10.1080/00396338.2022.2032984

if it were willing to learn them. Afghanistan has occupied various locales in the imagined terrain of US strategy, from the front lines of the Cold War in the 1980s to the eastern outpost of the 'war' on terrorism's 'Greater Middle East' after 2001. The George W. Bush administration even appointed a White House 'Iraq and Afghanistan' czar to take charge of that effort's main theatres. These were two countries nearly 2,000 miles apart with different languages, cultures and histories, neither of which had attacked the United States. The Obama administration announced plans for a 'New Silk Road' to link Central and South Asia through Afghanistan, though without allocating any funds to build it. The Trump administration's initial policy towards Afghanistan, announced in August 2017, situated the country in a 'South Asia strategy' based on pressuring Pakistan to cease harbouring the Taliban, in part by encouraging Indian involvement in the country. Geography, alas, dictated that India's access to Afghanistan depended on Iran, which the Trump administration sought to isolate and destabilise.

In April 2021, the Atlantic Council proposed a 'Transatlantic Charter' for Afghanistan – a partnership of the US with Europe 'to build on the long-term multinational policies in support of the Afghan state and its people'. The charter's vision of a transatlantic Afghanistan freed its authors from concern with the interests, goals or capabilities of any of the country's decidedly non-transatlantic neighbours. It encouraged them to end their support for 'non-state violent actors' and 'build regional consensus on the future of Afghanistan codified in specific multilateral and bilateral agreements on sovereignty, non-interference, economic cooperation, and dispute-resolution mechanisms', but considered neither why it would be in the neighbours' interest to do so, nor potential transatlantic obstacles to 'regional consensus', such as unilateral counter-terrorism strikes, great-power competition, maximum pressure on Iran, or sanctions on Russia and China.[2]

US national-security elites' escape from geography into geopolitical imagination derives from a security paradigm as obsolete as the liberal colonialism of 1884. The *New York Times* writer's belief in the progressive impact of imperial military adventures lives on among those who advocated a permanent military presence in Afghanistan to safeguard the unsustainable gains made during the US intervention. One needed only hear members of the US national-security establishment opine that the US must keep troops in Afghanistan for decades or more, as it has done in Germany, Japan and South Korea, to realise that for them, as Andrew Bacevich argues in *After the Apocalypse*, it is always 1945, when the US was the only nuclear power and produced half of global GDP.[3] The equating of Afghanistan with Germany, where the Soviet Union and the US destroyed the Nazi regime; Japan, where the emperor signed an instrument of unconditional surrender after history's only nuclear attack; and Korea, where a balance of nuclear deterrence with China has kept an armistice in place despite decades of challenges, shows that for some in the American policy establishment, the power and good works of America are context-free dogma, not capacities to be tested against historical reality.

The United States' relative decline

The US debate about the troop withdrawal and its aftermath ignored not only geographical reality – that Afghanistan is a landlocked country, access to which is controlled by powers that do not share US goals – but also fundamental geostrategic facts. In particular, the balance of power between the US and Afghanistan's neighbours shifted against the US during its 20-year intervention in Afghanistan. States with direct interests in Afghanistan include four nuclear powers – China, India, Pakistan and Russia – plus Iran, which could soon be capable of fabricating nuclear weapons.

During the two decades of the military effort in Afghanistan, the combined economies of the surrounding countries in the region grew from five-sixths the size of the US economy to almost twice its size. The decline of the combined transatlantic economies relative to those of the region was comparable: from well over twice as big in 2001 to barely equal by the US withdrawal.

The main cause of the change in relative power is the rise of China, which the US is trying to balance not only through the transatlantic alliances built to contain the Soviet Union, but also through the Quad, an association comprising Australia, India, Japan and the US. The combined economies of the Quad remain more than 50% larger than that of China, but the trend of relative decline is even more pronounced than that of the transatlantic partners. During the period from the Soviet withdrawal from Afghanistan in 1990 to

Table 1: **GDP (PPP) in current international US dollars (billions) and ratios**

Country	1990	2001	2019
United States	5,963	10,582	21,433
European Union	6,220	9,963	20,787
China	1,229	4,292	24,040
India	1,049	2,372	9,560
Iran	407	697	1,073
Pakistan	207	395	1,061
Russia	1,188	1,075	4,315
Australia	296	531	1,324
Japan	2,417	3,493	5,346
Region	4,080	8,831	40,131
Quad	9,725	16,978	37,663
US/Region	146.2%	119.8%	53.4%
US+EU/Region	298.6%	232.7%	105.2%
Quad/China	791.4%	395.6%	156.7%

Source: World Bank Data

the US withdrawal in 2021, the combined Quad economies diminished from nearly eight times China's to barely more than 50% larger. Japan's sluggish performance was the main reason for the rapid decline, which would have been greater without the now-stalled acceleration of the Indian economy.

Geographic edit

The Quad has become the focus of US policy in a region that the US now calls the 'Indo-Pacific', in what looks like an attempt to edit China out of geography through a change in nomenclature. Whatever the Quad's potential or shortcomings may be, the Indo-Pacific is hardly a substitute for Asia. Neither Afghanistan, China, Iran, Pakistan nor Russia are Indo-Pacific any more than they are transatlantic. Even India, with its lengthy Himalayan borders with China and Pakistan, and its defence and commercial ties to Russia and Iran, can hardly be defined by a maritime label.

The development of maritime trade between Europe and Asia after the invention of blue-water navigation technologies in the fifteenth century marginalised the land route from the Mediterranean to China, commonly known as the Silk Road. The relative isolation and decline of landlocked continental Asia, including Afghanistan, dates to that time. Today, Chinese naval expansion poses a potential challenge to the domination of those still-busy sea routes by the US, though from Beijing's point of view US naval dominance in the Indian Ocean also poses a challenge to China, 60% of whose trade travels by sea. In 2016, an estimated 64% of China's maritime trade, including 80% of its crude-oil imports, transited the vulnerable Malacca Strait, which links the South China Sea to the Indian Ocean.[4] Naval expansion, however, is only one part of China's response to this challenge. The other is the Belt and Road Initiative (BRI), which circumvents the Indo-Pacific by reviving Eurasian transcontinental land routes through the Silk Road Economic Belt.

The United States' Pacific-centric perspective on Asia, a product of US geography, has distracted it from appreciating the dynamism of continental Asia west of China. China's movement of trade and investment towards the old Silk Road land route across Eurasia has the potential to become one of the most significant geopolitical shifts of our time. The BRI, whatever its shortcomings, is the largest development plan in history and meets immense needs for infrastructure that the US and its allies have hardly addressed.[5]

The World Bank has estimated that the world needs $40 trillion of investment in infrastructure, but the US response to the BRI at first treated it almost entirely as a challenge to the US-led 'rules-based international order' without acknowledging that it addressed neglected needs. In remarks at the Wilson Center in Washington in November 2019, Alice Wells, principal deputy assistant secretary of state for South and Central Asia, characterised the BRI as 'the Chinese Communist Party promoting its own brand of development', which 'stands outside of global efforts including those of the IMF and World Bank to improve transparency that enhances policy-making, prevents fiscal crises and deters corruption'. She added that

> this lack of transparency also hides risk to borrowing countries that already face substantial fiscal challenges, particularly since Chinese state companies undertaking [BRI] projects have a clear incentive to inflate costs and encourage corruption. Failure to repay those huge loans raises roadblocks to further development and leads to a surrender of strategic assets and it diminishes sovereignty.[6]

Perhaps aware of the aphorism attributed to former lobbyist and convicted felon Jack Abramoff that 'you can't beat somebody with nobody', Wells went on to recount the programme of development that the US was proposing, including a new institution, the US International Development Finance Corporation, to be capitalised at $60 billion. In the regional breakdown of its work on its website, however, Asia slips through the cracks between the 'Indo-Pacific', 'Central Europe and Eurasia' and 'Africa and the Middle East'.[7] Connectivity is not listed as a priority. Wells spoke a lot about the problems of the China–Pakistan Economic Corridor, but the bottom line for many in Pakistan appears to be that the country is benefitting from its relationship with China. Notes *Dawn*, Pakistan's leading daily: 'After suffering decades of electricity shortages that left families and businesses in the dark, Pakistan finds itself with a new problem: more electricity generating capacity than it needs. Large-scale construction of new power plants – largely coal-fired ones funded by China – has dramatically boosted the country's energy capacity.'[8]

The Abramoff problem persists. On 4 May 2021, a senior State Department official en route to a G7 planning meeting remarked to reporters that some countries lack alternatives to 'Chinese economic coercion'.[9] The Biden administration's proposed alternative is the 'Build Back Better World' (B3W) programme approved in principle at the June 2021 G7 summit. If implemented, B3W would be a multinational set of public–private partnerships that, like the BRI, aims to 'help narrow the $40+ trillion infrastructure need in the developing world'. B3W, the administration claims, 'will collectively catalyze hundreds of billions of dollars of infrastructure investment for low- and middle-income countries in the coming years'.[10] Without mentioning the BRI, the White House's fact sheet on the US proposal for the B3W programme clearly means to contrast the two, asserting that B3W will be values-driven, transparent, carried out in consultation with local communities and in support of the goals of the Paris agreement on climate change and good governance. In a background press call, a senior administration official made explicit that 'the contrast between our approach and China's, on these and other issues … should speak for itself'.[11] The fact sheet states that the programme 'will be global in scope, from Latin America and the

Caribbean to Africa to the Indo-Pacific', but neither that document nor the G7 communiqué even mentions Asia.[12]

The need to cooperate with China

The senior administration official also said 'this is not about making countries choose between us and China; this is about offering an affirmative, alternative vision and approach that they would want to choose', but the US and G7 did not propose any cooperation with China on common goals. The United States could not only compete with but also engage with and try to influence China's BRI.[13] One way to do that would be for the US to join the Asian Infrastructure Investment Bank (AIIB), a multilateral development bank established in January 2016 with 103 member states and $21bn in investment.

The characterisation of the AIIB as a Chinese-inspired challenge to the international order is mistaken. India is the second-largest shareholder, and most NATO and EU members have joined. A 2018 study published by Chatham House concluded that 'the AIIB clearly does not challenge the global governance status-quo'.[14] The Brookings Institution has described joining the AIIB as 'an avenue of constructive cooperation to help stabilize the rocky US–China relationship and enhance the US economic presence in Asia'.[15] The addition of the United States and Japan could change the balance and increase the influence of the US and its allies and partners over investment in the BRI.

Cooperation with China is even more essential if the US is to succeed in limiting the damage of climate change. China produces nearly 30% of global carbon emissions, and the US 15%.[16] No other nations will need to sacrifice as much of their present economic activity or stand to gain as much from investment in renewable energy as these two. Combining cooperation with constructive competition would make the US claim that B3W is not mainly about competing with China more convincing.

The coal-fired power plants that China has built in Pakistan are a major source of carbon emissions, and in December 2020 Pakistani Prime Minister Imran Khan announced a moratorium on construction of such plants. China has also announced that it will not fund more coal-fired plants abroad.

This pledge could provide an opportunity for the US and its allies to help Pakistan – and China – 'build back better'. A little realistic humility is in order, however. The US may be concerned that Chinese assistance projects serve Chinese national interests, cater to Chinese domestic constituencies and sometimes seek to make others dependent on China, but it should hardly be surprised.[17] The US itself insisted on supplying the Afghan military with *Black Hawk* helicopters, placing the profits of the Lockheed Martin Corporation above the needs of the Afghan military, which had used Soviet-made M-17s for decades.[18]

China is a peer competitor such as the US has not had since it became a global power. This means that the US can no longer exercise leadership in the way it has for the past 80 years. Furthermore, as Michael Klare has pointed out, there may be a contradiction between insisting on US leadership and combatting climate change:

> If climate change is an existential threat and international collaboration between the worst greenhouse gas emitters key to overcoming that peril, picking fights with China over its energy behavior is a self-defeating way to start. Whatever obstacles China does pose, its cooperation in achieving that 1.5-degree limit is critical … The only way to avert catastrophic climate change is for the United States to avoid a new cold war with China by devising a cooperative set of plans with Beijing to speed the global transition to a green economy.[19]

Washington needs to learn how to cooperate with China on connectivity, climate security and regional security in Central and Northeast Asia, even as it competes with or opposes it on Taiwan, the South China Sea, trade and human-rights issues. No matter how difficult that may be, the alternative is worse.

*   *   *

Among the geography lessons that war can teach, none is more important than that global cooperation across geography is necessary to combat major existential threats to humanity. Nostalgia for a bygone America's leadership of a bygone international order may steer the US into ventures as misdirected as Gordon's attempt to remake Sudan, and with similar results. As the US faces a daunting struggle over its own future, partnership in the face of global threats, even with competitors, and honest recognition of some humbling geographic and economic realities should be the guiding principles of policy towards Asia and the world.

Notes

1   'From the Nile to the Congo', *New York Times*, 11 May 1884, p. 8, https://timesmachine.nytimes.com/timesmachine/1884/05/11/109777316.html?pageNumber=8.

2   See Atlantic Council, 'A Transatlantic Charter on Afghan Sovereignty, Security, and Development', South Asia Center, April 2021, https://www.atlanticcouncil.org/wp-content/uploads/2021/04/A-transatlantic-charter-for-peace-and-security-in-Afghanistan.pdf.

3   See Andrew Bacevich, *After the Apocalypse: America's Role in a World Transformed* (New York: Metropolitan Books, 2021).

4   See Center for Strategic and International Studies, 'How Much Trade Transits the South China Sea?', China Power Project, 2021, https://chinapower.csis.org/.much-trade-transits-south-china-sea/.

5   See, for example, James Crabtree, 'Competing with the BRI: The West's Uphill Task', *Survival*, vol. 63, no. 4, August–September 2021, pp. 81–8.

6   US Embassy & Consulates in Pakistan, 'Ambassador Wells' Remarks on the "China–Pakistan Economic Corridor"', 19 November 2019, https://pk.usembassy.gov/ambassador-wells-remarks-on-the-china-pakistan-economic-corridor/.

7   See US International Development Finance Corporation, 'Our Work – Regions', https://www.dfc.gov/our-impact/our-work.

8   'Pakistan's Unexpected Dilemma: Too Much Electricity', *Dawn*, 25 February 2021, https://www.dawn.com/news/1609241/pakistans-unexpected-dilemma-too-much-electricity.

9   US Department of State, 'Briefing with Senior State Department Officials to Traveling Press', 4 May 2021, https://www.state.gov/briefing-with-senior-state-department-officials-to-traveling-press/.

10 White House, 'Fact Sheet: President Biden and G7 Leaders Launch Build Back Better World (B3W) Partnership', 12 June 2021, https://www.whitehouse.gov/briefing-room/statements-releases/2021/06/12/fact-sheet-president-biden-and-g7-leaders-launch-build-back-better-world-b3w-partnership/.

11 White House, 'Background Press Call by Senior Administration Officials Previewing the Second Day of the G7 Summit', 12 June 2021, https://

www.whitehouse.gov/briefing-room/press-briefings/2021/06/12/background-press-call-by-senior-administration-officials-previewing-the-second-day-of-the-g7-summit/.

12 See White House, 'Fact Sheet'; and White House, 'Carbis Bay G7 Summit Communiqué', 13 June 2021, https://www.whitehouse.gov/briefing-room/statements-releases/2021/06/13/carbis-bay-g7-summit-communique/.

13 See Christopher Mott, 'Don't Fear China's Belt and Road Initiative', *Survival*, vol. 62, no. 4, August–September 2020, pp. 47–55.

14 See Shahar Hameiri and Lee Jones, 'China Challenges Global Governance? Chinese International Development Finance and the AIIB', *International Affairs*, vol. 94, no. 3, May 2018, pp. 573–93.

15 Madiha Afzal et al., 'A List of Specific, Actionable Foreign Policy Ideas for the Next President', Brookings Institution, 27 October 2020, https://www.brookings.edu/blog/order-from-chaos/2020/10/27/a-list-of-specific-actionable-foreign-policy-ideas-for-the-next-president/.

16 Pierre Friedlingstein et al., 'The Global Carbon Budget 2020', *Earth System Science Data*, vol. 12, no. 4, 2020, pp. 329–40.

17 On the strategic subtleties of the BRI, see, for instance, Jordan Calinoff and David Gordon, 'Port Investments in the Belt and Road Initiative: Is Beijing Grabbing Strategic Assets?', *Survival*, vol. 62, no. 4, August–September 2020, pp. 59–80.

18 See Thomas Gibbons-Neff, Helene Cooper and Eric Schmitt, 'Departure of U.S. Contractors Poses Myriad Problems for Afghan Military', *New York Times*, 19 June 2021, https://www.nytimes.com/2021/06/19/world/asia/Afghanistan-withdrawal-contractors.html.

19 Michael T. Klare, 'Biden's Tough Stance on China Will Lead to Global Climate Doom', *Nation*, 1 March 2021, https://www.thenation.com/article/world/biden-china-climate/.

India and US FONOPs: Oceans Apart

Rahul Roy-Chaudhury and Kate Sullivan de Estrada

Strategic convergence between the United States and India is proceeding apace. Yet in April 2021, the United States conducted a 'routine' freedom-of-navigation operation (FONOP) in India's exclusive economic zone (EEZ), contravening India's declared position that other states may carry out military exercises or manoeuvres in its EEZ only with prior notification. The US 7th Fleet swiftly publicised the FONOP and pointed to India's 'excessive maritime claims', drawing a volley of critical commentary from India's strategic elite and an official Indian statement that the operation of the USS *John Paul Jones* was unauthorised.[1]

India is a core partner in the Quadrilateral Security Dialogue ('the Quad') with Australia, Japan and the US, and endorses the rhetoric of a 'free and open Indo-Pacific', but its view on key aspects of coastal-state authority under maritime law is closer to that of China. US FONOPs targeting India therefore raise two key questions: to what extent do Washington and New Delhi share the same conception of the United States as an extra-regional maritime power in the Indian Ocean, and how can the United Nations Convention on the Law of the Sea (UNCLOS) accommodate the diverse demands of established and rising powers?

Kate Sullivan de Estrada, the lead author of this article, is Associate Professor in the International Relations of South Asia at the University of Oxford, a Fellow of St Antony's College and an Associate Fellow at the IISS. **Rahul Roy-Chaudhury** is Senior Fellow for South Asia at the IISS and author of two books on the Indian Navy and the Indian Ocean.

Survival | vol. 64 no. 1 | February–March 2022 | pp. 131–156   https://doi.org/10.1080/00396338.2022.2032989

The US and India: a growing defence and maritime partnership

Over the past three decades, bipartisan support in the United States for economic and strategic engagement with India has flourished. India's economic liberalisation in the early post-Cold War period and impressive economic growth drew the two countries closer on trade, investment and energy. In parallel, US interest in India's value as a major Asian democracy with the potential to offset Chinese influence led to bold strategic overtures. The most game-changing of these for the bilateral relationship was the US–India Civil Nuclear Agreement, signed in 2006 and operationalised in 2008, that sought to accommodate nuclear-armed India as a non-signatory of the Non-Proliferation Treaty (NPT) within the global nuclear order.[2]

At the same time, India's own compulsions to counter expanding Chinese influence in India's extended neighbourhood, on land and at sea, have increased appetites in New Delhi for strategic convergence with the United States. Cooperation has steadily advanced over the past six years. India became a 'Major Defense Partner' of the United States in 2016, a status that gives India licence-free access to a wide range of military and dual-use technologies regulated by the US Department of Commerce.[3] The two countries signed the Logistics Exchange Memorandum of Agreement (LEMOA) that same year, an accounting mechanism that allows both countries to access and offset logistical items and services from one another.[4] An annual US–India Maritime Security Dialogue was also inaugurated in 2016 to discuss maritime challenges, naval cooperation and multilateral engagement.[5]

In 2018, Indian defence minister Nirmala Sitharaman declared that defence cooperation had 'elevated India–U.S. relations to unprecedented heights'.[6] This was in the context of the two countries' first '2+2' dialogue, a bilateral mechanism between foreign and defence ministers. Both sides signed the Communications Compatibility and Security Agreement (COMCASA) that permits India to make optimal use, via encrypted communications systems, of India's multiple US-origin military platforms.[7] The third and most recent 2+2 dialogue took place in person in New Delhi, despite the constraints of the COVID-19 pandemic, in late 2020. A key outcome of the dialogue was the signing of the long-awaited Basic Exchange and Cooperation Agreement

(BECA) for geospatial cooperation. The United States is now India's fourth-largest arms supplier after Russia, Israel and France.[8]

Washington and New Delhi have begun to emphasise shared values around a rules-based international order in the maritime domain.[9] The United States seeks allies and partners to endorse the concept of a free and open Indo-Pacific as a bulwark against China's increasing assertiveness over its territorial claims in the South China Sea.[10] India's own concerns centre on Chinese ambitions in what New Delhi considers its 'maritime backyard'. China's connectivity plans in the Indian Ocean, expressed through the country's Maritime Silk Road initiative, foreshadow a possible incremental strategy of power projection: there are concerns that Beijing could, for example, establish a military presence and project combat power in maritime spaces adjoining Bangladesh, the Maldives, Pakistan or Sri Lanka.[11]

Normative consensus between the United States and India over a liberal, legal order for the oceans emerged during former US president Barack Obama's visit to New Delhi in January 2015. In their US–India Joint Strategic Vision for the Asia-Pacific and Indian Ocean Region, the two countries invoked a commitment to international law and UNCLOS, and affirmed 'the importance of safeguarding maritime security and ensuring freedom of navigation and overflight throughout the region, especially in the South China Sea'.[12] Indian Prime Minister Narendra Modi mapped these commitments onto the Indo-Pacific space in a major statement at the 2018 IISS Shangri-La Dialogue in Singapore that emphasised India's 'shared vision of an open, stable, secure and prosperous Indo-Pacific Region'.[13]

In parallel, from late 2017 a re-energised Quadrilateral Security Dialogue began to emerge after having been suspended in 2008.[14] In November 2020, Australia was incorporated into the long-standing *Malabar* series of US–Indian bilateral naval manoeuvres, which had started in 1992 and had added Japan as a permanent member in 2015. Thus, *Malabar* became a naval exercise of the four Quad nations. The first Quad Leaders' Summit took place in March 2021, albeit in a virtual format. In their first joint statement, the Quad partners declared that they would 'prioritize the role of international law in the maritime domain, particularly as reflected in the United Nations Convention on the Law of the Sea'.[15] The first in-person

Quad summit took place in Washington DC in September 2021. India and the United States have recently and rapidly consolidated a significant bilateral defence partnership, have a clear appetite for bilateral and quadrilateral maritime cooperation, and appear to share a common commitment to the rules and norms that govern the maritime domain.

The USS *John Paul Jones* FONOP

Amid so much concordant talk and action over matters at sea, the US decision to undertake and publicise a freedom-of-navigation operation targeting India on 7 April 2021 was both unexpected and, for some in India's strategic community, galling. India had been the target of US FONOPs before, but this time the US Navy broke with previous practice in deciding to make an immediate announcement rather than folding individual FONOPs into an annual report of all operations worldwide.

The central point of contention was US–Indian disagreement over whether, under each country's interpretation of UNCLOS, foreign warships are subject to the requirement of prior permission for military exercises or manoeuvres in a coastal state's EEZ.[16] The US Navy's public statement announced that the destroyer *John Paul Jones* had carried out a military exercise approximately 130 nautical miles west of the Lakshadweep islands, within India's EEZ in the Arabian Sea, 'without requesting India's prior consent'.[17] The exercise's stated objective was to assert US navigational rights and freedoms 'consistent with international law' to 'demonstrate that the United States will fly, sail and operate wherever international law allows'.[18]

The US Navy's clarification in its announcement that US FONOPs do not target any one country and are not intended to make 'political statements' did little to pacify observers who construed the *John Paul Jones* FONOP as an unnecessarily barbed challenge to India's interpretation of UNCLOS. Arun Prakash, a former chief of the Indian Navy, made the point starkly: 'this gratuitous public declaration, coming within weeks of the US-led Quad Leaders virtual meeting and on the heels of a major Indo-US naval exercise, can only be seen as an act of breath-taking inanity'.[19] In the storm that erupted across the Indian media, various interpretations of the FONOP were offered: it signalled a security challenge to India; it was encouragement to other navies to violate India's domestic maritime law; it was intended as a warning against India's acquisition of the Russian S-400 air-defence missile system; it symbolised the 'arrogance' of the United States despite close ties with India.[20] Other analysis simply noted that the FONOP challenged India's maritime claims while signalling to China that such 'non-political' actions were intended to uphold UNCLOS and the rules-based international order, and were not solely directed at China.[21]

In contrast to this heated public debate, the Indian Ministry of External Affairs released a relatively low-key statement in which it noted that 'India's stated position on [UNCLOS] is that the Convention does not authorise other States to carry out in the Exclusive Economic Zone and on the continental shelf military exercises or manoeuvres, in particular those involving the use of weapons or explosives, without the consent of the coastal State'.[22] This reiterated the position India had declared in ratifying UNCLOS in 1995.[23] The ministry's statement also noted that India had conveyed its concerns to the US administration through diplomatic channels.

Amid the fallout of the *John Paul Jones* FONOP, three core proposals began to emerge. The first was that India bring its interpretation of UNCLOS in line with that of the United States – which has not itself ratified the convention – by jettisoning the requirement of prior consent for military exercises or manoeuvres in India's EEZ.[24] Retired Indian Commodore Lalit Kapur, for example, suggested that India update its position and differentiate itself from China, arguing that India's caveated stance on freedom of navigation 'probably owes more to dogma and bureaucratic inertia, and risks placing India in the same revisionist position as China in the South China Sea'.[25]

A second position proposed that India double down by not only retaining its current stance but also codifying it more explicitly in domestic law.[26] An influential retired Indian foreign secretary, Kanwal Sibal, agreed that India should be differentiated from China, but suggested that the United States should make the distinction, and not use FONOPs as an indiscriminate tool.[27] Sibal argued that India and the United States 'cannot together support the principle of freedom of navigation if that freedom becomes a tool by the US for giving short shrift to India's legal position on its maritime rights'.[28]

A third set of suggestions called for no specific steps, but greater mutual understanding.[29] One US commentary, for example, proposed that the two countries avoid highlighting their public differences – in effect, sweeping the issue under the rug.[30] Yet the countries' divergent stances preclude a deep bilateral consensus on maritime order and a common multilateral position within the Quad.

US FONOPs and India

For the United States, the capacity to secure unimpeded access to maritime aerospace and to uphold intercontinental sea lines of communication is both a core US national-security interest and a fundamental precondition for its role as a manager of regional and global order.[31] President Jimmy Carter instituted the US Freedom of Navigation (FON) Program in 1979, and Ronald Reagan reaffirmed it in 1983.[32] Sustained by bipartisan support since then, the programme's aim is to offer tangible proof that the United States does not acquiesce to the maritime claims of coastal states where these appear excessive according to US interpretations of international maritime law.[33] Bilateral consultations and formal diplomatic protests can take place under the programme, but its most conspicuous tools are naval and aerial military operations.[34]

The United States' commitment to unimpeded access to the seas and maritime aerospace is a product both of the country's history and of its contemporary strategic priorities. James Kraska has observed that 'virtually every war in U.S. history involved some aspect of freedom of navigation, and the FON program was designed to ensure the issue did not fade during peacetime'.[35] Today, the power-projection capabilities of the US Navy and Air Force are predicated on their ability to freely exploit the global commons.[36]

In asserting the freedom of navigation and challenging so-called excessive maritime claims, the United States regularly invokes UNCLOS, despite never having ratified it. UNCLOS permits its 168 parties to lay claim to a territorial sea extending 12 nautical miles from their respective coastlines and to an EEZ of 200 nautical miles for the purposes of natural-resource extraction. Despite the outsize role played by the United States in negotiating the terms of UNCLOS, Reagan announced in 1982, under pressure from US mining corporations, that the US would not sign the convention due to its provisions relating to deep-seabed mining.[37] Instead, he clarified the US position through his 1983 'Statement on United States Oceans Policy', affirming that the US would accept and act in accordance with the provisions of UNCLOS relating to traditional (non-seabed) uses of the ocean. In particular, the statement declared that the United States would 'exercise and assert its navigation and overflight rights and freedoms on a worldwide basis in a manner that is consistent with the balance of interests reflected in the convention'.[38] The US would not, however, 'acquiesce in unilateral acts of other states designed to restrict the rights and freedoms of the international community in navigation and overflight and other related high seas uses'.[39]

The 'balance of interests' within UNCLOS is far from undisputed. In particular, there are differences of interpretation over the scope of activities permitted to military vessels in a country's EEZ. Coastal states hold the rights to natural resources in their EEZs, yet must give 'due regard' to the rights and duties of other states (Article 56).[40] In particular, all states enjoy the same freedom of navigation and overflight within EEZs as they do on the high seas (Article 58, with reference to Article 87). However, all states transiting through the EEZ of a coastal state must give 'due regard' to the rights and duties of that state and comply with its laws and regulations, insofar as these do not contravene the rules of the convention (Article 58).[41] Warships on the high seas have immunity from the jurisdiction of any state except for their own flag state (Article 95), yet the convention states that the high seas should be used for peaceful purposes (Article 88). States should also refrain from threatening the use of force against any state (Article 301).[42] Thus, the convention neither expressly authorises nor prohibits military activities in EEZs.[43] As Stephen Rose has observed, this ambiguity was the only way to achieve agreement between a 'large number of states with dissimilar history, unequal resources and different maritime interests'.[44]

The US position is that customary law favours the interests of international vessels and aircraft in EEZs, which enjoy the freedom of navigation and overflight associated with the high seas. This gives free rein, says Kraska, to foreign naval forces to conduct 'task force manoeuvring, flight operations, military exercises, surveillance, intelligence gathering activities, and ordnance testing and firing' within the EEZs of coastal nations, which in turn are understood to have no legal authority to restrict the high-seas freedoms of other states in their EEZs.[45]

As one of a number of littoral powers that assert the right to restrict the activities of foreign military vessels in their EEZs, India has long been a target of US FONOPs, 22 of which have taken place in India's EEZ in the past 30 years. More than half have taken aim at India's requirement for prior consent for military activities in its EEZ, with multiple FONOP challenges conducted annually against India between 2007 and 2017. In 2019, the US explicitly stated that that year's FONOP against India had been conducted to challenge India's requirement for prior consent for military exercises in its EEZ involving the use of weapons or explosives. A FONOP with the same rationale had previously taken place in 1999.[46]

India has long been a target of US FONOPs

This is not the only type of operation that the US has carried out against India. FONOPs have challenged Indian claims along four additional lines. Firstly, India's domestic law requires all foreign warships to give prior notification before entering the country's territorial sea for innocent passage. UNCLOS holds that ships of all states enjoy the right of innocent passage through countries' territorial seas (Article 17).[47] This clause does not differentiate between warships and commercial ships. By contrast, India's Territorial Waters, Continental Shelf, Exclusive Economic Zone and Other Maritime Zones Act, 1976 (hereafter the '1976 Maritime Zones Act') specifically excludes warships, including submarines and other underwater vehicles, from exercising the right of innocent passage through the country's territorial waters, requiring prior notice to be given to the central government.[48] Since the United States insists on an unconditional right of innocent passage through territorial seas, US FONOPs on this basis have taken place against India in 1992, 1994, 1996, 1997, 1999, 2000–03 and 2011.[49] Significantly, however, no FONOP asserting the right of innocent passage in India's territorial sea (as opposed to its EEZ) has taken place in the past decade.

Secondly, India requires all foreign warships to give prior notification to enter its 24-nautical-mile security/contiguous zone. This has been challenged by US FONOPs in 2000–03 and 2016. Thirdly, India claims the Gulf of Mannar as historic waters, an assertion that was challenged by US FONOPs in 1994 and 1999. Finally, though not the target of US FONOPs, India has declared straight baselines delineating zones around the Andaman and Nicobar islands, on the islands' western edge. Under UNCLOS, such lines can only be drawn around archipelagic nation-states (such as Indonesia), not island provinces or administrative regions of existing continental states.[50] India's 1976 Maritime Zones Act also contains provisions that permit the Indian government to establish a 'designated area' within the country's EEZ and continental shelf in which it can establish 'fairways, sealanes [and] traffic separation schemes', possibly infringing on others' right to navigate those waterways.[51]

In the early 2000s, India formally protested against US military survey vessels operating in its EEZ even though UNCLOS does not restrict the conduct of military survey operations. These protests were made on the basis that the US warships were conducting marine scientific research within India's EEZ, an activity prohibited by UNCLOS. India later shifted away from this position, however, perhaps as a means of distinguishing itself from China: Beijing does not differentiate between marine scientific research and military surveys, and seeks to restrict both in its EEZ.[52]

To date, the Indian Navy has never challenged US ships carrying out FONOPs against India, even within its territorial waters. Instead, in the most recent incident, the Indian Navy tracked the *John Paul Jones* from the time it emerged from the Gulf until it passed through the Strait of Malacca, but did not seek to interfere with its navigation.[53] India has thus far avoided an 'action–reaction dynamic' of the kind that has seen escalatory developments in the South China Sea with near-perilous results, such as the near collision in September 2018 between the USS *Decatur*, conducting a FONOP near Gaven Reef, and a Chinese People's Liberation Army Navy *Luyang* destroyer that demanded it leave the area.[54] The distinction, as Mohan Malik has argued, is that 'China is seeking to enforce its view, while others [including India] lack the will and capability to do so'.[55]

India, UNCLOS and freedom of navigation

US FONOPs of the kind undertaken by the *John Paul Jones* in April present at least three sets of interlinked issues for New Delhi. These relate to India's position on UNCLOS, its maritime security and its status in the Indian Ocean region.

India and coastal-state authority under UNCLOS

In recent years, India has signalled a strong commitment to UNCLOS, both in practice and through public statements. In 2014, the Indian government accepted the outcome of arbitration proceedings through UNCLOS over a decades-old maritime-boundary dispute with Bangladesh. Both countries benefited from the verdict, but Bangladesh, which had initiated the proceedings, was awarded additional maritime entitlements.[56] India's unqualified acceptance of the ruling compared favourably to China's rejection of a verdict in July 2016 that challenged a number of Chinese claims and activities in the South China Sea, following the Philippines' initiation of arbitration under UNCLOS. In September 2016, at the 11th East Asia Summit, Modi urged all parties to 'show utmost respect for the UNCLOS', adding that India's 'own track record in settling its maritime boundary with Bangladesh can serve as an example'.[57]

India's rejection of US FONOPs in its EEZ is not a rejection of UNCLOS, but of certain US interpretations of the convention and customary international law. The Indian position on coastal-state authority over military activities in EEZs has its origins in both the first and third UN Conferences on the Law of the Sea.[58] During the former, held in Geneva in 1958, India sought to secure the requirement of both prior notification and authorisation of the passage of foreign warships through the territorial sea of a coastal state. According to Indian accounts, the experience was unpleasant: despite backing from the International Law Commission, India's proposal was opposed 'by the major maritime powers' and did not secure a two-thirds majority.[59] For this reason, India did not ratify the 1958 Convention on the Territorial Sea and the Contiguous Zone. By the time of the Third UN Conference, held between 1973 and 1982, India – styling itself a 'growing maritime nation'[60] – had shifted from insistence on prior notification and authorisation of military vessels through the territorial sea to prior notifica-tion only. Since the 1958 convention did not expressly forbid notification, and since there had been no unanimity of opinion on the issue at the First UN Conference, India chose to read customary law as supporting notification.[61] As a result, India's 1976 Maritime Zones Act requires that foreign warships and submarines give prior notice before passing through India's territorial waters.[62] Indian newspaper reports at the time apprehended, however, that there would be controversy at the Third UN Conference between 'rich and powerful nations' and 'developing countries' over the issue.[63]

Importantly, India's 1976 Maritime Zones Act acted upon the emerging concept of the exclusive economic zone granting to coastal states sovereign rights over the living and non-living resources and economic uses of the sea within a certain distance from their coasts.[64] As well as new rights, this concept also imposed demanding obligations, with which the 1976 Maritime Zones Act attempted to grapple. In addition to requiring foreign warships to give notification before passing through India's territorial waters, Article 7(7) of the Act permits the extension of any pre-existing enactments to India's EEZ.[65] One legal expert commented that India's view of the EEZ as expressed in its legislation appeared 'simply to be another component of national territory', with India asserting direct authority to regulate naviga-tion in the zone.[66] While the 1976 Maritime Zones Act does provide, in Article 7(9), for the exercise of navigation rights in and over the EEZ, it nonetheless makes freedom of navigation and overflight dependent on India's claimed rights in the zone, which are expansive.[67]

The final text of UNCLOS takes an ambiguous stance on the military activities of foreign states in EEZs. Unofficial discussion took place on the issue during the Third UN Conference, but the major maritime powers, led by the United States and the Soviet Union, permitted no formal debate. Instead, they centred their negotiation strategies on protecting navigation rights in straits and new jurisdictional zones such as coastal-state EEZs.[68] O.P. Sharma, former judge advocate general of the Indian Navy and a representative of India at the conference, found the lack of open debate regrettable.[69] Positions polarised on the extent of coastal-state authority over EEZs and the related rights of other states. Brazil, Cape Verde and Uruguay were persistent and vocal proponents of prior authorisation, going so far as to claim that military exercises did not constitute a peaceful use of the oceans. The United States' objection to this stance was so strong that its representative issued a veiled threat to withdraw from the conference.[70] India was among the first wave of state signatories to UNCLOS, signing the convention on 10 December 1982 and ratifying it on 29 June 1995. Yet India lodged a formal declaration upon ratification conveying its understanding that military exercises or manoeuvres in an EEZ, in particular those involving the use of weapons or explosives, required not just prior notification but the consent of the coastal state.[71]

Due to the ambiguities inherent in UNCLOS, it is not tenable to argue that India has committed itself to unconditionally accept the military activities of another state's ships and aircraft in its EEZ simply by ratifying the convention. Yet the Indian position of requiring notification for all military activities may also be a stretch. Some legal experts argue that an international court would accept neither that states have an 'absolute' right to conduct military activities without prior notification of or consultation with affected coastal states, nor that all military activities are subject to the prior consent of coastal states.[72] Instead, the principle of 'due regard' – whereby coastal states must give due regard to the rights and duties of other states (Article 56), and other states must in turn give due regard to the rights and duties of coastal states (Article 58) – removes any 'automatic presumption in favour of the rights of the coastal state over a third state or *vice-versa*'.[73] A balanced approach would avoid a unilateral assessment of the scope of 'due regard' on both sides – in other words, a coastal state should not require prior consent or authorisation for all military activities in its EEZ, and other states should not engage in such activities without prior notice or consultation, in particular where operations could obstruct a coastal state in exercising its economic rights in its EEZ.[74]

This position supports India's preference for prior notification in all cases (to avoid a unilateral interpretation of 'due regard' by the visiting state) and authorisation in most, though not all, cases of military activities in its EEZ. Careful bilateral or multilateral discussion would be needed to establish the precise scope of such authorisation, which cannot be established through fixed, unilateral positions on how to interpret coastal-state authority under UNCLOS.

India and maritime security

India's contemporary concerns around military activities in its EEZ centre primarily on the potential for Chinese maritime activism in the mould of US navigation patrols in the South China Sea. As maritime expert Abhijit Singh has observed, 'the U.S. Navy's emphasis on navigational freedoms in the EEZs encourages other regional navies to violate India's domestic regulations in the waters surrounding the Andaman and Nicobar islands'.[75] These islands, as noted, do not enjoy the legal status of an archipelago under UNCLOS, and thus are vulnerable to intrusions by foreign military vessels.[76] This is a key reason why India has avoided participating in US patrols in the South China Sea, despite repeated invitations from Washington to do so.

India's position also has historical antecedents. The activities of the great powers in India's maritime environs during the Cold War have cast a long shadow over India's strategic thinking on the oceans. Disquiet over great-power naval activity in the Indian Ocean can be traced to the presence of Soviet warships in its waters from 1968, and the decision by the United Kingdom and United States to plan a military base on the Chagos Islands (the UK leased Diego Garcia to the US in 1970).[77] Seeking to limit further escalation and to discourage extra-regional powers from carrying out military or nuclear activities in the Indian Ocean, India supported a Sri Lankan initiative to establish a zone of peace in that ocean.[78] The UN General Assembly adopted Resolution 2832 (XXVI) on 16 December 1971, a day after the United States sent Task Force 74, a carrier battle group led by the nuclear-powered USS *Enterprise*, into the Bay of Bengal in an attempt to intimidate India in the closing days of the 1971 India–Pakistan War.

The deployment of the *Enterprise* sent shockwaves through India's political, diplomatic and strategic communities. As one former Indian naval commander explained in 2015, 'the significance attached to this incident can be gauged by the fact it continues to find repeated mention despite a larger Indo-US rapprochement, particularly while discussing the divisive aspects of bilateral relations'.[79] Accordingly, references to the 1971 incident surfaced in commentary on the *John Paul Jones* FONOP: Indian politician Manish Tiwari, for one, linked the two incidents, noting that 'American perfidy at that critical moment is indelibly imprinted in the collective Indian psyche'.[80]

Threats from within the Indian Ocean have also driven India's growing perceptions of its maritime security vulnerabilities. The 1965 Indo-Pakistani War saw Pakistani warships disguised as merchant ships approach and bombard the ancient coastal city of Dwarka in Gujarat, and the Indian Chief of the Naval Staff felt compelled to take measures for the defence of the Andaman and Nicobar islands against a possible Indonesian attack after then-president Sukarno offered military help to Pakistan's president Mohammad Ayub Khan.[81]

More recently, non-traditional security challenges have contributed to India's expanding concerns about the movement of vessels with dangerous cargoes – of any type, not just foreign military ones – in its coastal zones. The 26–28 November 2008 terrorist siege in Mumbai that killed 166 people and involved ten Pakistani nationals arriving by sea posed tough questions about India's coastal and maritime security. The major overhaul that followed made India's coastguard responsible for coastal security, with the navy placed in charge of overall maritime security. But key questions remained about how effective the coordination between those two forces would be in operational terms. Concerns have also been mounting about the growth of 'floating armouries' in the Indian Ocean. Following an upsurge in piracy in the western Indian Ocean from 2006 to 2009, commercial shipowners began to make use of privately contracted armed security personnel. Floating armouries offer a solution for private maritime-security companies to the challenges of moving arms and ammunition between vessels given the limitations on bringing weapons into the territorial seas of many of the region's coastal states. India fears these armouries could be seized by terrorists.[82]

To date, there is no single government organisation responsible for coordinating the activities and often competing priorities of the many stakeholders involved in maritime affairs in India. These include more than 20 ministries, departments and agencies of the central government, the maritime institutions of nine coastal states and four union-territory governments (including those of the Lakshadweep islands in the Arabian Sea and the Andaman and Nicobar islands in the Bay of Bengal), the navy, coastguard and marine police. The result has been a lack of coordination and cooperation that poses risks for maritime security. Indeed, some coastal states in India continue to perceive coastal security as the primary responsibility of the central government even though they are solely responsible for the marine police that patrol the shallow waters close to the coast.[83]

The announcement by India's Chief of Defence Staff in April 2021, in the wake of the *John Paul Jones* FONOP, that a federal body, the National Maritime Commission (NMC), was to be set up (subject to approval by the Cabinet Committee on Security), demonstrated fresh impetus to streamline India's policymaking and coordination on maritime affairs, although as of early January 2022 this had not formally taken place.[84] The origin of the NMC lies in the first comprehensive review of national-security management in India, which was commissioned by the first government of the Bharatiya Janata Party (BJP) in the aftermath of the 1999 Kargil conflict and released in February 2001. Titled 'Reforming the National Security System', the report recommended that 'an apex body for management of maritime affairs … be formed for institutionalized linkages between the Navy, Coast Guard and the concerned Ministries of the Central and the State Governments'.[85] Despite this recommendation being approved by the Cabinet Committee on Security in May 2001, it has taken more than two decades to materialise.

A lack of coordination poses risks for maritime security

Instead, the ruling congress-led United Progressive Alliance government proposed a Maritime Security Advisory Board, with a Maritime Security Advisor as its chief, but this was not approved by the Cabinet Committee on Security. Instead, it created a National Committee to Strengthen Maritime and Coastal Security (NCSMCS) in August 2009. Chaired by the cabinet secretary, the NCSMCS consists of representatives of relevant ministries, departments and organisations within the central government, as well as the chief secretaries or administrators of the coastal states and union territories.[86] But it has met only occasionally.

The current plan, for an NMC to be headed by a National Maritime Security Coordinator as the principal adviser to the government working under the National Security Advisor, follows a pledge in June 2014 by the newly elected BJP-led government to set up a National Maritime Authority.[87] Nothing came of this pledge until the announcement of the NMC in April 2021. It is not clear whether this body will coordinate among multiple maritime stakeholders or instead integrate all agencies operating along the coast as well as on the high seas under the navy.[88] Regardless, the move demonstrates New Delhi's growing prioritisation of India's maritime security. It may also lead to more coordinated and systematic thinking over how India will handle discrepancies between its own and others' interpretations of UNCLOS.

India and status in the Indian Ocean

In keeping with the views of twentieth-century Indian statesman K.M. Panikkar, who argued that India should control the Indian Ocean, the country opposed the presence of extra-regional powers in the Indian Ocean from the late 1960s, seeking instead to assert its own regional leadership.[89] This position started to change from the early 2000s, however, as India began to welcome the role of the United States and others, including (more recently) the UK, in helping to counter China. But just how much US influence is tolerable has emerged as a subject of debate, spurred in part by a US move in September 2020 to sign a defence- and security-cooperation agreement with the Maldives.[90] As one maritime commentator warned, the Indian Ocean faces the risk of becoming 'over-crowded … with defence pacts and multiple navies crisscrossing one another'.[91] Some Indian observers worry that the growing US military presence in the eastern Indian Ocean region could heighten rivalries and provoke China, while others fear that India's own regional influence and desire to consolidate its status as a 'net security provider' in the Indian Ocean stand to be diminished if the United States' strategic footprint grows.[92]

India's relative standing vis-à-vis the major powers in the Indian Ocean is clearly of importance to the country's decision-makers, which is one reason why the Quad grouping is an attractive prospect. Minilaterals such as the Quad are flexible, issue-driven and diversity-tolerant: they accord equivalent status to members despite the material differences between them.[93] Actions such as US FONOPs can degrade this veneer of equivalence, however, reminding India that the United States grants itself the right to unilaterally declare and uphold international legislation at the same time as it demonstrates its superior material status. In other words, US FONOPs underscore the fact that the US–India relationship remains far from an equal partnership. Some voices in India are also sensitive to any suggestion that India's status is not superior to that of China. This explains Sibal's protest that the US policy of treating India and China 'on an equal footing' with regard to freedom-of-navigation issues was 'politically absurd'.[94]

India's own maritime strategy in the Indian Ocean, encapsulated in the formulation 'SAGAR' – Security and Growth for All in the Region – reflects an aspiration not simply to provide regional public goods, such as serving as a 'first responder' in instances of natural and environmental disasters, but also to politically differentiate itself as a rising power from the powers of the past, by offering egalitarian and inclusive regional leadership.[95] This strategy makes sense for a country that cannot match the material power of China in the Indian Ocean and that is wary of extra-regional powers playing too great a role. To retain the Indian Ocean as its 'own backyard', India must build legitimacy. Its policies towards smaller, weaker littoral states in the coming decade will be of great importance. Responding to their human-security and development needs will be key.[96]

India and a free and open Indo-Pacific

A decade ago, one US scholar of maritime law argued that India was 'awakening to the importance of a liberal legal order of the oceans'.[97] A rules-based maritime order is today at the heart of India's strategy to manage its security and enhance prosperity in the Indian Ocean, a region in which China's influence is expanding. Given its distinctive regional status, security concerns and understanding of international maritime law, however, India does not view a self-appointed US role as custodian and guarantor of the maritime global commons as the only, or most desirable, route to regional peace and prosperity.

Calls persist for India to 'move on', to shed its 'historical baggage' and to share in the normative maritime commitments of the United States. But the US has 'history', too, as seen in the predominant role it has played in shaping the law of the seas and in the ways it has interpreted its role as a strategic actor in the Indo-Pacific. The United States' vision of 'free and open' oceans is closely linked to the unbridled projection of its power by enabling the unrestricted manoeuvrability of the US Navy and Air Force within the global commons, and their ability to shift rapidly between theatres. India currently has neither the capability nor the political will to share in such a vision: US readings of UNCLOS are not a natural destination for rising maritime powers. Moreover, the United States' refusal to ratify UNCLOS undermines its credibility and tacitly encourages the kind of great-power exceptionalism – or exemptionalism – that China has displayed in relation to its 'historic claims' in the South China Sea. If India can be asked to set aside its trepidation over the potential for powerful maritime states to challenge its security and vision for regional leadership, can the United States likewise be asked to shed its own baggage as an assertive, unipolar maritime state? The answer, in both cases, is likely to be 'not entirely'.

India is rising, but not quite according to the rulebook of a global order shaped to a significant degree by the United States. Both Washington and New Delhi need to determine how their countries' diverse positions on core institutions of global governance, including UNCLOS, can be managed. As Kyle Lascurettes and Sara Moller argue,

> if the international system of the near future is to be characterized by norm-governed order rather than competitive anarchy, it will have to be based on both great power consensus and the toleration of political diversity rather than Western primacy and the single-minded pursuit of the West's normative preferences.[98]

It is clear that New Delhi and Washington will need to find common ground on the issue of military activities in the EEZs of coastal states, as well as on other areas of UNCLOS where their interpretations diverge. On the former, one path could be to take seriously the concept of mutual 'due regard' as outlined in articles 56 and 58 of UNCLOS, and for the United States and India to pin down the details of a consensus over prior notification, which US military activities might be subject to prior authorisation and how information-sharing could support such an agreement.

A second consideration centres on what really lies behind India's efforts to seek accommodation for its distinctive views on certain institutions of global governance. In the case of UNCLOS, it is clear that India is seeking to manage China's maritime assertiveness through a rules-based international order and the concept of the freedom of the seas, and is doing so in partnership with the United States. But any tactic from New Delhi of using growing polarisation between the US and China to gain special accommodations would be only a short-term tactic: neither India nor the United States would move closer to finding a modus vivendi with China under these conditions. Eventually, if and when US security commitments and credibility in the Indian Ocean and wider Indo-Pacific wane, India will be left to manage its relations with China alone. A consensus approach between the United States and India, two countries that have friendly relations, on UNCLOS could aid in opening dialogue and managing some of the tensions with China: working through the ambiguities around the issue of 'due regard', for example, could deliver a midpoint between the US position that all states have the right to conduct military activities in the EEZs of coastal states and the Chinese position that all military activities by other states in coastal states' EEZs are potentially non-pacific and pose a security threat. Given that several Asian maritime nations – Bangladesh, Malaysia, Thailand and Vietnam among them – broadly converge on the position that greater coastal-state control should trump the freedoms and rights sought by other maritime states, India could seek to drive a regional understanding that satisfies Asian maritime powers and invites some flexibility on the part of the United States.[99]

Acknowledgements

The authors would like to thank Todd H. Hall for generous and thoughtful feedback on this article.

Notes

1   US 7th Fleet, '7th Fleet Conducts
    Freedom of Navigation Operation',
    7 April 2021, http://www.c7f.
    navy.mil/Media/News/Display/
    Article/2563538/7th-fleet-conducts-
    freedom-of-navigation-operation/;
    and Government of India, Ministry
    of External Affairs, 'Passage of USS
    John Paul Jones Through India's
    EEZ', 9 April 2021, https://www.mea.
    gov.in/press-releases.htm?dtl/33787/
    Passage_of_USS_John_Paul_Jones_
    through_Indias_EEZ.

2   See Shivshankar Menon, *Choices: Inside
    the Making of India's Foreign Policy*
    (Gurgaon: Penguin, 2016).

3   US Department of State, 'U.S. Security
    Cooperation with India: Fact Sheet', 20
    January 2021, https://www.state.gov/u-
    s-security-cooperation-with-india/.

4   See Snehesh Alex Philip, 'The 3
    Foundational Agreements with US
    and What They Mean for India's
    Military Growth', *Print*, 27 October
    2020, https://theprint.in/defence/
    the-3-foundational-agreements-with-
    us-and-what-they-mean-for-indias-
    military-growth/531795/.

5   US Embassy and Consulates in India,
    'U.S. and Indian Officials Meet for
    First Maritime Security Dialogue',
    16 May 2016, https://in.usembassy.
    gov/u-s-indian-officials-meet-first-
    maritime-security-dialogue/.

6   US Embassy and Consulates in India,
    'Closing Remarks at the U.S.–India
    2+2 Dialogue', 6 September 2018,
    https://in.usembassy.gov/closing-
    remarks-at-the-u-s-india-22-dialogue/.

7   See Dinakar Peri, 'What Is
    COMCASA?', *Hindu*, 6 September

2018, https://www.thehindu.com/
news/national/what-is-comcasa/
article24881039.ece.

8   See Antoine Levesques and Viraj
    Solanki, 'India–US Relations in
    the Age of Modi and Trump', IISS
    Analysis, 27 March 2020, https://www.
    iiss.org/blogs/analysis/2020/03/sasia---
    us-india-relations-trump-and-modi.

9   See Rahul Roy-Chaudhury and Kate
    Sullivan de Estrada, 'India, the Indo-
    Pacific and the Quad', *Survival*, vol. 60,
    no. 3, June–July 2018, pp. 181–94; and
    Iskander Rehman, *India, China, and
    Differing Conceptions of the Maritime
    Order* (Washington DC: Brookings
    Institution, 2017).

10 See Michael R. Pompeo, 'U.S.
    Position on Maritime Claims in
    the South China Sea', press state-
    ment, US Department of State, 13
    July 2020, https://2017-2021.state.
    gov/u-s-position-on-maritime-claims-
    in-the-south-china-sea/index.html.

11 See Abhijit Singh, 'India's Strategic
    Imperatives in the Asian Commons',
    Asia Policy, no. 22, July 2016, p. 39.

12 Government of India, Ministry of
    External Affairs, 'US–India Joint
    Strategic Vision for the Asia-Pacific
    and Indian Ocean Region', 25 January
    2015, https://www.mea.gov.in/
    bilateral-documents.htm?dtl/24728/
    USIndia_Joint_Strategic_Vision_
    for_the_AsiaPacific_and_Indian_
    Ocean_Region.

13 Narendra Modi, 'Prime Minister's
    Keynote Address at the Shangri-La
    Dialogue', Singapore, 1 June 2018,
    https://www.mea.gov.in/Speeches-
    Statements.htm?dtl/29943/Prime+Mini

sters+Keynote+Address+at+Shangri+La+Dialogue+June+01+2018.

14 See William T. Tow, 'Minilateral Security's Relevance to U.S. Strategy in the Indo-Pacific: Challenges and Prospects', *Pacific Review*, vol. 32, no. 2, 2019, pp. 232–44.

15 White House, 'Quad Leaders' Joint Statement: "The Spirit of the Quad"', 1 March 2021, https://www.whitehouse.gov/briefing-room/statements-releases/2021/03/12/quad-leaders-joint-statement-the-spirit-of-the-quad/.

16 See Lalit Kapur, 'Reading the USS John Paul Jones FONOP Right', *DPG Brief*, vol. 6, no. 13, 12 April 2021.

17 US 7th Fleet, '7th Fleet Conducts Freedom of Navigation Operation'.

18 *Ibid.*

19 Arun Prakash, 'US 7th Fleet's Patrol in India's EEZ Was an Act of Impropriety', *Indian Express*, 12 April 2021, https://indianexpress.com/article/opinion/columns/us-navy-warship-india-eez-area-freedom-of-navigation-lakshadweet-7269343/.

20 See Seshadri Chari, 'US Should Learn to Treat India as a Security Partner, Not a Sidekick', *Deccan Herald*, 18 April 2021, https://www.deccanherald.com/opinion/us-should-learn-to-treat-india-as-a-security-partner-not-a-sidekick-975637.html; Abhijit Singh, 'Not on the Same Page at Sea', *Hindu*, 13 April 2021, https://www.thehindu.com/opinion/op-ed/not-on-the-same-page-at-sea/article34304977.ece; Jeff M. Smith, 'America and India Need a Little Flexibility at Sea', *Foreign Policy*, 15 April 2021, https://foreignpolicy.com/2021/04/15/us-india-fonop-maritime-law/; and

Commodore Anil Jai Singh, 'US Navy FONOPS in India's EEZ More Than a Storm in a Teacup?', *Financial Express*, 12 April 2021, https://www.financialexpress.com/defence/us-navy-fonops-in-indias-eez-more-than-a-storm-in-a-teacup/2231445/.

21 Singh, 'Not on the Same Page at Sea'.

22 Government of India, Ministry of External Affairs, 'Passage of USS John Paul Jones Through India's EEZ'.

23 United Nations, 'United Nations Convention on the Law of the Sea – Declarations and Reservations: India', United Nations Treaty Collection, 10 December 1982, https://treaties.un.org/Pages/ViewDetailsIII.aspx?src=TREATY&mtdsg_no=XXI-6&chapter =21&Temp =mtdsg3&clang=_en#EndDec.

24 See Kapur, 'Reading the USS John Paul Jones FONOP Right'; and Sudarshan Shrikhande, 'UNCLOS & EEZ Violations: Is There a Grey Zone?', *Strat News Global*, 9 April 2021, https://stratnewsglobal.com/usa/unclos-eez-violations-is-there-a-grey-zone/.

25 Kapur, 'Reading the USS John Paul Jones FONOP Right'.

26 See Aditya Manubarwala and Bhavyata Kapoor, 'Why India Needs to Strengthen Its Maritime Laws and Regulatory Mechanisms', *Indian Express*, 28 June 2021, https://indianexpress.com/article/opinion/columns/why-india-needs-to-strengthen-its-maritime-laws-and-regulatory-mechanisms-7379949/.

27 Kanwal Sibal, 'US Navy FONOPS: Confused Messaging', Chanakya Forum, 14 April 2021, https://chanakyaforum.com/us-navy-fonops-confused-messaging/.

28 *Ibid*.

29 See Kapur, 'Reading the USS John Paul Jones FONOP Right'; and 'US Navy Could Have Avoided "Thumbing Its Nose" at India: Shashi Tharoor', NDTV, 14 April 2021, https://www.ndtv.com/india-news/us-navy-could-have-avoided-thumbing-nose-at-india-shashi-tharoor-2413209.

30 Smith, 'America and India Need a Little Flexibility at Sea'.

31 See Katherine Morton, 'China's Ambition in the South China Sea: Is a Legitimate Maritime Order Possible?', *International Affairs*, vol. 92, no. 4, 2016, pp. 909–40.

32 See Rachel Esplin Odell, 'Maritime Hegemony and the Fiction of the Free Sea: Explaining States' Claims to Maritime Jurisdiction', MIT Political Science Department Research Paper No. 2016-21, 30 June 2016, available at https://papers.ssrn.com/sol3/papers.cfm?abstract_id=2802204.

33 See James Kraska, 'IO 2.0: Indian Ocean Security and the Law of the Sea', *Georgetown Journal of International Law*, vol. 43, no. 2, 2011, p. 489.

34 See Odell, 'Maritime Hegemony and the Fiction of the Free Sea'.

35 Kraska, 'IO 2.0', p. 490.

36 See *ibid*.

37 Ronald Reagan, 'Statement on United States Actions Concerning the Conference on the Law of the Sea', 9 July 1982, https://www.reaganlibrary.gov/archives/speech/statement-united-states-actions-concerning-conference-law-sea.

38 Ronald Reagan, 'Statement on United States Oceans Policy', 10 March 1983, https://www.reaganlibrary.gov/archives/speech/statement-united-states-oceans-policy.

39 *Ibid*.

40 United Nations, 'United Nations Convention on the Law of the Sea', 10 December 1982, https://www.un.org/depts/los/convention_agreements/texts/unclos/unclos_e.pdf.

41 *Ibid*.

42 See Odell, 'Maritime Hegemony and the Fiction of the Free Sea'; and United Nations, 'United Nations Convention on the Law of the Sea'.

43 There is, however, the qualification on 'Marine Scientific Research' (Article 246) in EEZs, which some argue also applies to military surveillance and surveying. See Ioannis Prezas, 'Foreign Military Activities in the Exclusive Economic Zone: Remarks on the Applicability and Scope of the Reciprocal "Due Regard" Duties of Coastal and Third States', *International Journal of Marine and Coastal Law*, vol. 34, no. 1, 2019, p. 101.

44 Stephen Rose, 'Naval Activity in the Exclusive Economic Zone: Troubled Waters Ahead?', *Ocean Development & International Law*, vol. 21, no. 2, 1990, p. 129.

45 Kraska, 'IO 2.0', p. 453.

46 There was no FONOP against India in 2018 or 2020. See US Department of Defense, 'DoD Annual Freedom of Navigation (FON) Reports', https://policy.defense.gov/ousdp-offices/fon/.

47 United Nations, 'United Nations Convention on the Law of the Sea'.

48 Government of India, 'The Territorial Waters, Continental Shelf, Exclusive Economic Zone and Other Maritime Zones Act, 1976', articles 4(1) and 4(2), https://legislative.gov.in/sites/default/files/A1976-80_0.pdf.

49 US Department of Defense, 'DoD

Annual Freedom of Navigation (FON) Reports'.

50 United Nations, 'United Nations Convention on the Law of the Sea'.

51 Government of India, 'The Territorial Waters, Continental Shelf, Exclusive Economic Zone and Other Maritime Zones Act, 1976'; and Jeff M. Smith, 'UNCLOS: China, India, and the United States Navigate an Unsettled Regime', Heritage Foundation, Backgrounder No. 3608, 30 April 2021, p. 14.

52 See Andrew J. Thomson, 'Keeping the Routine, Routine: The Operational Risks of Challenging Chinese Excessive Maritime Claims', US Naval War College, 9 February 2004.

53 Government of India, Ministry of External Affairs, 'Passage of USS John Paul Jones Through India's EEZ'.

54 See Morton, 'China's Ambition in the South China Sea', p. 936; and Steven Stashwick, '"Unsafe" Incident Between US and Chinese Warships During FONOP', Diplomat, 2 October 2018, https://thediplomat.com/2018/10/ unsafe-incident-between-us-and-chinese-warships-during-fonop/.

55 Mohan Malik, 'The Indo-Pacific Maritime Domain: Challenges and Opportunities', in Mohan Malik (ed.), Maritime Security in the Indo-Pacific: Perspectives from China, India and the United States (Lanham, MD: Rowman & Littlefield, 2014), p. 27.

56 See Mark E. Rosen and Douglas Jackson, 'Bangladesh v. India: A Positive Step Forward in Public Order of the Seas', CNA Occasional Paper, September 2017, https://www. cna.org/cna_files/pdf/DOP-2017-U-016081-Final.pdf.

57 'India Backs Freedom of Navigation in SCS, Seeks Respect for Law', Deccan Chronicle, 8 September 2016, https://www.deccanchronicle. com/world/asia/080916/ india-backs-freedom-of-navigation-in-scs-seeks-respect-for-law.html.

58 The Second Conference deferred most substantive decisions until a later stage. See United Nations, 'United Nations Conference on the Law of the Sea', Codification Division, UN Office of Legal Affairs, https://legal.un.org/ diplomaticconferences/1958_los/.

59 Om Prakash Sharma cites the 27 May 1958 report of E.E. Jhirad, who was judge advocate general of the Indian Navy at the time. See O.P. Sharma, 'Enforcement Jurisdiction in the Exclusive Economic Zone: The Indian Experience', Ocean Development & International Law, vol. 24, no. 2, 1993, p. 168. See also Manjula R. Shyam, 'Maritime Zones Act, 1976 and the Draft Treaty: The Question of Ratification', California Institute of Technology, Social Science Working Paper No. 379, March 1981, https:// authors.library.caltech.edu/82135/1/ sswp379.pdf.

60 See O.P. Sharma, The International Law of the Sea: India and the UN Convention of 1982 (New Delhi: Oxford University Press, 2009), p. xv; and Sharma, 'Enforcement Jurisdiction in the Exclusive Economic Zone', p. 168.

61 See Shyam, 'Maritime Zones Act, 1976 and the Draft Treaty', p. 8.

62 Government of India, 'The Territorial Waters, Continental Shelf, Exclusive Economic Zone and Other Maritime Zones Act, 1976', Article 4(2).

63 See J.D. Singh, 'A Global Law of

the Sea: Many Hurdles Yet to Be Overcome', *Times of India*, 30 July 1976, p. 8; and 'Of Little Comfort', *Times of India*, 2 August 1976, p. 8.

64 See Sharma, 'Enforcement Jurisdiction in the Exclusive Economic Zone'.

65 See William T. Burke, 'National Legislation on Ocean Authority Zones and the Contemporary Law of the Sea', *Ocean Development & International Law*, vol. 9, nos 3–4, 1981, p. 297.

66 *Ibid.*, p. 305.

67 See Burke, 'National Legislation on Ocean Authority Zones and the Contemporary Law of the Sea'.

68 See Sharma, *The International Law of the Sea*; and William T. Burke, 'Customary Law of the Sea: Advocacy or Disinterested Scholarship', *Yale Journal of International Law*, vol. 14, 1989, p. 512.

69 Sharma, *The International Law of the Sea*, p. 157.

70 See *ibid.*

71 The government of India also 'reserves the right to make at the appropriate time the declarations provided for in articles 287 and 298, concerning the settlement of disputes'. United Nations, 'Declarations and Reservations: India'.

72 Prezas, 'Foreign Military Activities in the Exclusive Economic Zone', p. 115. See also Jing Geng, 'The Legality of Foreign Military Activities in the Exclusive Economic Zone Under UNCLOS', *Merkourios-Utrecht Journal of International and European Law*, vol. 28, no. 74, 2012, pp. 22–30.

73 *Ibid.*, p. 110, emphasis in original.

74 *Ibid.*, pp. 116, 106.

75 Singh, 'Not on the Same Page at Sea'.

76 See Abhijit Singh, 'Rules-based Maritime Security in Asia: A View from New Delhi', ORF Occasional Paper, August 2020, p. 18, https://www.orfonline.org/wp-content/uploads/2020/08/ORF_OccasionalPaper_266_RBO-Maritime.pdf.

77 See John Garver, *Protracted Contest: Sino-Indian Rivalry in the Twentieth Century* (Seattle, WA: University of Washington Press, 2002), p. 277.

78 United Nations Office for Disarmament Affairs, 'Declaration of the Indian Ocean as a Zone of Peace', available in *United Nations Disarmament Yearbook* (New York: United Nations, 1983), pp. 375–89.

79 Raghavendra Mishra, 'Revisiting the 1971 "USS Enterprise Incident": Rhetoric, Reality and Pointers for the Contemporary Era', *Journal of Defence Studies*, vol. 9, no. 2, 2015, https://idsa.in/jds/9_2_2015_Revisitingthe1971USSEnterpriseIncident.

80 Manish Tewari, 'US Naval Fleet's Defiance of Indian Law Is Not Unprecedented. India Must Heed the Message', *Indian Express*, 14 April 2021, https://indianexpress.com/article/opinion/columns/us-navy-fleet-warship-india-eez-area-7272626/.

81 See Satyindra Singh, *Blueprint to Bluewater: Indian Navy, 1951–65* (New Delhi: Lancer International, 1992), chapter 13; G.M. Hirananadani, *Transition to Triumph* (New Delhi: Lancer Publishers, 2000), pp. 24–5; and Vernon Hewitt, *The New International Politics of South Asia* (Manchester: Manchester University Press, 1997), p. 126.

82 See United Nations Office on Drugs and Crime, *Summary of Laws Regulating Floating Armouries and*

Their Operations (Vienna: United
Nations, 2020), https://www.unodc.
org/documents/Maritime_crime/19-
02073_Floating_Armouries.pdf.

83 See Lok Sabha Secretariat, 'Coastal
Security', Reference Note No.
29/RN/Ref./November/2013,
http://164.100.47.193/intranet/Coastal_
Security.pdf.

84 See Bipin Rawat, 'Shaping the Armed
Forces to Meet Likely Current and
Future Challenges', Vivekananda
International Foundation, 7 April
2021, https://www.youtube.com/
watch?v=QT-XlbZaX3c&ab_cha
nnel=VivekanandaInternational
FoundationNewDelhi; and Rajat
Pandit, 'India to Get Apex Body for
Maritime Challenges', *Times of India*,
14 April 2021, https://timesofindia.
indiatimes.com/india/india-to-get-
apex-body-for-maritime-challenges/
articleshow/82057894.cms.

85 Government of India, 'Reforming
the National Security System:
Recommendations of the Group of
Ministers', February 2001, p. 74. In
2000, a co-author of this article, Rahul
Roy-Chaudhury, also recommended a
coordinating body for maritime secu-
rity to be called a 'National Maritime
Commission'. Rahul Roy-Chaudhury,
India's Maritime Security (New Delhi:
Knowledge World-IDSA, 2000), p. 189.

86 See Pushpita Das, 'Coastal Security: The
Indian Experience', IDSA Monograph
Series No. 22, September 2013, p. 65.

87 India PRS Legislative Research,
'Address by the President of India,
Shri Pranab Mukherjee to Parliament',
9 June 2014, https://prsindia.org/
files/policy/Policy_President_
Speech/2014_0.pdf.

88 See Pandit, 'India to Get Apex Body
for Maritime Challenges'; and C. Uday
Bhaskar, 'Finally, a National Maritime
Sherpa', *Hindustan Times*, 15 July 2021,
https://www.hindustantimes.com/
opinion/finally-a-national-maritime-
sherpa-101626349928117.html.

89 See David Brewster, 'An Indian Sphere
of Influence in the Indian Ocean?',
Security Challenges, vol. 6, no. 3, 2010,
pp. 1–20.

90 See 'US Signs Defence Cooperation
Deal with Maldives Amidst China's
Growing Presence in the Indian
Ocean', *Times of India*, 12 September
2020, http://timesofindia.indiatimes.
com/articleshow/78075612.cms?utm_
source=contentofinterest&utm_
medium=text&utm_campaign=cppst.

91 N. Sathiya Moorthy, 'After Male's
Defence Pact with US, India Needs
to Check Over-crowding of Indian
Ocean Strategic Space', Observer
Research Foundation, 22 September
2020, https://www.orfonline.org/
expert-speak/after-defence-pact-us-
india-needs-check-over-crowding-
indian-ocean-strategic-space/.

92 See Abhijit Singh, 'The U.S. Navy
in the Indian Ocean: India's
"Goldilocks Dilemma"', *War on
the Rocks*, 11 May 2021, https://
warontherocks.com/2021/05/
the-u-s-navy-in-the-indian-ocean-
indias-goldilocks-dilemma/.

93 Kate Sullivan de Estrada, 'Can
Minilaterals Deliver a Security
Architecture in the Indian Ocean?', *Asia
Policy*, vol. 16, no. 3, July 2021, pp. 40–4.

94 Sibal, 'US Navy FONOPS'.

95 Kate Sullivan de Estrada, 'Putting the
SAGAR Vision to the Test', *Hindu*, 22
April 2020.

96 See Singh, 'Rules-based Maritime Security in Asia', p. 8.

97 Kraska, 'IO 2.0', p. 491.

98 Kyle Lascurettes and Sara Bjerg Moller, 'The Normative Foundations for a New Global Concert in an Age of Western Retrenchment', in Harald Müller and Carsten Rauch (eds), *Great Power Multilateralism and the Prevention of War* (Abingdon: Routledge, 2017), p. 111.

99 See Sam Bateman, 'Security and the Law of the Sea in East Asia: Navigational Regimes and Exclusive Economic Zones', Paper for SLS and BIICL Symposium on the Law of the Sea, London, 22–23 March 2005, https://www.biicl.org/files/1366_bateman_security_and_the_law_of_the_sea.doc. India's ambition and aptitude for this was displayed in August 2021, when it used its presidency of the UN Security Council to host the first stand-alone debate on maritime security and achieved a consensus that included China on a presidential statement endorsing UNCLOS as 'the legal framework applicable to activities in the oceans, including countering illicit activities at sea'. See Geeta Mohan, 'UNCLOS "Laws of the Seas" at Heart of UN Security Council Consensus, China Onboard', *India Today*, 10 August 2021, https://www.indiatoday.in/india/story/unclos-law-of-sea-un-security-council-maritime-security-open-debate-india-presidency-1838903-2021-08-10.

After Afghanistan: Intelligence Analysis and US Military Missions

Julia Santucci

As Kabul fell to the Taliban and the world was haunted by images of thousands of Afghans, American citizens and other foreign nationals rushing to Hamid Karzai International Airport, it was clear that the United States had overestimated the Afghan Army. The US intelligence community became an immediate target of accusations that it had failed to warn the Biden administration about the Taliban's strength relative to the Afghan Army and about how quickly the Taliban would take control of the country.

It is difficult to assess the veracity of these judgements, based as they are on vague references or brief leaks from intelligence assessments by unnamed US officials claiming to have read them. We are unlikely to understand the full picture until the relevant reports are declassified in 25 to 40 years, or as part of an earlier investigation into the end of America's longest war. The information available to the public, however, suggests that the Afghanistan case was similar to two previous cases in which the intelligence community was asked to provide assessments of a client army's ability to defeat an insurgency: Vietnam in 1963 and Iraq in 2014. In both of those cases, civilian intelligence officers and lower-level military personnel were in fact sceptical that US training and support programmes had fully prepared the respective armies to overcome their rivals and offered prescient

Julia Santucci is Senior Lecturer in Intelligence Studies and Director of the Johnson Institute for Responsible Leadership and Frances Hesselbein Leadership Forum at the University of Pittsburgh. She served as a CIA analyst for over a decade; as director for Egypt, Middle East and North Africa on the National Security Council staff from 2012 to 2014; and in the US State Department.

Survival | vol. 64 no. 1 | February–March 2022 | pp. 157–178   https://doi.org/10.1080/00396338.2022.2032994

assessments of the defeats that lay ahead, only to be overruled by senior officials who painted a far rosier picture of the opportunities for success.

Academic and policy experts for years have studied whether the US can effectively train a foreign military or engage in nation-building. This article considers how intelligence agencies can best support policymakers as they weigh military-policy options. Certain missions may be inherently hopeless, and policymakers' insistent assumptions that such missions will succeed could lead to the downplaying or suppression of candid intelligence analysis that would encourage them to consider other options. By understanding US policymakers' mistakes in Vietnam, Iraq and Afghanistan, and revising the intelligence–policy relationship to promote more objective analysis of US military missions, US leaders would be better able to assess the feasibility of success in challenging missions and to adjust policy accordingly.

Vietnam: those who 'know best'

The images of US planes and helicopters departing Afghanistan immediately evoked comparisons to the withdrawal from Vietnam in 1975, when Gerald R. Ford was president. Incidents from the Kennedy administration, however, provide a more instructive model for understanding the interplay between intelligence and military assessments on the prospects for US-backed counter-insurgency success. When John F. Kennedy took office in 1961, the United States had a small contingent of a few hundred military advisers serving in Vietnam, deployed as part of the Eisenhower administration's broader efforts to contain communism in Southeast Asia and globally. In May 1961, Kennedy approved the interagency Vietnam Task Force's recommendation that the US should seek 'to prevent Communist domination of South Vietnam; to create in that country a viable and increasingly democratic society, and to initiate, on an accelerated basis, a series of mutually supporting actions of a military, political, economic, psychological, and covert character designed to achieve this objective'.[1] Subsequently, the US began gradually increasing the number of military advisers supporting the South Vietnamese Army (ARVN), which reached around 16,000 members at the time of Kennedy's assassination in November 1963.

The Kennedy administration's theory in Vietnam was that preventing communist domination would require defeating the Viet Cong insurgency, best accomplished through a combined strategy of military support to increase the ARVN's capacity for providing security throughout the country, and diplomatic pressure on the government of South Vietnam to make meaningful political and economic reforms that would build public trust. This approach was broadly similar to the counter-insurgency strategies applied in Iraq and Afghanistan in the 2000s. In the case of Vietnam, senior US defence officials were confident that their strategy was working, although they acknowledged that progress was slow. In January 1963, for example, Robert McNamara, the secretary of defense, told Kennedy that there were reasons to believe that the government forces of South Vietnam were becoming stronger, including indications that about 800,000 villagers appeared to have shifted their allegiance from the Viet Cong to the government of South Vietnam, increased Viet Cong casualty rates compared to those of the government forces, and a decrease in Viet Cong 'incidents' in South Vietnam.[2] He did warn of 'disquieting indications of possible trouble to come', noting that the Viet Cong continued to successfully recruit new members and retain the support of a significant portion of the rural population, and cautioning that the government's political reforms were proceeding very slowly. Nevertheless, McNamara stated that he was 'pleased with the progress' the US had made, and would be sending a senior military delegation to Vietnam to explore additional ways the US might accelerate it.

Intelligence analysts, on the other hand, were sceptical of senior military and defence leaders' view of events in Vietnam and believed that much of the reporting from military sources in the field was too optimistic. Field-level military commanders and military intelligence analysts apparently shared this scepticism. A declassified study by former CIA officer Harold Ford of the agency's performance during the Vietnam era assessed that, at best, senior officials' optimism could be attributed to operational enthusiasm; at worst, it was due to their desire to appear competent to their bosses in Washington and, therefore, to withhold evidence that their training mission was falling short of the mark. In any case, Ford noted that the record was 'replete with instances where supervisors and field commanders, the men charged with demonstrating operational progress in the programs assigned to them, overrode their subordinates' negative facts and judgments'.[3]

In late 1962, the intelligence community's Office of National Estimates set out to produce a National Intelligence Estimate (NIE) on Vietnam. Estimative intelligence is forward-looking by definition, designed to help US policymakers determine how best to advance US interests abroad. NIEs are perhaps the most widely known estimative-intelligence products; they represent the intelligence community's coordinated assessments of issues of strategic importance to the United States. The particular purpose of the NIE on Vietnam was to help the administration understand developments since it had increased the number of military advisers and the amount of economic assistance to the government of South Vietnam, and to assess the likelihood of success in the ARVN's counter-insurgency campaign. At that time, NIEs were drafted by a group of seasoned analysts housed within the CIA, coordinated at the working level across the intelligence community, and then taken before the United States Intelligence Board (USIB), which consisted of principals from across the intelligence community and was chaired by the director of central intelligence.

In early 1963, the Office of National Estimates submitted its coordinated draft of NIE 53-63, 'Prospects in Vietnam', to the USIB for approval. It included this judgement: 'The struggle in South Vietnam at best will be protracted and costly [because] very great weaknesses remain and will be difficult to surmount. Among these are lack of aggressive and firm leadership at all levels of command, poor morale among the troops, lack of trust between peasant and soldier, poor tactical use of available forces, a very inadequate intelligence system, and obvious Communist penetration of the South Vietnamese military organization.'[4]

John McCone, then the director of central intelligence, summarily rejected the draft, criticising the analysts who produced it for having ignored the views of the 'people who know Vietnam best' – namely, senior military and policy officials. McCone instructed the analysts to seek out these officials' perspectives and produce a new, revised version of the NIE. According to Ford's study, after interviewing these officials, analysts remained pessimistic about the government of South Vietnam's ability to overcome the insurgency. Nevertheless, they were overruled by their intelligence-community bosses, and the final NIE, published on 17 April 1963, judged: 'We believe that Communist progress has been blunted and that the situation is improving … Improvements which have occurred during the past year now indicate that the Viet Cong can be contained militarily and that further progress can be made in expanding the area of government control and in creating greater security in the countryside.'[5]

This view was nearly identical to that provided by McNamara to Kennedy just months earlier and was a useful tool for policymakers in arguing for a continuation of their strategy in Vietnam. It suggested that, with enough military training and pressure on the government of South Vietnam to reform, the United States could stem the Viet Cong insurgency and prevent communism from taking hold there. In fact, administration officials, including Kennedy himself, used the NIE's assessment to support a drawdown in the number of US personnel in Vietnam. Ultimately, instability resulting from the coup against South Vietnamese president Ngo Dinh Diem in November 1963 precluded implementation of the drawdown. But the pattern of scrubbing strategic intelligence products to support more optimistic policy assessments continued.

Iraq: the Iraqi Army vs the 'JV team'

One month into his presidency, on 27 February 2009, Barack Obama outlined US plans to end the war in Iraq. He said that all US combat troops would be removed from Iraq by 31 August 2010 and that, once they had left, the mission would shift to one of 'supporting the Iraqi government and its Security Forces as they take the absolute lead in securing their country'.[6] The president promised to leave a transitional force in place for another year to serve three functions: (1) training, equipping and advising Iraqi security forces as long as they remained non-sectarian; (2) conducting targeted counter-terrorism missions; and (3) protecting ongoing US civilian and military efforts within Iraq.[7] Recognising that the ultimate source of stability in Iraq was political rather than military, Obama pledged to reinforce these security efforts with sustained diplomacy to develop Iraq's civilian institutions, encourage its leaders to resolve differences peacefully, and support the millions of refugees and displaced persons who were still in need of assistance.

The emphasis on training the Iraqi security forces was nothing new. Between 2003 and 2012, the United States spent over \$25 billion to train, equip and support them, according to the final report of the Special Inspector General for Iraq Reconstruction.[8] The Iraqi Ministry of Defence received just over 57% of those funds and the Ministry of the Interior 38%, with the remaining portion spent on programmes that benefitted both ministries. But given that the US programmed these funds primarily through the Department of Defense, it is unclear whether it accurately evaluated prospects for the Iraqi security forces to successfully confront internal and external threats. US officials' surprise at the quick collapse of the Iraqi Army in 2014 suggests that it did not.

US officials did not seem to recognise the threat from ISIS

In early 2013, the Islamic State in Iraq, the successor of al-Qaeda in Iraq, merged with the al-Qaeda-affiliated Nusra Front in Syria, forming Islamic State in Iraq and Syria (ISIS). By the end of that year, the group had conducted attacks that killed thousands of civilians, launched a campaign to target Iraqi security forces, freed 500–1,000 prisoners from Abu Ghraib prison and secured control of the Iraqi city of Fallujah and parts of Ramadi.[9] While US officials were concerned with ISIS's apparent build-up of strength and Iraqi prime minister Nouri al-Maliki's increasingly sectarian policies, which alienated Iraqi Sunnis from the government, they did not seem to recognise the full extent of the threat ISIS posed to stability in Iraq and beyond its borders. In a January 2014 interview with the *New Yorker*'s David Remnick, Obama compared ISIS to a junior varsity ('JV') sports team, explaining: 'I think there is a distinction between the capacity and reach of a [Osama] bin Laden and a network that is actively planning major terrorist plots against the homeland versus jihadists who are engaged in various local power struggles and disputes, often sectarian.'[10]

Yet, throughout the first half of 2014, ISIS continued its land grabs in both Syria and Iraq, taking control of the Syrian city of Raqqa in January and the Iraqi city of Mosul – the country's second-largest city – in June, and announced the establishment of a caliphate in the territory it controlled. In August, ISIS seized the towns of Sinjar and Zumar, perpetrating genocide against the Yazidi population there, raping women and girls, and forcing thousands into sexual slavery. Many of the group's battlefield successes in Iraq came with little resistance from the Iraqi security forces; in some cases, Iraqi soldiers abandoned their posts, leaving behind weapons, materiel and even uniforms for ISIS to commandeer. US airstrikes against ISIS began just a few days after its attack on Sinjar, and in September the US announced the creation of a broad international coalition to defeat ISIS, which would provide support to Iraqi and Kurdish forces fighting against the group on the ground.

As the US assembled the coalition, many questioned how Obama could have been caught so off guard by ISIS's successes, pointing to his 'JV' comments just a few months earlier. In an 18 September interview with *60 Minutes*, Obama seemed to blame the intelligence community.[11] The president pointed to comments that James Clapper, the director of national intelligence, had made in an interview with the *Washington Post* just a few days earlier, in which Clapper said that while intelligence analysts had accurately reported on ISIS's emergence and capability, 'what we didn't do was predict the will to fight. That's always a problem. We didn't do it in Vietnam. We underestimated the Viet Cong and the North Vietnamese and overestimated the will of the South Vietnamese. In this case, we underestimated [ISIS] and overestimated the fighting capability of the Iraqi army … I didn't see the collapse of the Iraqi security force in the north coming. I didn't see that.'[12] According to the *New York Times*, some unnamed intelligence officials pushed back on Obama's comment, claiming that they did warn of both the growing threat posed by ISIS and the Iraqi security forces' shortcomings, but that the White House ignored those reports.[13]

At this stage, less than eight years removed from the events of 2014, with most documents still classified, it is difficult to assess whether the president had been adequately warned by the intelligence community and, if not, whether the blame lies with analysts' failed assessments or with senior officials' interference in the presentation of the intelligence. Several unclassified statements by senior intelligence officials in early 2014 suggest that the intelligence community was tracking the potential for increased violence in Iraq and Syria, but that senior officials did not include pointed warnings that the Iraqi security apparatus could collapse. For example, in January 2014, Clapper delivered the intelligence community's annual Worldwide Threat Assessment to Congress. His unclassified statement for the record to the Senate Select Committee on Intelligence made no reference to ISIS by name, nor did it refer to the group's late 2013 battlefield successes in Iraq.[14] The statement did warn that Syria had become 'a significant location for independent or al-Qa'ida-aligned groups to recruit, train, and equip a growing number of extremists, some of whom might conduct external attacks'. He added that 'hostilities between Sunni and Shia' were 'also intensifying in Syria and spilling into neighboring countries', which was 'increasing the likelihood of a protracted conflict'.[15] He went on to say that 'Iraq's trajectory in 2014 will depend heavily on how Baghdad confronts the rising challenge from al-Qa'ida in Iraq (AQI) and manages relations with the country's disenfranchised Sunni population', and he noted that the conflict in Syria had facilitated the movement of terrorists between Syria and Iraq and increased AQI's capabilities.[16]

In an 11 February statement before the Senate Armed Services Committee, General Michael Flynn, then director of the Defense Intelligence Agency (DIA), was more direct, referring to ISIS by name and saying that the group 'probably will attempt to take territory in Iraq and Syria to exhibit its strength in 2014'.[17] While Flynn also said that ISIS's ability to hold territory would depend in part on the Iraqi security forces' response, he did not offer an assessment (at least in the unclassified version of his statement) of whether it would be able to effectively do so.

At least in the unclassified environment, senior intelligence officials were not sounding the alarm about ISIS's growing strength in Iraq or the Iraqi military's inherent weaknesses in early 2014. But were these views shared by working-level analysts? Here again, there is very little evidence available in the public sphere, but an unclassified report by the Defense Department's inspector general investigating US Central Command's (CENTCOM) intelligence products at that time shared an incident that strongly suggests that at least some analysts believed the situation in Iraq was worsening. According to the inspector general's report, analysts in the Joint Intelligence Center CENTCOM's Iraq Branch recommended on 8 May that the Iraq Internal Stability Indications and Warning level (WATCHCON) be raised to the highest level. This would have indicated to military planners and policymakers that analysts were not confident in the Iraqi government's ability to maintain order, giving them time to prepare for that eventuality or possibly intervene to mitigate or prevent it. But CENTCOM's director of intelligence initially rejected the analysts' recommendation, which was not implemented until after the fall of Mosul in June.

The WATCHCON episode formed the basis for one in a series of complaints that two CENTCOM analysts brought to the inspector general related to their perception that senior CENTCOM officials distorted intelligence assessments to present a more negative impression of ISIS's capabilities and a more positive impression of the Iraqi security forces. The complainants alleged

Two analysts claimed CENTCOM officials distorted intelligence

that this approach continued throughout 2014 and the first half of 2015, with senior intelligence officials editing reports to sound less critical of Iraqi forces, imposing a higher burden of proof on assessments that presented a negative impression of their performance, and insisting that analysts integrate the views of operators on the ground, which were generally more positive about Iraqi forces than other intelligence sources. Two bodies – a House Joint Task Force on CENTCOM Intelligence and the Pentagon inspector general's office – investigated these complaints. The inspector general interviewed dozens of CENTCOM analysts and leaders up the chain, including its commander at the time, General Lloyd J. Austin III (now the secretary of defense), as well as officials from other intelligence agencies. In addition, the inspector general reviewed selected drafts and final versions of CENTCOM intelligence assessments to examine the alleged editorial changes analysts regarded as inaccurate. The House Joint Task Force interviewed a smaller number of CENTCOM analysts and leaders and also reviewed a sampling of finished intelligence assessments.

The two separate investigations ultimately reached different conclusions. The House Joint Task Force's initial report, published in August 2016, concluded that CENTCOM's published analytic products were inconsistent with the judgements of many senior analysts and were more optimistic than assessments from other intelligence agencies, and than actual events warranted.[18] The report pointed to survey data from the Director of National Intelligence's (DNI) annual Analytic Objectivity and Process survey, in which more than 50% of CENTCOM respondents said that CENTCOM procedures hampered objective analysis and 40% responded that they had 'experienced an attempt to distort or suppress intelligence in the past year'.[19] The inspector general's report, published in January 2017, determined that CENTCOM leaders had not deliberately suppressed or distorted intelligence assessments, noting that while its review of analytic products did reveal examples that were consistent with the whistle-blowers' complaints, those incidents were not statistically significant.[20] However, that report did raise substantial concerns about the perception among analysts that senior leaders were suppressing or distorting intelligence, noting that of the 82 analysts interviewed, 49% believed CENTCOM leaders imposed a narrative on their assessments, or required a higher burden of proof or greater sourcing requirements, if an intelligence assessment was contrary to that of the operational reporting.[21] Such a perception among analysts is deeply problematic in the intelligence world because it could lead to self-censorship – that is, analysts revising their assessments before submitting them for review based on what they think reviewers will allow to be published.

Afghanistan: repeating mistakes

Since the start of the war in Afghanistan in 2002, the US has spent more than $88bn in support of Afghanistan's security sector. For over a decade, US policy in Afghanistan centred around preparing for an eventual withdrawal of US forces by building effective Afghan National Defense and Security Forces (ANDSF).[22] In his July 2021 quarterly report to Congress, the Special Inspector General for Afghanistan Reconstruction (SIGAR) noted that throughout this time, senior military officials had displayed a pattern of making overly optimistic assessments of the effectiveness of training programmes, citing public comments and congressional testimony from generals David Petraeus (2011), John Campbell (2015) and John Nicholson (2017), and from Pentagon press secretary John Kirby (2021).[23] The SIGAR report views these statements as consistent with an overall unwarranted sense of optimism that beleaguered monitoring and evaluation of Afghan reconstruction efforts, noting:

> Over the years ... other data points (or the lack thereof) recommended greater skepticism. SIGAR has expressed serious concerns about the corrosive effects of corruption within the ANDSF (including the existence of ghost soldiers and police); the questionable accuracy of data on the actual strength of the force; the inability of assessment methodologies to account for the influence on combat readiness of intangible factors such as the will to fight; the shaky sustainability of the ANDSF given its dependencies on advanced equipment and the initial lack of focus on ministerial-level capabilities; and the discontinuation of critical data, such as assessments of district control, that could be used to help measure the ANDSF's performance in recent years.[24]

SIGAR interviews with military trainers obtained and published by the *Washington Post* confirmed that those working closely with the ANDSF recognised its many flaws. These trainers described their Afghan counterparts as incompetent and corrupt, pointing to high levels of desertion among troops; police recruits' theft of US-provided supplies, especially fuel; and commanders' practice of pocketing the salaries of thousands of 'ghost soldiers' who existed only on paper.[25] According to the *Post*'s review of the interviews, none of the trainers expressed confidence 'that the Afghan army and police could ever fend off, much less defeat, the Taliban on their own'.[26]

Here, as in Vietnam and Iraq, it seems that senior US military officials did not objectively assess the capability of the forces they trained and equipped. And as in Iraq, they were surprised by the ANDSF's quick collapse in the face of the Taliban, which occurred as the US was completing its withdrawal. In late September, Secretary of Defense Austin confirmed this reaction in congressional testimony, saying that 'the fact that the Afghan army we and our partners trained simply melted away – in many cases without firing a shot – took us all by surprise. It would be dishonest to claim otherwise.'[27] Remarks by some senior administration officials and members of Congress suggest that the intelligence community was similarly surprised by the ANDSF's collapse, and that it did not warn policymakers that the Taliban could take over control of Afghanistan in a matter of days or weeks. During an 18 August press briefing, Chairman of the Joint Chiefs of Staff General Mark Milley said:

> Let me make one comment on the intelligence, because I am seeing all over the news it that there were warnings of a rapid collapse. I have previously said from this podium and in sworn testimony before Congress that the intelligence clearly indicated multiple scenarios were possible. One of those was an outright Taliban takeover following a rapid collapse of the Afghan security forces and the government. Another was a civil war. And a third was a negotiated settlement. However, the timeframe of a rapid collapse, that was widely estimated and ranged from weeks to months and even years following our departure. There was nothing that I or anyone else saw that indicated a collapse of this army and this government in 11 days.[28]

Did the intelligence community understand the limitations of the ANDSF during the war, and did it predict Afghan forces' rapid collapse? Nearly all intelligence assessments related to Afghanistan remain classified. However, comments by both named and anonymous intelligence officials in the media suggest that at least some intelligence agencies had been pessimistic for decades about the train-and-equip mission in Afghanistan and about the ANDSF's prospects overall. The *New York Times* reported in August that intelligence agencies had been divided on this point for years, with CIA analysts being more doubtful about the training of Afghan security forces than their counterparts at the DIA and in other parts of the military.[29] A former CIA counter-terrorism chief for South and Southwest Asia, Douglas London, who retired in 2019, wrote that the agency had assessed different scenarios for Afghanistan's future that were shared with national-security policymakers in both the Trump and Biden administrations. He said that in a scenario 'without any US military and intelligence presence beyond the Embassy in Kabul, faced with a Taliban military and propaganda offensive, and undermined by [Afghan president Ashraf] Ghani's fractious relationship with his own national political partners, the intelligence community warned the government could dissolve in days. And so it went.'[30]

Comments by former DNI Clapper published in *The Hill* provide perhaps the most telling insight about the intelligence community's analysis and policy support regarding the ANDSF. He said that 'during the six-plus years I was DNI, the [intelligence community] consistently assessed the Afghan government and the Afghan military and security forces with a much more pessimistic outlook than did [the Defense Department] generally, and [the International Security Assistance Force] specifically. Invariably, we were criticized for being too negative, uninformed or both.'[31] Clapper's remarks imply an intelligence community that once again was at odds with the military commanders responsible for a mission to train and equip a foreign military, and that once again was scolded for coming to a different conclusion than those viewed in Washington as closest to the mission. Clapper's subsequent remark was even more revealing about the dynamic: 'The point is here that making such judgments would not be the exclusive province of the [intelligence community]. In fact, the military and the embassy would be in a far better position to make such judgments.' Just as the director of central intelligence told analysts in 1962 to defer to those who 'know Vietnam best', Clapper seemed to believe that those serving in Afghanistan were better placed to evaluate the capability and will of the Afghan government and security services.

Lessons

The three cases presented here span nearly 60 years. Across four generations, tens of thousands of American soldiers, many of their allies and hundreds of thousands of Vietnamese, Iraqis and Afghans have fought and died in the three wars. Despite the long time frame between these cases and their geographic diversity, they share four characteristics that contributed to the failure of the US missions. Firstly, in each case, intelligence and policy officials relied too heavily on operational information from those whom they presumed to know the most about the foreign militaries. In Vietnam, McCone's deference to those who 'know Vietnam best' resulted in an altered key judgement in the NIE and reaffirmed policymakers' views that the US role in the country was nearly complete. In Iraq, the Pentagon inspector general concluded that CENTCOM intelligence leaders over-emphasised operational reporting when evaluating reports on Iraqi security forces, which contributed to many analysts' perception that these leaders favoured such reporting at the expense of other intelligence sources.[32] And in Afghanistan, Obama-era intelligence leaders – in particular, DNI Clapper – viewed military and embassy officials as better positioned to provide assessments on the ANDSF's capability and resolve, though the full effect of Clapper's position on analytic assessments of the situation in Afghanistan then or now remains unclear.

Senior commanders tend to be overly optimistic

Secondly, the prevailing deference to the military's view did not seem to consider the fact that the military's assessments of train-and-equip missions sometimes exclude the perspectives of soldiers on the ground in preference for those of senior commanders, who tend to be overly optimistic about the prospects for success. In the case of Vietnam, Harold Ford wrote that the military leaders were especially sensitive to analysis in the draft NIE that was critical of the ARVN and pointed to its mistreatment of civilians as a factor that undermined the counter-insurgency campaign. Military intelligence analysts who coordinated on the draft noted that these views of ARVN transgressions were shared by nearly every field-grade returnee they had interviewed. However, senior military commanders strongly pushed back on these assessments, either denying them outright or attributing them to 'inexperienced and youthful American officers' who did not understand that ARVN brutality was considered 'acceptable' in the Vietnamese context.[33] SIGAR interviews with military trainers working in Afghanistan similarly revealed a degree of pessimism that senior commanders' public comments did not reflect.

Thirdly, intelligence leaders' concerns about bureaucratic marginalisation seemed to affect their thinking in each of these cases, in some instances leading them to revise assessments or overemphasise military reporting precisely to avoid this fate. As Lloyd Gardner has noted, 'the analyst is the modern messenger … who does risk "banishment" of sorts if his conclusions fail to serve a policymaker's need to appear in control of events. Once around that corner, the analyst can qualify optimistic assessments with reference points that nudge the reader to reconsider assumptions. The danger is that no one reads beyond page one.'[34] Gardner's point was that while bureaucratically astute analysts may slip pessimistic caveats into their assessments, these tend not to make it into the key findings of the executive summary. McCone himself was sceptical of US progress in Vietnam, but he still chose to soften the intelligence community's judgements in lieu of risking that the NIE would be trashed or ignored by senior policymakers. Clapper's comment that during his tenure, pessimistic assessments meant that 'we were criticized for being too negative, uninformed, or both' suggests that this trend had not abated during the Iraq and Afghanistan military operations.

Finally, in these cases the practice of red-teaming – that is, designating selected analysts to challenge consensus assessments – was not effectively used by the intelligence or policy communities. In the Vietnam era, disagreements between the intelligence community and the military might have led to red-team examinations of both the intelligence analysts' assessments that the ARVN was not gaining traction among the Vietnamese population and the military's more optimistic line of thinking. Policymakers might have then considered options for either scenario. But there is little indication that analysts or policymakers considered alternative hypotheses of how events might play out. In early 2014, Obama seemed to believe that Iraqi forces – with billions of dollars' worth of US equipment and training – would not fall apart when facing a few thousand extremists with far more limited resources. That was not an unreasonable assessment. Nevertheless, the intelligence community should have prepared alternative scenarios that factored in indicators that the Iraqi forces might not succeed, and policymakers should have planned for such a possibility, however unlikely they thought it might be.

We do not know the full extent of intelligence-community analysis on Iraq, and the CIA has a robust red cell that routinely prepares assessments on high-impact, low-probability scenarios.[35] But according to the Pentagon inspector general's report, CENTCOM disbanded its intelligence red team in 2013, suggesting that the analysts most closely tied to military planners responsible for Iraq were not considering alternative perspectives. In the case of Afghanistan, the limited information emerging from intelligence officials who have spoken to the press suggests that analysis of alternative scenarios was prepared and delivered to policymakers, including a scenario in which the government quickly collapsed. Secretary Austin told Congress that US troops were able to deploy quickly to assist in the Afghan evacuation efforts precisely because the Pentagon had prepared for such a contingency, indicating that the military did utilise analyses of alternative scenarios for the US drawdown. Yet policymakers seem to have been caught completely off guard by the speed with which the Taliban took control of the entire country. Clearly there is more wisdom to be digested on this front.

Remedial measures

For decades, scholars and policymakers have debated the merits of US support for foreign armies. Despite the failures of train-and-equip missions in Vietnam, Iraq and Afghanistan, the United States continues to commit significant resources to supporting militaries and security services around the world.[36] If that investment in foreign security assistance is unlikely to change in the near term, US officials should make a concerted effort to better ensure it pays off in terms of achieving American objectives.

A key task is to reassess the role that intelligence plays in supporting such policy endeavours. The intelligence community exists to provide objective insights and analysis to policymakers to help inform their decisions. Yet, as the Vietnam, Iraq and Afghanistan cases demonstrate, in assessing the capability and will of foreign armies the US is supporting, policy and intelligence leaders alike too often turn to the very military commanders who are responsible for designing the training missions. These commanders have proven to be too invested in the success of those missions to objectively analyse foreign militaries' flaws. Three specific changes to the intelligence–policy relationship could ameliorate this persistent problem.

Firstly, operational reporting should come from operators themselves and carry equal weight in all-source intelligence analysis. In each of the cases discussed here, military personnel working on the ground recognised the shortcomings of their Vietnamese, Iraqi and Afghan counterparts. Yet the military command structure meant that their input was often altered before being sent to Washington in order to present a more positive view of the training programmes' effectiveness. The military should provide a channel for the views of lower-level personnel to be systematically captured and represented, especially to intelligence analysts, without their commanders' interference. Once that information reaches analysts, it should carry weight equal to that of information from other sources.

The intelligence community's analytic standards dictate that analysis be informed by all relevant information available.[37] When information from different sources conflicts, it is the analysts' job to make judgements about which sources are more likely to be correct. Intelligence analysts in all three cases did this, but were often overruled by their managers and senior leaders, and urged to disproportionately credit reporting from the senior field officers, which overstated the success of the training missions. As with military commanders and military reporting, intelligence-community managers and leaders should resist the urge to insinuate themselves into the analytic process, permitting more objective consideration of all sources of information by the analysts who know the content best.

Secondly, senior officials should take care to avoid sending prejudicial signals to the intelligence community, even implicitly, that bad news is not wanted. Lyndon Johnson once said of the intelligence community:

> Let me tell you about these intelligence guys. When I was growing up in Texas, we had a cow named Bessie. I'd go out early and milk her. I'd get her in the stanchion, seat myself and squeeze out a pail of fresh milk. One day I'd worked hard and gotten a full pail of milk, but I wasn't paying attention, and old Bessie swung her shit-smeared tail through the bucket of milk. Now, you know that's what these intelligence guys do. You work hard and get a good program or policy going, and they swing a shit-smeared tail through it.[38]

While most presidents lack Johnson's colourful language and gift for metaphor, nearly all of them – including those who have genuinely valued intelligence analysis – have sent skewed signals to the intelligence community at one point or another during their administrations. This has been especially true in times of war, when the United States has been most deeply invested in a policy's success. But even offhand comments from the president or his senior advisers can prompt intelligence leaders to moderate the community's views. For example, the inspector general's investigation into allegations of intelligence distortion at CENTCOM concluded that the use of the term 'narrative' by the then-commander Austin without a clear explanation of what he meant by the term contributed to the perception among analysts that he and other CENTCOM leaders wanted them to spin their assessments in accordance with the command's preferred vision.[39]

To avoid this pitfall, the president and senior policymakers should consistently reinforce to the intelligence community that they welcome objective assessments and take great care to avoid language that might suggest otherwise. Furthermore, they should find ways to demonstrate to the intelligence community that they value 'bad news' assessments as much as 'good news' ones. This would mean, for example, integrating such assessments into policy discussions and considering new approaches that might avert the worst-case outcomes predicted by intelligence analysts.

Finally, the policy process should make better use of alternative intelligence analysis and integrate consideration of divergent assessments at both the planning and the implementation stages of a given policy. In the aftermath of the failure to find the predicted weapons of mass destruction in Iraq, the intelligence community placed a new premium on alternative hypotheses, and on applying the use of structured analytic techniques to consider different outcomes or worst-case scenarios. Analyses that consider alternative views are routinely produced by the CIA's red team and 'mainline' analytic units on a range of topics of strategic importance to US national-security and foreign policy. Yet national-security policymakers have not yet figured out how to integrate them into the decision-making process, which limits such products' utility in preventing surprise, as most recently seen in Afghanistan.

The National Security Council (NSC) should consider options for integrating alternative analyses into its work and preparing for high-impact, low-probability scenarios identified by the intelligence community around areas of strategic concern. Such work could be led by the NSC's Strategic Planning directorate or, better still, woven into the deliberations of regional and functional directorates that are typically the policy leads. In either case, the NSC could prompt decision-makers from all of the agencies involved in the NSC inter-agency process to consider whether, if an alternative scenario played out, the US would still pursue a given policy; if so, how that policy might be implemented differently; and how to prepare for such a contingency.

*   *   *

From the early 1960s to the present day, the US has repeated the same mistakes regarding aiding and training foreign militaries fighting insurgencies, especially by failing to objectively analyse their prospects for success once US support ends. After 60 years, major adjustments in the intelligence–policy relationship are overdue. By creating a channel for operational information to flow directly from military personnel in the field to intelligence analysts, allowing that information to be integrated with other intelligence sources without political interference, embracing bad news as well as good news, and incorporating analysis of alternative scenarios into the policymaking process, the president and senior decision-makers would develop a better understanding of developments on the ground. This would increase the likelihood that viable policies would succeed as well as the likelihood that futile policies would be abandoned.

Notes

[1] McGeorge Bundy, 'Report of the Vietnam Task Force', National Security Action Memorandum 52, 6 May 1961, p. 1, availale at the John F. Kennedy Presidential Library and Museum, https://www.jfklibrary.org/asset-viewer/archives/JFKNSF/330/ JFKNSF-330-002.

[2] Robert McNamara, 'Briefing to President Kennedy and Members of the Bipartisan Legislative Leaders Meeting', 8 January 1963, quoted in 'The Kennedy Commitment', Miller Center,

University of Virginia, 18 September
2017, https://millercenter.org/the-
presidency/educational-resources/
kennedy-commitment.

3   Harold P. Ford, *CIA and the Vietnam
Policymakers: Three Episodes, 1962–1968*
(Washington DC: Center for the Study
of Intelligence, 1998), pp. 10–11.

4   *Ibid.*, p. 6.

5   *Ibid.*

6   Barack Obama, 'Remarks on
Responsibly Ending the War in Iraq',
White House Archives, 27 February
2009, https://obamawhitehouse.
archives.gov/the-press-office/
remarks-president-barack-obama-
ndash-responsibly-ending-war-iraq.

7   *Ibid.*

8   See 'Learning from Iraq: A Final
Report from the Special Inspector
General for Iraq Reconstruction',
March 2013, p. 93, https://www.
globalsecurity.org/jhtml/jframe.
html#https://www.globalsecurity.
org/military/library/report/2013/
sigir-learning-from-iraq.
pdf|||Learning%20From%20Iraq:%20
A%20Final%20Report%20from%20
the%20Special%20Inspector%20
General%20for%20Iraq%20
Reconstruction.

9   See Sarhang Hamasaeed and Garrett
Nada, 'Iraq Timeline: Since the
2003 War', US Institute of Peace, 29
May 2020, https://www.usip.org/
iraq-timeline-2003-war.

10 Quoted in David Remnick, 'Going
the Distance: On and Off the Road
with Barack Obama', *New Yorker*,
19 January 2014, https://www.
newyorker.com/magazine/2014/01/27/
going-the-distance-david-remnick.

11 See Steve Kroft, 'President Obama:

What Makes Us America', *60
Minutes*, 28 September 2014,
https://www.cbsnews.com/news/
president-obama-60-minutes/.

12 Quoted in David Ignatius, 'James
Clapper: We Underestimated the
Islamic State's "Will to Fight"',
Washington Post, 18 September
2014, https://www.washingtonpost.
com/opinions/david-ignatius-we-
underestimated-the-islamic-state-
james-clapper-says/2014/09/18/
f0f17072-3f6f-11e4-9587-5dafd96295f0_
story.html.

13 See Peter Baker and Eric Schmitt,
'Many Missteps in Assessment of
ISIS Threat', *New York Times*, 29
September 2014, https://www.nytimes.
com/2014/09/30/world/middleeast/
obama-fault-is-shared-in-misjudging-
of-isis-threat.html.

14 See James Clapper, 'Statement for
the Record: Worldwide Threat
Assessment of the US Intelligence
Community', Senate Select Committee
on Intelligence, 29 January 2014,
https://www.dni.gov/files/documents/
Intelligence%20Reports/2014%20
WWTA%20%20SFR_SSCI_29_Jan.pdf.

15 *Ibid.*, p. 4.

16 *Ibid.*, p. 15.

17 Michael Flynn, 'Annual Threat
Assessment: Statement Before the
Senate Armed Services Committee',
11 February 2014, p. 9, https://www.
armed-services.senate.gov/imo/media/
doc/Flynn_02-11-14.pdf.

18 See US House of Representatives,
'Initial Findings of the US House of
Representatives Joint Task Force on
US Central Command Intelligence
Analysis', 10 August 2016, p. 11,
https://news.usni.org/2016/08/11/

document-report-congress-u-s-nuclear-weapons-turkey.

19 *Ibid.*, p. 9.

20 See Inspector General, US Department of Defense, 'Unclassified Report of Investigation on Allegations Relating to USCENTCOM Intelligence Products', 31 January 2017, pp. 82–3, https://irp.fas.org/agency/dod/ig-centcom.pdf.

21 See *ibid.*, pp. 55–6.

22 See Special Inspector General for Afghanistan Reconstruction, 'Quarterly Report to Congress', 30 July 2021, p. 62, https://www.sigar.mil/pdf/quarterlyreports/2021-07-30qr.pdf.

23 *Ibid.*

24 *Ibid.*

25 See Craig Whitlock, 'The Afghanistan Papers: At War with the Truth', *Washington Post,* 19 December 2019, https://www.washingtonpost.com/graphics/2019/investigations/afghanistan-papers/afghanistan-war-confidential-documents/.

26 *Ibid.*

27 Secretary of Defense Lloyd J. Austin III, 'Prepared Remarks before the Senate Armed Services Committee', 28 September 2021, https://www.armed-services.senate.gov/imo/media/doc/20210927%20-%20SecDef%20Written%20Testimony%20-%20AFG%20hearings.pdf.

28 Secretary of Defense Austin and Chairman of the Joint Chiefs of Staff Gen. Milley, Press Briefing, US Department of Defense, 18 August 2021, https://www.defense.gov/News/Transcripts/Transcript/Article/2738086/secretary-of-defense-austin-and-chairman-of-the-joint-

chiefs-of-staff-gen-mille/.

29 See Mark Mazetti, Julian Barnes and Adam Goldman, 'Intelligence Warned of Afghan Military Collapse, Despite Biden's Assurances', *New York Times,* 17 August 2021, https://www.nytimes.com/2021/08/17/us/politics/afghanistan-biden-administration.html.

30 Douglas London, 'CIA's Former Counterterrorism Chief for the Region: Afghanistan, Not an Intelligence Failure – Something Much Worse', *Just Security,* 18 August 2021, https://www.justsecurity.org/77801/cias-former-counterterrorism-chief-for-the-region-afghanistan-not-an-intelligence-failure-something-much-worse/.

31 Quoted in Morgan Chalfant and Rebecca Beitsch, 'Afghanistan Disaster Puts Intelligence Under Scrutiny', *Hill,* 18 August 2021, https://thehill.com/policy/national-security/568475-afghanistan-disaster-puts-intelligence-under-scrutiny.

32 See 'Learning from Iraq', p. 175.

33 Ford, *CIA and the Vietnam Policymakers,* p. 14.

34 Lloyd Gardner, 'Introduction', in David F. Gordon et al. (eds), *Estimative Products on Vietnam, 1948–1975* (Washington DC: National Intelligence Council, 2005), p. xx.

35 See Micah Zenko, *Red Team: How to Succeed in Thinking Like the Enemy* (New York: Basic Books, 2015), pp. 90–8.

36 According to the FY22 Congressional Budget Justification, the State Department alone requested more than $9.5bn in foreign military and security assistance for the current fiscal year. See US Department of State, 'Congressional

Budget Justification, Department of State, Foreign Operations, and Related Programs', Fiscal Year 2022, https://www.state.gov/wp-content/uploads/2021/05/FY-2022-State_USAID-Congressional-Budget-Justification.pdf.

37 See 'Intelligence Community Directive 203: Analytic Standards', 2 January 2015, https://www.dni.gov/files/documents/ICD/ICD%20203%20 Analytic%20Standards.pdf.

38 Quoted in Robert Jervis, *Why Intelligence Fails: Lessons from the Iranian Revolution and the Iraq War* (Ithaca, NY: Cornell University Press, 2010), p. 156.

39 See Inspector General, US Department of Defense, 'Unclassified Report of Investigation on Allegations Relating to USCENTCOM Intelligence Products', p. 89.

Why Have Chinese Diplomats Become So Aggressive?

Nien-chung Chang-Liao

Sir Henry Wotton, the seventeenth-century British diplomat, reportedly once remarked that an ambassador is 'an honest gentleman sent to lie abroad for the good of his country'.[1] Many Western commentators have been astonished that Chinese diplomats have discarded the professionalism and courtesy that have facilitated China's engagement with the world for more than four decades. Their offensive rhetoric and behaviour are often at odds with the facts and even with Beijing's diplomatic line. From the war of words over foreign criticism of China's handling of COVID-19 to the scuffle with their Taiwanese counterparts in Fiji, their behaviour is not what would be expected of professional diplomats seeking to improve China's international image in the wake of the pandemic. Why have Chinese diplomats become so aggressive?

There are three possible explanations for why Chinese diplomats are so belligerent these days. Firstly, their more assertive behaviour may be calculated to persuade international audiences to accept China's narrative regarding responsibility for the pandemic. Secondly, their bluster could be designed to appeal to nationalist attitudes at home, thus bolstering the legitimacy of the Chinese Communist Party (CCP). Thirdly, they might just be following instructions and demonstrating their loyalty to President and CCP General Secretary Xi Jinping. All three explanations may be valid to some extent.

Nien-chung Chang-Liao is an assistant research fellow at the Institute of Political Science at Academia Sinica in Taiwan. His work has been published in various academic journals, including *Global Policy*, *International Affairs* and the *Washington Quarterly*.

Survival | vol. 64 no. 1 | February–March 2022 | pp. 179–190   https://doi.org/10.1080/00396338.2022.2032997

Shirking responsibility

Some analysts speculate that Chinese diplomats are attempting to distract foreign audiences rather than persuade them.[2] Their controversial statements might be part of a strategy to divert international attention away from Beijing's mishandling of COVID-19. The Chinese government initially covered up the extent and severity of the coronavirus outbreak in Wuhan, although there have since been calls worldwide for Beijing to be held accountable.[3] Chinese diplomats, knowing that they cannot make a strong case in their country's defence, have perhaps turned to provocative narratives about the weakness of other states. One example is Chinese Foreign Ministry spokesman Zhao Lijian, whose Twitter blasts include a conspiracy theory claiming that the coronavirus originated from the US military and an allegation of war crimes on the part of Australian soldiers.[4] He and others seem to believe that by disseminating a high volume of disinformation, they can divert public attention from the facts.

Such an approach appears short-sighted. The main task of diplomats is to maintain dialogue and conduct negotiations across different political, cultural and ideological boundaries, resolving disagreements and trying to reconcile conflicting national interests.[5] This requires pragmatism, sophistication and a willingness to compromise in order to reach common ground. A strategy of distraction may protect their government's authority and legitimacy in the short run, but it could derail communication and cooperation on the long-term priorities of bilateral relationships. One example is the investment pact between the European Union and China reached in December 2020, which the European Parliament has refrained from ratifying due to the row between Beijing and Brussels over human-rights violations in Xinjiang. Chinese diplomats have done nothing to smooth the ratification process.[6]

A diplomat who uses undiplomatic language will find it difficult to help his or her country maintain foreign support. China's international popularity has been in free fall since the beginning of the COVID-19 crisis, despite Beijing's offers of medical supplies and economic aid to afflicted countries.[7] In contrast, during the 2003 SARS outbreak in Guangdong, Chinese leaders and officials responsibly facilitated international coordination, helping to limit the spread of the virus.[8]

China's diplomacy, however, was becoming inflammatory even before the pandemic. For example, in 2019, Lu Shaye, then the Chinese ambassador to Canada, accused the Canadian government of 'white supremacy' when it detained Meng Wanzhou, the Huawei executive charged with violating US sanctions against Iran. After Lu became China's ambassador to France, a post on the Chinese Embassy's website claimed care staff in a French nursing home were abandoning residents and leaving them to starve during the pandemic.[9] Although the post was withdrawn after French Foreign Minister Jean-Yves Le Drian protested, it appears to have been calculated not to make points with a foreign audience but rather to impress the Chinese public.

Nationalist impulses

Chinese diplomats may also be playing hardball in their dealings with their foreign counterparts out of fear of repercussions at home, as nationalism surges in China.[10] They might worry that domestic audiences would interpret moderation and restraint as weakness and collaboration, threatening their political careers. China's diplomatic corps has in fact been criticised at home for being 'either conservative or pusillanimous' on global issues and 'too weak-kneed' in promoting China's sovereignty claims.[11]

Many Chinese people buy into the idea of 'wolf-warrior' diplomacy – a reference to a popular Chinese movie franchise featuring a Chinese soldier who defeats foreign mercenaries. Over 70% of respondents to a *Global Times* survey said they thought it improved China's global image.[12] A large proportion of the population sees foreign narratives as unfairly discrediting their country. 'I don't see any problem in living with that "wolf-warrior" title', said Chinese Foreign Ministry spokeswoman Hua Chunying, because 'we are fighting for China's sovereignty, security and development interests, national dignity and honour, and international fairness and justice'.[13] Such emotive language may be sincere, but it is not diplomatic.

Patriotic assertions of China's rights and position in the world may constitute a response to Xi Jinping's emphasis on the need for confidence in China's developmental path, political system, guiding doctrines and culture.[14] The political chaos and mismanagement experienced in Western countries during the COVID-19 crisis have only reinforced that confidence. But Chinese diplomats may now be overplaying the nationalist card. Especially after the pandemic was brought under control in China but was still rampant elsewhere, there was a strong sense of triumphalism among Chinese elites and media. They felt that China's rigid epidemiological control measures had been vindicated, while the more permissive and improvisational Western approach had failed. This led to a series of propaganda campaigns praising China as a major contributor to the worldwide fight against COVID-19.[15] These campaigns were diplomatically counterproductive, as it appeared that Beijing was seizing on the West's vulnerability to boost its national image.[16] Yan Xuetong, a hawkish Chinese scholar of international relations, warned against such hubris, arguing that it could fuel rising anti-Chinese feelings abroad, particularly in the United States and Europe.[17]

Nationalism is a double-edged sword. It placates domestic audiences but limits diplomatic manoeuvrability. In the past, Beijing consistently resorted to public expressions of grievance to signal diplomatic resolve, but carefully calibrated them.[18] Chinese diplomats' ultimate aim was to defuse rather than stoke nationalist sentiment. Examples include their handling of the popular protests over the United States' accidental bombing of the Chinese Embassy in Belgrade in 1999, and the collision between a US surveillance plane and Chinese fighters over the Chinese island of Hainan in 2001. Prominent Chinese diplomats, though publicly condemnatory and insistent on apologies from the US, behaved in a deliberately restrained manner, reiterating the importance of solidarity and stability, and preventing nationalists from escalating the tension.[19] More recently, when Chinese and Indian troops clashed on the border between the two countries in 2020, Chinese diplomats, though laying the blame on India, softened their tone and refrained from provoking public anger.[20] This restraint was exceptional, however, and reflects Chinese sensitivity and nuance with respect to a unique issue of sovereignty and security close to home.

Showing loyalty

Sir Henry Wotton did not mention that diplomats also lie for their own benefit, to promote their careers or exploit political opportunities. Thus, what economists Georgy Egorov and Konstantin Sonin call a loyalty–

competence trade-off is another reason for Chinese diplomats' jingoism.[21] To demonstrate loyalty to superiors, officials often feel compelled to do whatever they are asked to do, regardless of whether it is ineffectual or even outrageous. An extreme American instance of this arose when Sean Spicer, then the White House press secretary, publicly defended blatantly false estimates of the size of the turnout for Donald Trump's presidential inauguration in 2017.[22] The pugnacity of Chinese diplomats is a sign of loyalty to their leader, showing that they are prepared to burn bridges in his service. The stronger the pushback they receive, the more credible is their display of loyalty from a domestic point of view. This dynamic is common in authoritarian regimes, where insecure leaders prefer loyal but inept subordinates who can help them consolidate power. Josef Stalin's purge of the Red Army in the 1930s yielded him a docile military leadership, but it was incapable of repelling the 1941 German invasion.[23]

For Chinese bureaucrats, political loyalty has long been a prerequisite for career advancement, and the requirement has intensified with the shift from collective leadership to personalist rule under Xi.[24] In addition to taking policy-related matters into his own hands, he has centralised the party's authority over government personnel.[25] This has affected the Chinese Foreign Ministry and other institutions involved in foreign affairs.[26] The importance of China's foreign-policy establishment in the decision-making process has greatly decreased, and its role has been redefined to serve the leader's own diplomatic agenda.[27]

In 2017, Xi ordered China's diplomats to be 'absolutely loyal to the Party, to the country and to the people', and demanded their 'strict compliance with political discipline'.[28] His tone was markedly different from that of the 2009 Law of the People's Republic of China on Diplomatic Personnel Stationed Abroad, under which diplomats were required to be loyal to the constitution, the motherland and the people. Senior Chinese diplomats have since ensured that China's foreign affairs were guided by Xi.[29] Shortly before Yang Jiechi became the first diplomat in two decades to be elected to the Politburo, in 2017, he admonished his colleagues 'to study and achieve a deep understanding of General Secretary Xi Jinping's thought on diplomacy … in conducting China's foreign affairs and diplomacy'.[30] Young and ambitious Chinese diplomats have increasingly answered Xi's call to achieve a national renaissance with 'fighting spirit' (*douzheng jingshen*).[31] Foreign Ministry spokesman Zhao is one prominent example.

For Otto von Bismarck, foreign policy was an extension of domestic policy. For Chinese diplomats, it would seem to be the extension of their leader's will. Xi has clearly shaped the world view of Yang and other Chinese.[32] Those in power during the Cultural Revolution did the same, favouring dramatic and extreme behaviour, and sweeping aside those who were more diplomatically inclined.[33] Contemporary Chinese diplomats do not lack skills or talent, but they are constrained from providing advice that questions Xi's policy. As a result, the tradition of professionalism that the Chinese Foreign Ministry has nurtured since the 1970s is beginning to break down.[34] Chinese diplomats are becoming more like an 'organizational weapon' of the party and its leader than rational agents acting on behalf of the state.[35]

The relative influences of distraction, nationalism and leadership preference on the conduct of Chinese diplomats are unclear and require more political science. If distraction is the dominant motivation, Chinese diplomats should cool down once the COVID-19 controversy has subsided.[36] If nationalism is the primary factor, Chinese leaders may be willing to restrain their diplomats to subdue nationalist sentiment. If leadership preference is key, however, Chinese-initiated disputes that risk serious international repercussions seem likely to become more frequent.

In any case, the muscularity of Chinese diplomats does not mean that they have greater sway over China's foreign policy. On the contrary, as Jing Sun points out, China's top diplomats' 'combative performance could paradoxically reveal a struggling ministry, a diplomatic corps that is getting increasingly nervous enough to heed rather than to advise the top leadership'.[37] In other words, their outward assertiveness may be a performance put on to satisfy an increasingly demanding domestic audience, be it the nationalistic public or Xi and like-minded senior officials. That seems the most appropriate reading of Chinese officials Yang Jiechi and Wang Yi's public confrontation of their US counterparts Antony Blinken and Jake Sullivan during the high-level Alaska meeting in March 2021.[38] In short, Chinese diplomats today are 'speaking global but thinking domestic'.[39]

* * *

The radicalisation of Chinese diplomats clearly signifies that pragmatism in Chinese foreign policy is waning. For decades, Chinese diplomats avoided public attention unless they were voicing their opinion on international matters as part of the foreign-policy process. As recently as 2013, US China expert David Shambaugh described the Chinese Foreign Ministry as exhibiting 'commendable professionalism and sophistication' and as having 'earned the respect of diplomats around the world'.[40] Today, as Chinese diplomats have become more combative in defending their country's policies and less tolerant of foreign criticism, China is more unpopular internationally than it has been since the 1989 Tiananmen Square crackdown.[41] The late Chinese diplomat Wu Jianmin's admonition to his peers to 'remain modest, keep a cool head, and be rational' (*qianxu, danding* and *lixing*) has fallen on deaf ears.[42]

Since his accession to power in 2012, Xi has launched a series of diplomatic campaigns that highlight China's regional leadership and global influence. From the New Asian Security Concept to a regional 'community of common destiny' (*mingyun gongtongti*) to the Belt and Road Initiative that connects Europe and Asia, Xi's diplomatic activism is unprecedented among Chinese leaders.[43] Departing from Deng Xiaoping's low-profile foreign policy, Xi has not shied away from taking a leading role in world affairs and assuming greater global responsibility.[44] The ultimate goal of his extroversion is domestic: to enhance the CCP's legitimacy and secure his regime. In placing himself at the apex of the hierarchy, however, possibilities for missteps have increased while opportunities for correction have diminished, as they did in the Mao era.[45] Jessica Weeks notes that personalist leaders who face fewer domestic constraints are more inclined to undertake reckless and risky international behaviour.[46]

In seeking to avoid responsibility for its actions, China is bound to increase international distrust. Assertive nationalism limits Beijing's scope for compromise. Eagerness among Chinese diplomats to demonstrate their loyalty to Xi could do lasting damage to China's external relations. As China's wolf-warrior diplomacy alarms more and more foreign leaders, their resistance to it is becoming stronger and more cohesive.[47] For them to formulate considered responses that might moderate Chinese behaviour, it is crucial to understand the reasons behind it.

Notes

1   See, for example, Eloise Davis, 'Honest Men Lying Abroad', *London Review of Books*, 19 July 2019, https://www.lrb.co.uk/blog/2019/july/honest-men-lying-abroad.

2   As Suisheng Zhao points out, Chinese diplomats have tried to 'deflect the blame on China and counter Western accusations that coronavirus originated in China'. Suisheng Zhao, 'Rhetoric and Reality of China's Global Leadership in the Context of Covid-19: Implications for the US-led World Order and Liberal Globalization', *Journal of Contemporary China*, vol. 30, no. 128, July 2020, p. 243. See also Dingding Chen and Junyang Hu, 'Is China Really Embracing "Wolf Warrior" Diplomacy?', *Diplomat*, 9 September 2020, https://thediplomat.com/2020/09/is-china-really-embracing-wolf-warrior-diplomacy/; and Kyoko Kuwahara, 'China's "Wolf Warrior Diplomacy": The Limitations and Challenges Exposed by the Corona Crisis', *JIIA Strategic Comments*, Japan Institute of International Affairs, 16 May 2020, https://www.jiia.or.jp/en/strategic_comment/2020/05/jiia-strategic-comments-2020-11.html.

3   See François Heisbourg, 'From Wuhan to the World: How the Pandemic Will Reshape Geopolitics', *Survival*, vol. 62, no. 3, June–July 2020, pp. 7–24.

4   See T.S. Allen, 'China's Pandemic Public Opinion Warfare Alienates Global Audiences', *China Brief*, vol. 20, no. 21, 6 December 2020, p. 30, https://jamestown.org/program/chinas-pandemic-public-opinion-warfare-alienates-global-audiences/.

5   See Jean-Robert Leguey-Feilleux, *The Dynamics of Diplomacy* (Boulder, CO: Lynne Rienner Publishers, 2009), p. 153.

6   See Philip Blenkinsop, 'EU–China Deal Grinds into Reverse After Tit-for-Tat Sanctions', Reuters, 23 March 2021, https://www.reuters.com/article/us-eu-china-trade-idUSKBN2BF276; and Stuart Lau, 'China Throws EU Trade Deal to the Wolf Warriors', *Politico*, 22 March 2021, https://www.politico.eu/article/china-throws-eu-trade-deal-to-the-wolf-warriors-sanctions-investment-pact/.

7   See Bates Gill, 'China's Global Influence: Post-Covid Prospects for Soft Power', *Washington Quarterly*, vol. 43, no. 2, Summer 2020, pp. 97–115; and Brian Wong, 'China's Mask Diplomacy', *Diplomat*, 25 March 2020, https://thediplomat.com/2020/03/chinas-mask-diplomacy/. On China's international popularity ratings, see Laura Silver, Kat Devlin and Christine Huang, 'Unfavorable Views of China Reach Historic Highs in Many Countries', Pew Research Center, 6 October 2020, https://www.pewresearch.org/global/2020/10/06/unfavorable-views-of-china-reach-

historic-highs-in-many-countries/.

8   See, for example, Joseph Kahn, 'China Discovers Secrecy Is Expensive', *New York Times*, 13 April 2003, https://www.nytimes.com/2003/04/13/weekinreview/china-discovers-secrecy-is-expensive.html.

9   See Jiangtao Shi, 'Coronavirus: They're Only Answering Xi Jinping's Call but Are China's "Wolf Warrior" Diplomats Doing More Harm than Good?', *South China Morning Post*, 27 April 2020, https://www.scmp.com/news/china/diplomacy/article/3081592/coronavirus-theyre-only-answering-xi-jinpings-call-are-chinas. In common with most Chinese ambassadors, China's envoy in Canada holds a bureau-level post. The ambassadors to Brazil, France, Germany, India, Japan, North Korea, Russia, the United Kingdom and the United States are ranked at vice-ministerial level.

10 See Min Ye, 'Wolf Warriors Blow Hot Before Cooling Down', *Global Asia*, vol. 15, no. 3, September 2020, pp. 103–6. As Jessica Chen Weiss points out, 'nationalism creates pressure for the government to talk tough and placate domestic audiences'. Jessica Chen Weiss, 'China's Self-defeating Nationalism', *Foreign Affairs*, 16 July 2020, https://www.foreignaffairs.com/articles/china/2020-07-16/chinas-self-defeating-nationalism. See also Chen and Hu, 'Is China Really Embracing "Wolf Warrior" Diplomacy?'; and Zhiqun Zhu, '"Wolf-warrior Diplomacy": China's New Normal?', *ThinkChina*, 4 May 2020, https://www.thinkchina.sg/wolf-warrior-diplomacy-chinas-new-normal.

11 François Godement, 'China's Foreign Policy and the Leadership Transition: Prospects for Change Under the "Fifth Generation"', in Gilbert Rozman (ed.), *China's Foreign Policy: Who Makes It, and How Is It Made?* (New York: Palgrave Macmillan, 2013), p. 232.

12 Qi Wang, 'Over 70% Respondents Believe China's Global Image Has Improved, "Wolf Warrior Diplomacy" a Necessary Gesture: GT Poll' , *Global Times*, 25 December 2020, https://www.globaltimes.cn/content/1211003.shtml.

13 *Ibid.*

14 See Lanxin Xiang, 'Xi's Dream and China's Future', *Survival*, vol. 58, no. 3, June–July 2016, pp. 53–62; and Zhu, 'Wolf-warrior Diplomacy'.

15 See Yanzhong Huang, 'Xi Jinping Won the Coronavirus Crisis', *Foreign Affairs*, 13 April 2020, https://www.foreignaffairs.com/articles/china/2020-04-13/xi-jinping-won-coronavirus-crisis.

16 See Gill, 'China's Global Influence'.

17 See Catherine Wong, 'Too Soon, Too Loud: Chinese Foreign Policy Advisers Tell "Wolf Warrior" Diplomats to Tone It Down', *South China Morning Post*, 14 May 2020, https://www.scmp.com/news/china/diplomacy/article/3084274/too-soon-too-loud-chinese-foreign-policy-advisers-tell-wolf.

18 See Weiss, 'China's Self-defeating Nationalism'.

19 See Jessica Chen Weiss, *Powerful Patriots: Nationalist Protest in China's Foreign Relations* (New York: Oxford University Press, 2014), pp. 45–81.

20 See M. Taylor Fravel, 'China's Sovereignty Obsession', *Foreign Affairs*, 26 June 2020, https://www.foreignaffairs.com/

articles/china/2020-06-26/
chinas-sovereignty-obsession.

21 Georgy Egorov and Konstantin
Sonin, 'Dictators and Their Viziers:
Endogenizing the Loyalty–
Competence Trade-off', *Journal of the
European Economic Association*, vol. 9,
no. 5, October 2011, pp. 903–30.

22 See Ashley Parker, Philip Rucker
and Matea Gold, 'The First Days
Inside Trump's White House:
Fury, Tumult and a Reboot',
Washington Post, 23 January 2017,
https://www.washingtonpost.com/
politics/the-first-days-inside-trumps-
white-house-fury-tumult-and-a-
reboot/2017/01/23/7ceef1b0-e191-11e6-
ba11-63c4b4fb5a63_story.html.

23 See Peter Whitewood, *The Red Army
and the Great Terror: Stalin's Purge of
the Soviet Military* (Lawrence, KS:
University Press of Kansas, 2015).

24 See Hanzhang Liu, 'The Logic of
Authoritarian Political Selection:
Evidence from a Conjoint
Experiment in China', *Political
Science Research and Methods*, vol. 7,
no. 4, July 2019, pp. 853–70.

25 See Dimitar Gueorguiev, 'Dictator's
Shadow: Chinese Elite Politics Under
Xi Jinping', *China Perspectives*, vol. 1,
no. 2, July 2018, pp. 17–26.

26 See Linda Jakobson and Ryan
Manuel, 'How Are Foreign Policy
Decisions Made in China?', *Asia &
the Pacific Policy Studies*, vol. 3, no. 1,
January 2016, pp. 101–10. As Susan
Shirk has pointed out, 'how they
operate domestically spills over into
how they operate internationally'.
Quoted in Steven Lee Myers, 'China's
Aggressive Diplomacy Weakens Xi
Jinping's Global Standing', *New York
Times*, 19 October 2020, https://www.
nytimes.com/2020/04/17/world/asia/
coronavirus-china-xi-jinping.html.

27 See Jing Sun, 'Growing Diplomacy,
Retreating Diplomats: How the Chinese
Foreign Ministry Has Been Marginalized
in Foreign Policymaking', *Journal of
Contemporary China*, vol. 26, no. 105,
November 2016, pp. 419–33.

28 'Xi Calls for More Efforts in Major-
country Diplomacy with Chinese
Characteristics', Xinhua, 28 December
2017, http://www.xinhuanet.com/
english/2017-12/28/c_136858028.htm.

29 See 'Xi Urges Breaking New Ground
in Major Country Diplomacy with
Chinese Characteristics', Xinhua, 24
June 2018, http://www.xinhuanet.com/
english/2018-06/24/c_137276269.htm.

30 Jiechi Yang, 'Study and Implement
General Secretary Xi Jinping's
Thought on Diplomacy in a Deep-
going Way and Keep Writing
New Chapters of Major-country
Diplomacy with Distinctive Chinese
Features', Ministry of Foreign Affairs
of the People's Republic of China, 17
July 2017, https://www.fmprc.gov.
cn/mfa_eng/wjdt_665385/zyjh_91/
t1478497.shtml.

31 'Xi Focus: Xi Emphasizes "Struggles"
to Achieve National Rejuvenation',
Xinhua, 3 September 2019, http://
www.xinhuanet.com/english/2019-
09/03/c_138362482.htm.

32 See Dylan M.H. Loh, 'Institutional
Habitus, State Identity, and China's
Ministry of Foreign Affairs',
International Studies Review, vol. 22,
no. 4, December 2020, p. 891; Sun,
'Growing Diplomacy, Retreating
Diplomats', p. 427; and Peter Martin,
China's Civilian Army: The Making of

Wolf Warrior Diplomacy (New York: Oxford University Press, 2021), pp. 9–10.

33 See Barbara Barnouin and Changgen Yu, *Chinese Foreign Policy During the Cultural Revolution* (London: Kegan Paul International, 1998); and Xiaohong Liu, *Chinese Ambassadors: The Rise of Diplomatic Professionalism Since 1949* (Hong Kong: Hong Kong University Press, 2001), p. 126.

34 Some did see that development as brittle. See A. Doak Barnett, *The Making of Foreign Policy in China: Structure and Process* (Boulder, CO: Westview, 1986), p. 92.

35 See Philip Selznick, *The Organizational Weapon: A Study of Bolshevik Strategy and Tactics* (New York: McGraw-Hill, 1952).

36 See Ye, 'Wolf Warriors Blow Hot Before Cooling Down'.

37 Jing Sun, *Red Chamber, World Dream: Actors, Audience, and Agendas in Chinese Foreign Policy and Beyond* (Ann Arbor, MI: University of Michigan Press, 2021), p. 66.

38 See Rachel Cheung and Benjamin Wilhelm, 'Why China's "Wolf Warriors" Won't Back Down', *World Policy Review*, 7 April 2021, https:// www.worldpoliticsreview.com/ trend-lines/29554/china-s-wolf- warrior-diplomacy-is-here-to-stay; and 'China's "Wolf-warrior Diplomacy"', in 'Alaska Meeting Impresses World; Behind It Is the West–East Battle: Observers', *Global Times*, 25 March 2021, https://www.globaltimes.cn/ page/202103/1219387.shtml.

39 Author's email correspondence with Jing Sun, 14 April 2021.

40 David Shambaugh, *China Goes Global: The Partial Power* (Oxford: Oxford University Press, 2013), p. 66.

41 See 'Exclusive: Internal Chinese Report Warns Beijing Faces Tiananmen-like Global Backlash over Virus', Reuters, 4 May 2020, https://www.reuters.com/article/ us-health-coronavirus-china- sentiment-ex-idUSKBN22G19C.

42 See Jianmin Wu, *Ru he zuo da guo: shi jie zhi xu yu Zhongguo jue se* [How to Be a Great Power: The World Order and China's Role] (Beijing: China CITIC Press, 2016).

43 See 'Jet-setting Xi: With 14 Global Trips This Year, China's President Is the Country's Most-travelled Leader Since Foundation of Communist State', *South China Morning Post*, 26 December 2015, https://www.scmp. com/news/china/policies-politics/ article/1894878/jet-setting-xi-14-global- trips-year-chinas-president.

44 See Nien-chung Chang-Liao, 'China's New Foreign Policy Under Xi Jinping', *Asian Security*, vol. 12, no. 2, June 2016, pp. 82–91.

45 See Jakobson and Manuel, 'How Are Foreign Policy Decisions Made in China?', p. 108.

46 See Jessica L.P. Weeks, *Dictators at War and Peace* (Ithaca, NY: Cornell University Press, 2014).

47 See Dali L. Yang, 'The COVID-19 Pandemic and the Estrangement of US–China Relations', *Asian Perspective*, vol. 45, no. 1, Winter 2021, pp. 7–31.

Review Essay

From 11 September to 6 January: A Vexingly Dotted Line

Jonathan Stevenson

Reign of Terror: How the 9/11 Era Destabilized America and Produced Trump
Spencer Ackerman. New York: Viking, 2021. $30.00. 444 pp.

Subtle Tools: The Dismantling of American Democracy from the War on Terror to Donald Trump
Karen J. Greenberg. Princeton, NJ: Princeton University Press, 2021. £25.00/$29.95. 289 pp.

Two things about political extremism and democracy in America are by now clear. Firstly, the national mobilisation prompted by 9/11 against cresting transnational jihadism distracted American law-enforcement and intelligence agencies from residual but simmering domestic right-wing extremism, emblematised by the Oklahoma City bombing six years earlier and latent in the white-supremacist mindset since the republic's founding. Secondly, this mobilisation has involved diminishing individual liberties purportedly for the sake of increasing security, sometimes to the point of state criminality. Far less clear is whether the attacks on the Twin Towers and the Pentagon led inexorably to the mainstreaming of the far right and Donald Trump's abject degradation of American governance. In *Reign of Terror*, Spencer Ackerman says they did. In *Subtle Tools*, as the title suggests, Karen Greenberg provides a more nuanced and credible analysis.

Jonathan Stevenson is IISS Senior Fellow for US Defence and Managing Editor of *Survival*.

Survival | vol. 64 no. 1 | February–March 2022 | pp. 191–200   https://doi.org/10.1080/00396338.2022.2033001

Potted history

Ackerman is an able journalist, and here he proves adept at potting contemporary history into a readable narrative. His basic argument is that 9/11 led directly to the Capitol insurrection on 6 January 2021 by impelling the George W. Bush administration and an obeisant Congress to expand the reach, and martialise the methodology and mentality, of American law-enforcement and intelligence agencies. The apparent resilience, adaptability and transnational appeal of jihadism, he says, encouraged an aggressive and generational approach to countering Islamist terrorism, which led to the permanent structural entrenchment of what he calls the 'Security State', a term he repeats throughout the book as though it signified a revelatory epiphany. The intolerant and coercive mindset this state engendered in both government officials

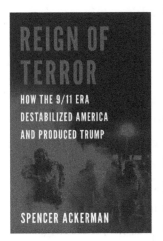

REIGN OF TERROR

HOW THE 9/11 ERA
DESTABILIZED AMERICA
AND PRODUCED TRUMP

SPENCER ACKERMAN

and the American public, so he contends, caused them to embrace right-wing extremism and authoritarianism, and enabled Trump to effectively turn the state into an instrument of regime security.

The author bends his analysis to fit his thesis, deploying suggestive juxtapositions and loaded terms – the ahistorically loose iteration of 'exceptionalist' is a pronounced tic – and glossing over inconvenient points. An early passage reflects the author's teleological approach, as well as pandering fealty to reflexive critics of US foreign policy:

> It was in this context – outwardly receiving deference from a frightened public; threatened with scapegoating for 9/11 by fearful politicians; expected to act as an instrument of both vengeance and deterrence – that the Security State constructed what became known as the War on Terror. Its name reflected what both [Susan] Sontag and [Joan] Didion had diagnosed: exceptionalist euphemism that masks a boundless, direful ambition. (p. 24)

He also selectively ignores political context: Bill Clinton asserted 'an inchoate exceptionalist right to humanitarian-premised military intervention. Following in a liberal-imperial tradition they seemed not to recognize, the

Clintonites tacitly premised their Balkans air strikes on enforcing standards of civilized behavior' (p. 93). Serbian misconduct goes unmentioned.

Relentlessly scolding and sanctimonious, Ackerman complains that Trump was able to use the unwinnability of the 'war on terror' as a 'cudgel' (p. 245) against his opponents, as if insusceptibility to clear victory were not a strong tendency of any religious and ideological conflict waged by true believers.[1] In a particularly tortuous line of reasoning, he portrays Democratic support for investigating Trump's possible enlistment of Russian help in the 2016 election as a 'conspicuous' symptom of the Security State that allowed Trump to appear the persecuted target of a 'shadow coup' (pp. 290–1). The book may reinforce the views of those predisposed to trace a through-line of malign government intent from Bush to Trump.[2] But there are major gaps in the argument.

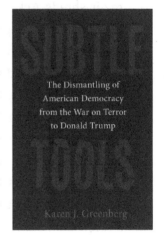

Indisputably, the US government committed myriad excesses in the name of 9/11 on the pretext of protecting the American homeland: 'rendering' suspected terrorists to 'black sites', torturing them – sometimes to death – and incarcerating hundreds for years without due process; visiting massive and intrusive electronic surveillance on American citizens; waging strategically perverse and absurdly over-ambitious wars in Iraq and Afghanistan; raining down drone strikes that killed hundreds of innocent civilians in Muslim countries; and adopting a broadly pre-emptive, legally and ethically dubious approach to security. These transgressions profoundly damaged the United States' standing as a liberal and humane state, and compromised any claim it might have had to exemplary status. And they yielded both greater state power to suppress terrorism and wider state tolerance for xenophobia and bigotry.[3]

Contra Ackerman, however, it does not follow that these missteps so corroded US governance and democracy as to guarantee Trump's ascendancy and the events of 6 January. In fact, this argument effectively relieves Trump and his supporters of the agency they have demonstrated and the blame they deserve. Take the war on terror away; do you still get Trump? We can never know for sure, but it's more than plausible that you do.

US opinion surveys showed that terrorism, though still a major worry, did not rank highest on most voters' lists of concerns in 2016.[4] Al-Qaeda had dispersed and become focused on regional conflict, and although the Islamic State (ISIS) had surged as a transnational terrorist player, the Obama team had established a plan for rolling it back in Iraq and Syria that was working. To be sure, expeditionary wars do take a toll on domestic politics and can move those who fight them to 'bring the war home' if they feel insufficiently appreciated.[5] During his campaign, Trump certainly exploited veterans' alienation, the broader resentment towards Muslims that 9/11 engendered and general war fatigue. He also vigorously defended torture, claiming that it worked and that techniques like waterboarding were 'not nearly tough enough'.[6] Nevertheless, Occam's razor shreds Ackerman's argument: Trump's presidential win is amply explained by a range of factors other than the war on terror. They include a steady decline in real wages, massive wealth inequality, globalisation, immigration, media manipulation, party-sorting and, consequently, white working-class disaffection with Democrats. These enabled Trump to cast the Democratic Party as the party of the rich and the Republican Party as that of the poor, and himself as a kind of post-Cold War, Reagan-style populist.[7]

Probably the deepest and most toxic source of Trump's success is percolating racism with origins long pre-dating 9/11.[8] Ackerman strains to draw a connection between that racism and the war on terror. For example: 'The longer the Forever War persisted, the more it fostered a nativist undercurrent, one that would never trust technocrats' (p. 108). Yet, in 2008, American voters elected Barack Obama – if not a technocrat, a liberal institutionalist par excellence, and a black man at that – and re-elected him in 2012. They appeared to be expressing their view that securing the American homeland against jihadists through perpetual external aggression was a mistake, and their desire to revert to the liberal ideals celebrated, if too triumphally, at the end of the Cold War. War-weary impulses, not an unquenchable thirst for using counter-terrorism tools to advance nativist objectives, led to Obama's election.[9] Indeed, he used his opposition to the Iraq War to considerable if not decisive electoral effect.[10]

Another rhetorically talismanic construct – the 'Sustainable War on Terror' (again, author's caps) – enshrines Ackerman's point that Obama was unable to abandon the war on terror and merely made it more manageable and less consuming. This is true.[11] Ackerman might also be correct that Bush's fulsome mobilisation against jihadism made counter-terrorism a jingoistically distorting American obsession that poisoned the American psyche.[12] But it remains unclear just what these policies had to do with Trump's elevation. The final paragraph of *Reign of Terror* – a last stab at linking the post-9/11 counter-terrorism push to Trumpism – is reductionist sophistry. 'Never would America acknowledge that the violent, reactionary dangers that it attributed to its enemies were also part of its own history', he writes.

> That was the meaning of Oklahoma City. It was the meaning of January 6. A white man with a flag and a gun, the man who had made America great, was not a terrorist. The 9/11 era said he was a counterterrorist. America had never been the sort of place that would tell him he was anything else. (p. 338)

Much earlier in the book, the author admits that 'only white supremacy can truly explain the depth of right-wing fury at Obama' (p. 157). Later, he observes that what supporters of Trump's 'Make America Great Again' (MAGA) agenda resented most about the Black Lives Matter movement 'was its demand to reckon with MAGA's cherished past, during which white supremacy was understood to be either meritocratic or natural' (p. 324). Obama's election and re-election signalled that the putative white majority was no longer secure, unearthing and energising deep-seated racism, which made the Republican Party increasingly obstructionist. Trump figured that by adopting an insular but selectively muscular foreign policy, tormenting immigrants who already lived in the United States, callously keeping out aspiring ones and encouraging far-right extremism, he could make America look great again and nail down the adulation of a large base sufficient, with gerrymandering and voter suppression, to preserve his electability. This approach has been lamentably effective. From this perspective, the practical inevitability of the white majority's evaporation is far more likely than the war on terror to have been the prime mover of Republicans' anti-democratic effort, with Trump as their main instrument, to coercively entrench minority rule, turbocharge replacement theory and harness the global far right.[13]

Measured and constructive

For Ackerman, 9/11 – or at least America's reaction to it – predestined Trumpism. On this point he overreaches. He may be onto something in his more modest suggestion that the national response produced institutional tools that Trump, once elected, was able to nefariously manipulate. The author seems to regard this too as an inexorable part of an irredeemable American package. For others, what makes America's dire prospects potentially so tragic is that they are avoidable.

Early in her even-toned book *Subtle Tools*, Karen Greenberg, director of the Center on National Security at Fordham Law School, notes that at the outset of Obama's presidency 'optimism abounded over the opportunities to reverse course on post-9/11 policies', while admitting that 'making progress proved harder than Obama had anticipated' (p. 3). For her, the policy and statutory responses to 9/11 did not inexorably lead to 1/6. Rather, the 'subtle tools' that evolved from them – the degradation of language, 'bureaucratic porousness', knee-jerk secrecy and rejection of precedent (p. 5) – simply helped Trump and his inner circle to stoke right-wing extremism and effectuate an authoritarian government. While her ambitions are more circumscribed than Ackerman's, she focuses a more discerning and salutary eye on the executive branch's conduct of national-security affairs.

Greenberg does permit herself the panoramic observation that post-9/11 presidents – especially Bush and Trump – have used these subtle tools to help skew once cyclically offsetting trends of progressive and conservative government, postulated by Arthur Schlesinger, Jr, in favour of the latter. The perversely Orwellian use of terms such as 'war', 'homeland' and 'enhanced interrogation' afforded statutory and other government terminology dangerous elasticity. By way of the USA PATRIOT Act and the Authorization for Use of Military Force (AUMF), Congress relinquished to the executive branch much of its authority over practices intimately affecting civil liberties and over waging war, respectively. Greenberg credits Obama with tightening executive-branch accountability for kinetic military action under the AUMF – pointedly, targeted killings – by means of the 'Obama Framework', an internal guidance document setting out specific criteria to be met and decision procedures to be followed before taking such action. This guidance was ignored, she notes, in the National Security Council's decision process leading to the January 2020 drone strike killing senior Iranian general and intelligence chief Qasem Soleimani. In terms of international fallout, the Trump administration more or less got away with it, but this only emboldened it to take even greater licence on the domestic front during the last year of Trump's presidency.

Although consolidating domestic law-enforcement agencies under one bureaucratic roof – namely, the Department of Homeland Security (DHS) – may have seemed sensibly efficient, in practice the new bureaucracy had little coordinative sinew and afforded opportunistic officials latitude to remake domestic security policies with insufficient accountability. Trump exploited subtle tools to unleash the two agencies in the DHS family responsible for immigration enforcement – Immigration and Customs Enforcement and Customs and Border Protection – on immigrants within the United States. Greenberg highlights not only the cynical political calculation of the policy but also 'the bureaucratic creep evidenced in using DHS for purposes well beyond terrorism, coupled with the reliance on vague and imprecise language to broaden the pool of those subjected to the most onerous application of the law' (p. 109).

Trump's misuse of federal law-enforcement agencies reached an extreme in summer 2020, as largely non-violent Black Lives Matter protests – triggered by the death of George Floyd, a black man, under the knee of a white Minneapolis policeman – burgeoned. In June, having made 'law and order' the centrepiece of his re-election campaign and tried but failed to enlist the active-service US military for domestic law enforcement, Trump issued an expansive executive order authorising the DHS and the Department of Justice to dispatch federal civilian personnel unilaterally to protect federal property. Pursuant to that order, the DHS established the Protecting American Communities Task Force. To populate it, the administration drew on myriad federal agencies with unrelated missions for personnel with inappropriate training and dispatched them to Portland (where they were especially exuberant), Albuquerque, Chicago, Cleveland, Detroit, Kansas City and Milwaukee. In many instances, they deployed in unmarked vehicles wearing combat fatigues with obscured insignia, like Russia's 'little green men' in Crimea. They frequently ranged well outside federal property, detaining protesters without cause and applying excessive force. In effect, Trump had mustered a praetorian guard, with the DHS as its leading element. Its purpose was not to maintain order and the rule of law through conventional policing, but rather to bolster his presidency with grey-zone paramilitary tactics.[14]

It is reasonable to speculate that Trump had hoped for a credible pretext to use the force on a larger scale for direct voter suppression during the presidential election that November.[15] The electorate provided him with no such opportunity. Trump did, of course, plant the false narrative of a rigged election to furnish a pretext for the 6 January insurrection and provide fuel for his political resurgence. But there were some signs of relief. In October 2020, a federal appeals court, upholding a district court's injunction arising from events in Portland, prohibited the DHS and the US Marshals Service from using force against journalists and legal observers without probable cause. According to Greenberg, the decision signified that 'the use of government agents as an "occupying force," violating rules and norms through secretive behavior and the spread of disinformation' was unlawful. It also 'constituted the most resounding rejection of the subtle tools to date' (p. 171).

*   *   *

Whereas *Reign of Terror* ends with a despondent thud, *Subtle Tools* strikes a concluding note of guarded hope for the rule of law against populist lawlessness. This hope resides in honouring 'clarity, transparency, bureaucratic integrity, and respect for law and norms' as opposed to 'imprecision, secrecy, bureaucratic porousness, and the violation of law and custom' (p. 209). Like any prescriptive reform, this remedy – essentially, institutionalised insistence on plain truth – is exasperatingly programmatic and sheepishly idealistic, far easier recommended than implemented. And it may be tempting to default to Ackerman's grim fatalism on the basis of the conviction that the United States has been irredeemably toxic from the start and fated to fall to its founding iniquity. But most Americans, still more inspired by the Obama administration's promise than flattened by its shortcomings, don't appear ready to concede that point; at least not yet.

Notes

[1] For more measured perspectives on the war on terror, see Hal Brands and Michael O'Hanlon, 'The War on Terror Has Not Yet Failed: A Net Assessment After 20 Years', *Survival*, vol. 63, no. 4, August–September 2021, pp. 35–54; and Audrey Kurth Cronin, 'US Counter-terrorism: Moving Beyond Global Counter-insurgency to Strongpoint Defence', *Survival*, vol. 63, no. 5, October–November 2021, pp. 97–120.

[2] See Jennifer Szalai, '"Reign of Terror" Brilliantly Traces the Course from 9/11 to President Trump', *New York Times*, 10 August 2021, https://www.nytimes.com/2021/08/10/books/review-reign-of-terror-9-11-era-trump-spencer-ackerman.html.

[3] See, for example, Thomas Hegghammer, 'Resistance Is Futile: The War on Terror Supercharged State Power', *Foreign Affairs*, vol. 100, no. 5, September/October 2021, pp. 44–52; and Cynthia Miller-Idriss, 'From 9/11 to 1/6: The War on Terror Supercharged the Far Right', *Foreign Affairs*, vol. 100, no. 5, September/October 2021, pp. 54–64.

[4] See, for example, John Lapinski and Stephanie Psyllos, 'Poll: One in Four Americans Rank Terrorism as Top Issue but Americans Split on Muslim Ban', NBC News, 16 June 2016, https://www.nbc-news.com/politics/2016-election/poll-one-four-americans-rank-terror-ism-top-issue-americans-split-n593886; and Pew Research Center, 'Top Voting Issues in 2016 Election', 7 July 2016, https://www.pewresearch.org/politics/2016/07/07/4-top-voting-issues-in-2016-election/.

[5] See Kathleen Belew, *Bring the War Home: The White Power Movement and Paramilitary America* (Cambridge, MA: Harvard University Press, 2018).

[6] Quoted in, for example, Ali Vitali, 'Donald Trump: "Torture Works"', NBC News, 17 February 2016, https://www.nbcnews.com/politics/2016-election/donald-trump-torture-works-n520086.

[7] See Michael Hirsh, 'Why Trump and Sanders Were Inevitable', *Politico*, 28 February 2016, https://www.politico.com/magazine/story/2016/02/why-donald-trump-and-bernie-sanders-were-inevitable-213685/; Michael McQuarrie, 'The Revolt of the Rust Belt: Place and Politics in the Age of Anger', *British Journal of Sociology*,

vol. 68, no. 1, November 2017, Special
Issue: The Trump/Brexit Moment:
Causes and Consequences, pp. S121–
52; George Packer, *The Unwinding:
An Inner History of the New America*,
2nd ed. (New York: Farrar Straus &
Giroux, 2014); and Eduardo Porter,
'How the GOP Became the Party of
the Left Behind', *New York Times*, 27
January 2020, https://www.nytimes.
com/interactive/2020/01/27/business/
economy/republican-party-voters-
income.html.

8   See, for example, Steven Simon and
Jonathan Stevenson, 'How Can We
Neutralize the Militias?', *New York
Review of Books*, vol. 68, no. 13, 19
August 2021; and Steven Simon,
'Trump's Insurrection and America's
Year of Living Dangerously', *Survival*,
vol. 63, no. 1, February–March 2021,
pp. 7–16.

9   On these impulses, see, for instance,
David Axelrod, *Believer: My Forty
Years in Politics* (New York: Penguin
Press, 2015).

10 See Gary C. Jacobson, 'George W.
Bush, the Iraq War, and the Election
of Barack Obama', *Presidential Studies
Quarterly*, vol. 40, no. 2, June 2010,
Special Issue: The 2008 Presidential
Election, Part I, pp. 207–24.

11 But the author studiously minimises
the considerable political obstacles
Obama faced in curtailing counter-
terrorism, fatuously taking him
to task for 'having deprived the
country of a chance at closure'
(p. 151) by not declaring victory
and going home after US special-
operations forces killed bin Laden in
May 2011 – a dubious position given
al-Qaeda's apparent resilience at the
time and the eventual emergence of
the Islamic State.

12 Quite a few others have made this
observation. See, for example, Alex
Lubin, *Never-ending War on Terror*
(Oakland, CA: University of California
Press, 2021).

13 See Belew, *Bring the War Home*;
Cynthia Miller-Idriss, *Hate in the
Homeland: The New Global Far Right*
(Princeton, NJ: Princeton University
Press, 2020); and Jonathan Stevenson,
'Hatred on the March', *New York
Review of Books*, vol. 66, no. 18, 21
November 2019.

14 See, for example, Jonathan Stevenson,
'Trump's Praetorian Guard', *New
York Review of Books*, vol. 67, no.
16, 22 October 2020, https://www.
nybooks.com/articles/2020/10/22/
trump-law-order-praetorian-guard/.

15 See, for instance, John W. Dean,
'Trump Has Been Comparing Himself
to Nixon. That's Hooey', *New York
Times*, 31 July 2020, https://www.
nytimes.com/2020/07/31/opinion/
trump-nixon-authoritarianism.html.

Book Reviews

Africa
Karen Smith

Born in Blackness: Africa, Africans, and the Making of the Modern World, 1471 to the Second World War
Howard W. French. New York: Liveright Publishing
Corporation, 2021. £25.00/$35.00. 499 pp.

Although there has been increased interest in Africa among Western scholars and policymakers from the perspective of new security threats, scholarship on Africa's role in the shaping of global order has been conspicuously absent. In response to this marginalisation of Africa, Howard French sets out to centre Africa and Africans in the making of the modern world, challenging a deterministic account of Western ascendancy based on science and reason. He effectively rewrites history, unsettling common-sense assumptions and breaking what he claims are deliberate and enforced silences in the study of history and international relations, in which Europeans always take centre stage and black and brown people play at most a supporting role.

In illuminating the 'deeply twinned and tragic history of Africa and Europe' (p. 3), French reimagines African agency by building on existing work that shows how the rise of Europe – associated with increased prosperity and scientific advances based on a supposedly innate superiority – is inextricably linked to its encounters with Africa. By inviting the reader to look beyond Europe's colonial conquests of the late nineteenth century, he convincingly makes the point that the infamous scramble for African territory was preceded by a scramble for its people (culminating in the transatlantic slave trade involving an estimated 12 million people), which not only became the foundation of a new economic system but profoundly transformed societies, making the development of the

Survival | vol. 64 no. 1 | February–March 2022 | pp. 201–207   https://doi.org/10.1080/00396338.2022.2033004

West possible. Turning some deep-seated beliefs on their heads, including the perception that, prior to contact with Europe, Africa was an undeveloped, primitive and uncivilised continent, he also challenges the idea that it was Europe's search for a maritime route to Asia that led to the so-called Age of Discovery, in which the African continent was merely an obstacle to be circumnavigated. He claims, instead, that West African gold was the driving motivation for European maritime exploration, led by Portugal. By exploring examples such as the role of the Kongo Kingdom in fuelling the war between Holland and Spain/Portugal, French further underlines the pivotal role that Africa has played in the global arena, and shows how the competition for control over Africa and Africans was at the heart of inter-European warfare for centuries.

French writes in an accessible way that draws the reader in with personal snippets based on his own life and experiences as a journalist for the *New York Times* in Africa and the Caribbean, yet his work is still underpinned by meticulous research. He explicitly engages with the work of well-known scholars such as Charles Tilly and Frederick Cooper, but also introduces lesser-known black intellectuals such as Eric Williams. His sometimes vivid depictions of sights and sounds rival those of great novelists, and yet the story he tells is, disturbingly, not one of fiction. The book is not entirely chronological: the pieces of the story fit together like intricate puzzle pieces. In some cases the same events or ideas are discussed in different parts of the book, resulting in some repetition and occasional jumps in the narrative, but the author can be forgiven for wanting to make sure that his point is driven home. Spanning five centuries and four continents, the content is inevitably selective and not exhaustive, something the author acknowledges.

Born in Blackness makes a valuable contribution to ongoing efforts to move beyond a Eurocentric account of history, which continues to influence how we understand global order and Africa's role in shaping it. The book is essential reading for anyone interested in understanding how the West came into being, and hoping to make sense of the challenges it faces.

Cyril Ramaphosa: The Path to Power in South Africa
Ray Hartley. London: C. Hurst & Co., 2018. £16.99. 238 pp.

Published in the year that Cyril Ramaphosa replaced Jacob Zuma as president of South Africa, this volume is a journalistic account of the chequered ascent to the highest political office of a man in whom South Africans placed their hopes to lift the country from the ashes of the previous era. South Africa was in dire straits: the Zuma years had left in their wake a trail of corruption, mismanagement and what became known as 'state capture'. The question was whether the new president could rise above the structural challenges facing the liberation-movement-turned-government, the African National Congress (ANC). Three years on, with South Africa's socio-economic crisis and its related woes having worsened as a result of the COVID-19 pandemic, including record unemployment (officially at 35%), the answer tends towards the negative. This sentiment was reflected in the ANC's dismal results in recent local elections.

Expectations of the new president were based on him being seen first and foremost as a successful businessman. At the time of his inauguration, almost 25 years after the end of apartheid, many had perhaps forgotten – or had not been aware of – the crucial role he had played as the ANC's chief negotiator during the transition to democracy, and subsequently as head of the committee leading the drafting of the new constitution. In fact, Nelson Mandela openly favoured him as his successor, but the party decided instead to offer the position of deputy president to Thabo Mbeki, who would eventually become South Africa's second democratic president. Without a leadership role in government, Ramaphosa shifted his focus to building a business empire on the back of a flurry of black-empowerment deals that followed the ANC's coming to power. This resulted in the former trade unionist becoming one of the wealthiest men in the country, something that still sits uneasily with some commentators on the left. His (mis)handling of the 2012 Marikana massacre – in which 34 striking miners were shot dead by police at a mine in which Ramaphosa held a small stake and on whose board he served – was undoubtedly the low point of his political life and bolstered those who criticised him for having sold out to capitalism. Yet his capitalist credentials were the reason why many middle-class South Africans, members of the local business community, and Western business and political elites welcomed his return to politics. Ramaphosa's close association with Mandela and stated commitment to Mandela's values also counted in his favour.

Ray Hartley writes in a journalistic, accessible style, which makes for an easy read. At the same time, he often shifts rapidly from one subject to the next, mentioning some milestone events – such as the 1976 Soweto uprisings – almost in passing, an approach which, for readers less familiar with the contours of South Africa's political history, might be puzzling. Aimed at a general audience, the book draws heavily on primary research published elsewhere, and lacks depth in parts, while going into considerable detail about specific events in others. For those preferring a more substantive analysis, Anthony Butler's 2007 biography *Cyril Ramaphosa*, to which Hartley frequently refers, and which was recently released in an updated edition, remains the gold standard.

Regional Economic Communities and Peacebuilding in Africa: Lessons from ECOWAS and IGAD
Victor Adetula, Redie Bereketeab and Cyril Obi, eds. Abingdon: Routledge, 2021. £120.00. 226 pp.

In the post-Cold War era, regional institutions have become increasingly relevant in responding to regional threats to peace and security, with the African continent leading this trend. This collection, which brings together an impressive list of (regrettably all male) contributors spanning the academic and policy worlds, largely sidesteps the African Union, drawing instead on the cases of the Economic Community of West African States (ECOWAS) and the Intergovernmental Authority on Development (IGAD) to provide a critical assessment of the role of African regional economic communities (RECs) in peacebuilding. Originally created to promote regional economic cooperation and integration, RECs have progressively diversified into other governance areas, notably peace and conflict. An important conclusion of the book, however, is that the RECs' increased focus on peace and security has ultimately come at the cost of economic integration and development, which, in turn, does not augur well for the prospects of sustainable peace.

The book is broadly divided into three parts, the first dealing with general conceptual and theoretical questions; the second focusing on the different elements of peacebuilding in ECOWAS; and the third on case studies revealing the impact of individual member states on ECOWAS's and IGAD's efforts, including a focus on the influence of leading states within these groupings. The inclusion of a chapter on the role of civil society in the promotion and implementation of regional peace and security agendas serves as a reminder that, within regional contexts, it is not just state actors and intergovernmental organisations that play a role. At the same time, the respective chapters on ECOWAS and IGAD highlight the differences between the two institutions in this regard, with the former's partnership with civil-society organisations much better developed than the latter's.

In their assessments, the authors take a critical approach, engaging not only with the successes but also with the significant challenges facing RECs, and acknowledging that the record is a mixed one. They similarly do not shy away from reflecting on the diverging interests of various regional actors, divergences that are further complicated by the agendas of powerful external actors and the constraints domestic challenges place on the ability of regional powers to engage effectively in regional peace and security efforts. The question of dependence on external funding is a key theme throughout, with an emphasis on the challenges this can pose to the legitimacy and effectiveness of peacebuilding efforts.

It would be interesting to apply the lessons of the book to other RECs on the continent, and to other regions of the world. Given an ongoing dependence on external donors, the ways in which the peacebuilding efforts of African RECs differ from those driven by Western actors remains an open question. *Regional Economic Communities and Peacebuilding in Africa* will be of particular use to anyone interested in (sub-)regional responses to peacebuilding or the peace–development nexus. In addition, at a time when international actors are reflecting on the effectiveness of their approach to peacebuilding in places like Afghanistan, policymakers in both African and Western institutions would benefit from engaging with the points raised by the authors, specifically regarding the critique of liberal peacebuilding aimed at state-building, and the importance of context-specific approaches that take seriously local histories, culture and regional dynamics.

Indigenous Discourses on Knowledge and Development in Africa
Edward Shizha and Ali A. Abdi, eds. Abingdon: Routledge, 2017. £125.00. 244 pp.

Based on the title, I was expecting critical engagement with African indigenous knowledge, particularly as it pertains to development, something that remains an understudied topic in international relations. This expectation was only partly met. The promising introduction provides a critical overview of how contemporary post-colonial practices continue to marginalise indigenous knowledge systems, and undertakes to disrupt the 'global ethnoracial hierarchy' by 'anchoring African knowledge and development in indigenous discourses' (p. 3). By including in its conceptualisation of indigenous knowledge 'all ideas, perspectives and epistemic connections that are about Africa and especially constructed by Africans' (p. 1), however, the project loses focus early on, and essentially opens itself to including anything written about Africa (or by Africans) about knowledge, education and development. As a result, the book suffers from a familiar plight of edited volumes: not all of its well-written and readable chapters are clearly related to the book's stated themes, nor is there sufficient explicit connection between them.

The first six chapters will be of most relevance to readers interested in international relations. In particular, George J. Sefa Dei's reflection on African development within the context of indigenous forms of knowledge is a powerful plea to challenge dominant Western understandings of development that claim universality in their beliefs about what constitutes development and how it can and should be achieved, and that serve to infantilise Africa while refusing to admit to the West's complicity in the continent's developmental challenges. Dei calls on us not only to question the legacy of North–South developmental practices, but to be equally critical of more recent South–South relations. His understanding of indigenous knowledge (which he distinguishes from 'local knowledge') encompasses the elements generally associated with it, including the view that humans are not separate from but an integral part of the natural world, recognition of the importance of spirituality as a knowledge base, and a philosophy of circularity, which has implications for development thinking. Gloria T. Emeagwali's chapter on the intersections between indigenous knowledge and economic development in Africa is equally thought-provoking. Reminding us of the essential importance of African resources such as gum arabic and columbite-tantalite (coltan) for the global soft-drink, pharmaceutical and microchip industries, she provides an overview of African indigenous-knowledge systems in the fields of textiles, engineering and medicine (among others), and expresses concern about the lack of indigenous participation in these areas, as well as the underuse of indigenous skills and expertise being repeated in the China–Africa model of development. Some of the chapters in the second part of the book focusing on education (particularly those by Ali A. Abdi and Edward Shizha) emphasise the importance of indigenising education with the goal of achieving inclusive, sustainable and holistic development, and the potential contribution of indigenous science to African development.

The book parallels work on indigenous knowledge from other parts of the world, especially Latin America, in rethinking what we understand by development, including how the relationship between humans and nature can be reimagined to find alternative solutions to global challenges such as climate change. Engaging with these debates is increasingly relevant for anyone frustrated with the limitations of existing (Western) frameworks of knowledge for providing effective solutions to social, economic and environmental crises.

An Emerging Africa in the Age of Globalisation
Robert Mudida. Abingdon: Routledge, 2021. £120.00. 150 pp.

Part of Routledge's *Innovations in International Affairs* series, this collection of short essays provides a broad overview of a range of issues facing Africa in the twenty-first century. Situating itself in the context of the 'Africa rising' narrative and the progress that has been made on the continent in recent decades, the book considers topics ranging from regional economic integration to technological innovation. While each chapter discusses a different subject, it becomes clear that the various issues are interrelated and require a holistic approach. The book provides a historical overview as well as an outline of challenges, followed by recommendations and policy prescriptions. In some sections, however, considerable space is devoted to describing the philosophical and conceptual foundations of the phenomenon being discussed (for example, peacebuilding or human rights), with substantive questions about their manifestation in the African context treated more as an afterthought.

While the introduction mentions Africa's attempts to assert itself on the global stage, this is less of an explicit focus in the individual chapters. Similarly, the linkages between African challenges and the rest of the world (also referred to in the introduction), and the stated importance of non-state actors, are not elaborated on in subsequent chapters, which are almost exclusively state-centric. The at times inexplicable emphasis on certain themes at the expense of others that might be deemed more important by a general readership is also reflected in the author's treatment of African states' engagement with non-traditional, emerging actors. While this topic is given some attention in the chapter on Africa's diplomacy, India is granted only five lines, and Japan and South Korea a combined four. At the same time, some chapters try to include too much, leading to related but essentially distinct issues being conflated in a way that obscures important differences. The chapter on the challenges of human-rights jurisprudence in Africa, for example, includes sections on Africa's relationship with the International Criminal Court and atrocity prevention, but ends up discussing conflict prevention. Similarly, in the chapter on conflict and the regional security architecture, the discussion shifts from South Sudan to Ethiopia to the Democratic Republic of the Congo and Sierra Leone, before moving on to the Grand Ethiopian Renaissance Dam and the Sahel.

The book's strength lies in its breadth rather than its depth – its mostly descriptive overview provides little by way of deep analysis. As a result, for readers familiar with the international relations of Africa, there is not much that is new. For more general readers aiming to gain a sweeping overview of Africa, this accessible volume will serve their purpose.

Russia and Eurasia
Angela Stent

Negotiating the New START Treaty
Rose Gottemoeller. Amherst, NY: Cambria Press, 2021.
$39.99. 218 pp.

Rose Gottemoeller, who served as undersecretary of state for arms control in the Obama administration, was tasked with negotiating the first comprehensive bilateral nuclear-arms-control treaty between the United States and Russia in more than a quarter of a century, and to do so in less than a year – an unprecedentedly short time. Despite the enormity of this task, she successfully negotiated the 2010 New START treaty. This book is a highly readable and engaging personal account of the process, which intermingles complex technical material about arms-control negotiations with personal reflections about these difficult negotiations and the three challenging interlocutors she faced: the Russians, the White House and the US Senate.

Gottemoeller was the first woman to lead a major arms-control negotiation and she describes how many of the Russians (and some Americans) did not take her seriously. Nevertheless, she developed a good working relationship with her Russian counterpart, Anatoly Antonov, now ambassador to the United States. Antonov was a tough negotiator, but he was also caught between the conflicting agendas of president Dmitry Medvedev and then-prime minister Vladimir Putin. Major issues of contention between Moscow and Washington involved telemetry, on-site inspections and the US missile-defence programme. Presidents Medvedev and Barack Obama personally pushed forward the negotiations but, at a crucial point, Putin suddenly intervened, claiming the treaty was weak and inadequate, and made new demands that were unacceptable to the Americans. Somehow, his criticism disappeared from public media. The author is convinced that on this occasion Medvedev defied Putin.

A recurring problem was that the timetables of the Russian and American sides were very different. Gottemoeller was under pressure to complete the agreement within a year; the Russians were under no such pressure. This led to several severe reprimands from the White House, so much so that the author thought she might be relieved of her job. But her diplomatic skills enabled her to calibrate the competing demands of the White House and the Kremlin, and to produce a treaty that was acceptable to both sides.

Then came the third challenge: persuading the Senate to ratify the treaty. The Democrats, with a majority of the seats, had sent several delegations to Geneva to monitor the negotiations. A two-thirds majority was needed to ratify

Survival | vol. 64 no. 1 | February–March 2022 | pp. 208–214   https://doi.org/10.1080/00396338.2022.2033005

the treaty, and a number of senators held the vote hostage to the administration promising a major nuclear-weapons modernisation programme. Gottemoeller and her colleagues had to embark on a full-scale public-relations campaign to secure enough support, but they succeeded and the treaty remains in force until 2026.

Gottemoeller enumerates several 'gold standard treaty lessons learned' (p. 171): to have carefully defined national-security objectives when embarking on negotiations; to understand the Russians' political imperatives and the pressures they are under; to not engage in 'drive-by' negotiations; and to keep the Russians informed during the Senate ratification process.

We Shall Be Masters: Russian Pivots to East Asia from Peter the Great to Putin
Chris Miller. Cambridge, MA: Harvard University Press, 2021.
£23.95/$29.95. 361 pp.

Russia has pursued increasingly close ties with China since its relationship with the West sharply deteriorated after its annexation of Crimea in 2014. Does this represent a break with Russia's past pattern of paying only intermittent attention to Asia? Chris Miller provides answers in this comprehensive and informative account of Russia's historical outreach to Asia. His conclusion: 'There is an enduring gap between Russia's periodic bursts of enthusiasm about Asia and the reality that its interests and its capabilities are anchored in the West' (p. 13). Russia has launched its various forays into Asia with excessive optimism, only to abandon them when they failed to yield results.

Miller's narrative begins in 1702, when Peter the Great received the first Japanese man to visit St Petersburg and encouraged him to teach Japanese to his subjects. It moves to Alexander I's (1801–25) vision of an empire centred on Alaska and spreading to California, Hawaii and Japan; Russians settled in Alaska and Fort Ross in California. The king of Kauai, a Hawaiian island, and his subjects even became Russian citizens for a short time. But there were enduring problems supplying the settlers with food and, in the end, the Russians left Fort Ross and the Americans purchased Russian Alaska.

Russia's complex encounters with China began in the seventeenth century on the Amur River, 'Russia's Mississippi'. Defeated by the Qing dynasty, Russia ceded the Amur Valley to China, only to reconquer it two centuries later and acquire the land that now constitutes the Russian Far East. But few Russians were willing to move there. After the Bolshevik Revolution, the Soviets supported forces loyal to Sun Yat-sen in China's ongoing civil war, and eventually lent their support to Chiang Kai-shek's nationalist forces against Mao Zedong's communists, a legacy that ultimately led to the Sino-Soviet split and the subsequent armed clashes in 1969 on the Soviet–Chinese border.

Russia's relations with Japan were historically defined by rivalry over Manchuria and Korea. The Russians' humiliating defeat in 1905 by Japan in the Russo-Japanese War led to the first popular uprising against the tsars. In the 1930s, there were intermittent military skirmishes between the USSR and Japan but, once the Nazis attacked, Josef Stalin understood the necessity of a neutrality pact with Japan, which lasted until April 1945. Thereafter, Red Army troops took Sakhalin and the Kuril Islands. Russia and Japan have never signed a peace treaty and Japan continues to claim the four southernmost Kurils as its own.

Vladimir Putin became the latest Russian leader to pursue a pivot to Asia from 2014. Yet, argues Miller, there are limits to this strategy. Its economic underpinnings are questionable – Russia's population is clustered on its western border, and the infrastructure connecting those lands to the underpopulated Far East and Asia is dysfunctional. Neither China nor Japan has been willing to make significant investments in Russia's underdeveloped Far East. Can Russia really find a 'Eurasian exit' from its crisis in relations with the West? The historical record suggests not.

Collapse: The Fall of the Soviet Union
Vladislav M. Zubok. New Haven, CT: Yale University Press,
2021. $35.00. 535 pp.

In this provocative, deeply researched and exhaustive retelling of Mikhail Gorbachev's turbulent six years in the Kremlin, Vladislav Zubok challenges the conventional wisdom that the USSR was destined to collapse. He attributes its demise to Gorbachev's ideological messianism, his failed reforms and repeated policy zigzags. 'History is never a sequence of inevitabilities', he writes, 'and the Soviet demise was no exception: it was full of contingencies' (p. 6).

Thirty years after the collapse, it remains challenging to understand how a nuclear superpower whose landmass extended over 12 time zones could have imploded without having been defeated in a war. Hence the prevalence of conspiracy theories about the role of outside agents, particularly the United States and its 'special services'. Zubok, while placing most of the blame for the collapse on Gorbachev and his inconsistent and contradictory policies, also focuses on the role of the United States. During the USSR's final years, he argues, US soft power played an outsize role in influencing the Soviet elite's view of how to transform society. Indeed, he believes that the US could have been more imaginative in wielding its soft power.

Zubok argues that had Soviet leader Yuri Andropov not succumbed to illness so soon after succeeding Leonid Brezhnev, the USSR could have successfully modernised under an enlightened authoritarian regime, and would not have collapsed. Andropov, he argues, fully understood the need for far-reaching reforms of the dysfunctional, sclerotic economy. Instead, Gorbachev chose first to open up the political space in the Soviet Union, making thoroughgoing economic reform more difficult. Zubok quotes one of Deng Xiaoping's sons, who said that his father considered Gorbachev an 'idiot' because he introduced glasnost before perestroika (p. 60). Yet he also writes that Gorbachev believed economic modernisation was impossible under the existing dysfunctional institutions, and sought to unleash people's creative energies in order to embark on economic reforms. When he did begin to reform, he had to contend with the aftermath of the 1986 oil-price collapse and the harsh impact of low oil prices on the Soviet economy.

The book highlights how Gorbachev became increasingly unpopular domestically in inverse proportion to his growing popularity in the West after 1989, when he allowed Eastern Europe to break free and Germany to be reunified. It was much more congenial to be feted in Bonn, London or Washington than to face his domestic challengers and failing reforms. Indeed, Western officials, especially during the negotiations on German reunification, were amazed by how much Gorbachev was willing to concede. Between 1989 and 1991 he made all the important foreign-policy decisions, bypassing the usual Communist Party channels and his own foreign minister, Eduard Shevardnadze.

In arguing that the Soviet Union's collapse was not inevitable, Zubok believes that the nationalities issue could have been resolved and that the country did not have to break up into 15 separate states. As the current crisis between Russia and Ukraine shows, the Soviet Union may have broken up, but, 30 years on, the final contours of that collapse have yet to be determined.

Russia and the Right to Self-determination in the Post-Soviet Space
Johannes Socher. Oxford: Oxford University Press, 2021.
£80.00. 250 pp.

In this extensively researched monograph, Johannes Socher examines why Russia's attitude toward self-determination differs substantially from widely accepted legal norms, and why much of Russia's scholarly legal discourse on these issues mirrors the Kremlin's views rather than those of other scholars of international law. He argues that Russia's unique approach to self-determination in the post-Soviet space is the product of the lasting legacy of

Soviet international-law doctrine. Contemporary Russian attitudes toward self-determination in Russia's neighbourhood reflect the country's hegemonistic ambitions in what it considers its 'sphere of privileged interests'.

The Soviet view of self-determination, explains Socher, was highly contradictory. On the one hand, Moscow championed the right of colonies to declare their independence and secede from their colonial masters, even if independence leaders, such as India's Jawaharlal Nehru, were considered 'bourgeois'. Indeed, the USSR competed with China to burnish its anti-imperialist credentials. However, when it came to the Soviet bloc the Kremlin's approach toward self-determination was totally different: it played a 'perverted role *inside* the Eastern bloc', says Socher (p. 35, emphasis in original). Attempts by Hungary and Czechoslovakia to chart distinctive paths were crushed by Soviet troops, leading to the articulation in 1968 of what became known as the Brezhnev Doctrine of limited sovereignty. The USSR claimed the right to prevent – using force if necessary – any deviations from Soviet-style socialism among its Warsaw Pact allies.

Post-Soviet Russia has continued to pursue a dualistic and contradictory approach to self-determination. On the one hand, Russia has supported the de facto independence of entities in neighbouring states that it seeks to dominate: Abkhazia, the Donetsk and Luhansk people's republics, Nagorno-Karabakh, South Ossetia and Transnistria. On the other hand, it fought two wars to prevent Chechnya's secession. It also bitterly denounced Kosovo's declaration of independence from Serbia, subsequently using the 'Kosovo precedent' to justify its recognition of Crimea's quest for self-determination and vote to join Russia in 2014. Socher highlights the inconsistences in Russia's position and the fact that Crimea's declaration of independence was illegal – as was the referendum by which Russia annexed Crimea. He claims that Russia has abused the right to self-determination as a pretext to justify territorial acquisitions by the threat and actual use of force.

Vladimir Putin has also tried to implement a doctrine of limited sovereignty in the former Soviet states. He demands that no former Soviet state – especially Ukraine – seek to join Euro-Atlantic structures. He insists that Russia is entitled to a sphere of interest in the post-Soviet space, including a veto right over the foreign-policy orientation of its neighbours. And in the Ukrainian case, he has threatened to use military force again if these demands are ignored.

Socher's conclusion is sobering: '"Crimea" arguably marks a shift away from legal arguments towards eclectic historical claims and restoration of hegemonic power' (p. 176).

Germany's Russia Problem: The Struggle for Balance in Europe
John Lough. Manchester: Manchester University Press, 2021.
£20.00. 296 pp.

In this trenchant analysis, John Lough traces three decades of what he views as highly consistent but ineffective German policy toward Russia informed by 'fear, sentimentality, ambivalence, economic complementarity, residual *Ostpolitik* reasoning and a sense of obligation to Moscow for allowing Germany to reunify' (p. 245).

Surveying the evolution of the complex German–Russian relationship over several centuries, Lough highlights patterns of confrontation and cooperation, both benign and malign. Germans and Russians were bound to come into conflict, he argues, because both countries had historically undefined borders and a shared fear of encirclement, leading both to expand territorially and create overlapping spheres of interest. After fighting each other in two world wars, the twentieth century ended with German reunification and recognition of the debt owed to Russia for allowing the country to do so – a debt which, Lough argues, Vladimir Putin has been quick to exploit.

The settlement of the German question in 1990 raised a new Russia question: 'how should Russia, an expanding EU and the Europe in between (*Zwischeneuropa*) relate to each other and what institutional arrangements should support these relationships?' (p. 151). Since reunification, Berlin has sought to answer the question of where Russia belongs by engaging Moscow in a variety of bilateral and multilateral political dialogues, and promoting its modernisation. Berlin has reiterated the mantra of *Wandel durch Handel* (change through trade), which was at the core of 1970s-era Ostpolitik. Economic interdependence, it was argued, would promote closer political ties. But the Kremlin has increasingly tried to separate economic ties from political ones, and the various partnerships for modernisation have failed. The current Russian–Ukrainian crisis reminds us that institutional arrangements have also failed to give the Kremlin a stake in the post-Cold War Euro-Atlantic security system.

From 1991 to 2014, argues Lough, Germany believed that Russia could be an economic and security partner for Europe. But Berlin consistently failed to understand the difference between the Russia it wished to see and the Russia with which it was actually dealing. The Germans persuaded themselves that Russia was generally moving in the right direction, even as it became clear that Russia did not share either the values or the interests that underlaid Germany's optimistic view of Russia's integration into Europe.

Moscow's annexation of Crimea and launch of a war in the Donbas region finally ended the period of optimism triumphing over realism. Putin's Russia had shattered German chancellor Angela Merkel's vision of a peaceful post-Cold War European order in which Russia could be a security partner. She led Europe in imposing a new sanctions regime and managed to maintain solidarity among European Union member states on Russia sanctions. Nevertheless, she continued to support the controversial Nord Stream 2 gas pipeline.

Will the new German government develop a more realistic strategy toward Russia? Lough's advice for Berlin includes abandoning dialogue for dialogue's sake, investing more in hard-power capabilities and paying more attention to Russia's growing influence operations in Germany. Above all, Germany and its allies must understand how to defend their interests.

Latin America
Russell Crandall and Britta Crandall

Conservative Party-building in Latin America: Authoritarian Inheritance and Counterrevolutionary Struggle
James Loxton. Oxford: Oxford University Press, 2021.
£47.99. 279 pp.

On 11 September 1990, the leaders of Chile's Independent Democratic Union (UDI), a rightist political party, crafted a statement extolling Augusto Pinochet, their esteemed head of state who had seized power that day 17 years earlier. The statement emphasised Pinochet's heroism in sparking the euphemistically phrased 'liberating military action' that removed his Marxist predecessor, Salvador Allende (p. 1). In his highly original, rigorous book *Conservative Party-building in Latin America*, political scientist James Loxton notes this was a puzzling development in a country that had just completed a chequered transition back to democracy. How, the author asks, could any party expect to win elections in a democratic era after engaging in such a public courtship of a bloodthirsty dictator? Yet within a decade the UDI had garnered more total votes than any other party, an enviable record that it held until 2017.

According to Loxton, the UDI's trajectory was far from unique. The so-called third wave of democracy in the 1980s and early 1990s witnessed the departure of rightist military regimes not only in Chile but also in Argentina, Bolivia, Brazil, El Salvador and Guatemala. As democracy strengthened in these countries, right-wing parties also emerged that, paradoxically, had 'deep roots' in the preceding dictatorships – the author labels these 'authoritarian successor parties' (p. 2). Chile's UDI, for one, was established in 1983 by senior *pinochetistas*. Two years prior, the rightist National Republican Alliance (ARENA) party was organised in El Salvador by death-squad boss Roberto D'Aubuisson, a maniacal figure who had been an intelligence operative in the military regime. Meanwhile, conservative parties that had less autocratic baggage and were more grounded in the rule of law, such as Guatemala's National Advancement Party (PAN) and Argentina's Union of the Democratic Center (UCEDE), did not seem to perform as well. The author sets out to explain the unexpected successes and failures of these post-military parties.

He finds that the authoritarian successor parties thrived 'not despite their roots in dictatorship, but because of them' (p. 2). Much of their bountiful 'authoritarian inheritance', such as brand recognition and organisational networks, proved useful in a modern democracy. An equally critical factor, according to Loxton, was that regime-linked parties were seen as embodying a

Survival | vol. 64 no. 1 | February–March 2022 | pp. 215–220   https://doi.org/10.1080/00396338.2022.2033006

'counterrevolutionary struggle', meaning that they were perceived not as mere political parties, but as the defenders of *la patria* against existential Marxist threats. The parties' 'formative experiences', writes Loxton, 'endowed them with a powerful sense of mission and esprit de corps, leaders with undisputed internal authority, and a deep hostility toward their adversaries, which together served as an effective source of cohesion' (p. 3). The author provides four painstakingly researched chapters offering historically rich narratives on the successes of the ARENA and UDI parties and the struggles of their Argentine and Guatemalan counterparts. This is comparative political science at its best.

City of Omens: A Search for the Missing Women of the Borderlands
Dan Werb. New York: Bloomsbury, 2019. $28.00. 304 pp.

In 2018, more than 2,300 people were killed in Tijuana, Mexico, setting a record for the city that roughly doubled the previous year's tally and represented a homicide rate of 135 per 100,000 citizens. The Mexican metropolis also experienced a 50% increase in the death rate of female residents. Directly across the border in San Diego, however, the murder rate dipped to 2.2 per 100,000, the lowest rate in decades. As recently as ten years ago, the two cities had had comparable levels of violence. What was going wrong in Tijuana, particularly for women?

Dan Werb, a native of Vancouver, Canada, and a former journalist, was a freshly minted professor of epidemiology when he received an invitation from a colleague and mentor at the University of California to travel to Tijuana to help observe the HIV epidemic among residents who injected drugs in makeshift encampments along the city's infamous river canal. As he writes in *City of Omens*, Werb was eager not to engage in the type of 'shock tourism' he'd witnessed in Downtown Eastside, a crime- and drug-ridden neighbourhood of Vancouver, where curious outsiders came to slum with the natives. 'I vowed to avoid the temptation to treat Tijuana like a dark and titillating ride, and instead recognize the visit for what it was: a scientific excursion into a field research site beset by a public health crisis' (p. 5).

Having honed his research skills in Downtown Eastside, Werb thought he was prepared to endure unsightly and difficult circumstances. Yet Tijuana's mostly dry, occasionally flash-flooding canal was of an entirely different order. 'Here at the bottom of the canal, a few hundred yards from the world's busiest border crossing, there was no energy at all', he writes (p. 15).

> As we approached the encampment we passed a solitary man in the center of the canal, shirtless in the sun and standing ankle-deep in the noxious brown wastewater. His old pants were cinched up above his knees and

slick white foam spread in clumps along the water's oily surface and
circulated around his bare legs. He leaned down, drenched his T-shirt in
the sewage, and splashed it across his bare chest. (p. 9)

What Werb begins to understand is that the health crisis in Tijuana is
rooted in addiction and sex. The location of the red-light district Zona Norte,
which butts up against the border and the canal, facilitates flows of women
into the city, which in turn fuels the HIV epidemic. The author estimates that
around half of the city's drug-injecting women have traded sex for drugs, and
of these, one in six has tested positive for HIV. Thus, HIV transmission, environmental toxins and drug overdoses, in addition to gang-related violence,
were fuelling a horrifying surge in female deaths.

Werb describes himself and other epidemiologists as 'scientists with labo-
ratories that just happen to be located in the real world' (p. 10). He explains
that epidemiologic field research requires looking at population-level trends to
prevent epidemics, as opposed to treating individuals. By making Tijuana his
laboratory, Werb was able to uncover the complex dynamics behind the city's
alarming statistics.

Garibaldi in South America: An Exploration
Richard Bourne. London: C. Hurst & Co., 2020. £25.00. 232 pp.

Born in Nice (or Nizza, as it was known under Italian dominion) in 1807,
Giuseppe Garibaldi is remembered as the champion of Italian unification in
the nineteenth century. Yet, as long-time British journalist Richard Bourne tells
us in his latest work, the legendary Italian figure also made a name for himself
in Latin America. Exiled to the Western Hemisphere after being condemned to
death in 1834 following an unsuccessful operation by the Young Italy outfit he
had joined, he spent more than a dozen years learning to be an effective and
charismatic leader in the breakaway republic of Rio Grande do Sul in southern
Brazil and civil-war-ravaged Uruguay.

Along the way, Garibaldi met and, in 1839, eloped with the redoubtable
young Brazilian Anita Ribeiro. That same year, the newlyweds fought together
in the naval battle of Imbituba. In the late 1840s Garibaldi returned to Europe
with his bride to work for Italian unification. Sadly, what the author describes
as one of the 'greatest romances' of the time would end in 1849 with Anita's pre-
mature death at the age of 28 from a disease she contracted during the couple's
retreat from the Roman Republic (p. xi). The couple's offspring stayed true to
the cause, however, and were still fighting for what Bourne calls an 'international brand of liberty and international fraternity' into the 1900s (p. xiii).

While the author acknowledges Garibaldi's personal faults – his womanising, vanity and ideological inconsistencies – as well as his military and political setbacks, the author also displays a deep respect for this outsized figure 'who was both a nationalist and an internationalist; a freethinker who fought for the underdog' (p. xiii). He notes, for example, that in 1843 alone, Garibaldi marched to Montevideo, 'now facing extreme danger and siege after [Fructuoso] Rivera's defeat at Arroyo Grande' by Manuel Oribe, the leader of the *colorados* faction in Uruguay's civil war; issued a proclamation to form an Italian Legion and raised funds for 'four small craft and six guns'; won a battle at sea against William Brown, the Irish-born Argentine general whose forces had been deployed by Juan Manuel de Rosas to support his friend Oribe; and helped to turn the legion's volunteers into a 'fighting unit, recognisable with red shirts' (p. xvii). That same year, his second child, Rosita, was born (p. xvii). There would be many more exploits to come.

Persuasive Peers: Social Communication and Voting in Latin America

Andy Baker, Barry Ames and Lúcio Rennó. Princeton, NJ:
Princeton University Press, 2020. $29.95. 336 pp.

Brazil's 2014 presidential election was a fascinating and intense contest, displaying 'all the drama of a telenovela and a closely fought soccer match' (p. 1). At the beginning of the year, sitting president Dilma Rousseff of the left-wing Workers' Party (PT) held a formidable lead; polls showed a gap so large that many observers assumed that she would receive a majority of ballots, and hence be re-elected, in the election's first round in October. The same polls showed Aécio Neves of the rightist Brazilian Social Democratic Party (PSDB) in a distant second place. The party affiliations of the two leading contenders were only too predictable: in the previous five presidential elections, the top-two first-round finishers had come from the same two parties, despite the fact that there were more than 30 parties contesting elections in Brazil.

It came as a surprise, then, when Eduardo Campos of the Brazilian Socialist Party (PSB) started closing in on Neves, meaning the dark-horse candidate would advance to what, by now, looked like a second-round run-off against Rousseff. Yet in another unexpected twist, Campos died suddenly in a plane crash on 13 August; his running mate, Marina Silva, quickly replaced him on the ticket and, buoyed by an outpouring of public sympathy, surged in the polls, opening up a 20-point lead over Neves and drawing even with Rousseff. In the last month of the campaign, however, Silva's standing evaporated, resulting in a pitiful showing in the first round of the election, in which she garnered a meagre 12% of the vote.

In their well-considered work exploring voter preferences in Brazil (and Latin America more generally), three political scientists, Andy Baker, Barry Ames and Lúcio Rennó, conclude that the 2014 Brazilian presidential election, in which a remarkable four in ten voters changed their party preference, poses a 'major puzzle' (p. 5). Despite all the churn during the course of the campaign, a majority of voters still backed the two conventional-party candidates in October's first round. Contrary to what we might assume, these voters, having considered and at least for a while backed other parties, didn't necessarily return to the candidate of their initial preference. Rather, those voters who initially intended to back, say, Rousseff at the start of the year were 'very different' from those who ultimately backed her in October (p. 7). To help us understand the paradox of 'short-term volatility' in an election campaign that produces a conventional outcome on election day, the authors turn to the concepts of 'horizontal social ties' and informal political discussion. It seems that 'knowledgeable peers' or social influencers, who themselves are inclined toward the mainstream candidates, play an underappreciated role in Brazilian politics. Their influence on voters who may be less informed or just too busy to follow the campaign helps to explain why dark-horse candidates flame out. Political-opinion leaders, the authors note, tend to have more traditional preferences, hence the return to the established political parties. These social influences, much more than any partisan predispositions, determine political outcomes in Brazil.

Republics of Knowledge: Nations of the Future in Latin America
Nicola Miller. Princeton, NJ: Princeton University Press, 2020.
$39.95. 320 pp.

A visitor to Argentina's Mendoza province in the early nineteenth century may well have been surprised by the graciousness of the province's eponymous capital city. Located more than 1,000 kilometres from Buenos Aires, Mendoza City nevertheless boasted tree-shaded avenues, irrigated vineyards, a large hospital, and both public and parochial schools, all established by the 1820s. Several newspapers and magazines offered information and debate on the major questions of the day.

What one historian has called Mendoza's 'age of enlightenment' (p. 2) was catalysed by the city's involvement in the region's wars for independence against colonial Spain. On 7 September 1814, the Argentine general José de San Martín arrived in the city, shortly followed by 3,000 Chileans. They plotted to use Mendoza as a base from which to cross the Andes and liberate Chile. Remarkably, San Martín mandated that the city establish its first printing press so that news of the republican rebels' victories could be disseminated far and wide. In fact, throughout the independence wars that raged from Mexico to Chile in the 1810s and 1820s, one of the most valued items in rebels' arsenals was the mobile press (*imprenta volante*). As UK-based historian Nicola Miller writes in *Republics of Knowledge*, these 'gleaming' gadgets were easily operated with one lever:

> Reports of the campaigns, proclamations of victory and rallying calls to hastily designed flags, as well as military orders and policy edicts, were cranked out onto single sheets of scarce paper, snatched from the miniature press and borne away to be read – often out loud – wherever people gathered. (p. 5)

Pro-independence civilians and officers selectively but effectively used ideas and information to further their cause, contrasting their own readiness to spread information with the so-called Black Legend, the belief that Madrid intentionally kept its colonies ignorant to secure its rule. The nations of Latin America, writes Miller, were 'born in smudgy print' (p. 5). All republican constitutions provided for a free press, and a majority, unlike their US counterpart, had clauses on public education. A few went so far as to stipulate that the constitution was a tool with which to promote the country's 'general enlightenment' (p. 6).

This sense that knowledge lies at the heart of a country's political battles and national life has endured into the twentieth and twenty-first centuries. During the Cold War, rightist military dictatorships burned books. In a more recent (and positive) example, Colombia in 2017 funded mobile libraries as part of its state-building efforts in parts of the country that had been ravaged by 50 years of internal conflict. To be sure, these so-called 'republics of knowledge' have not always been as enlightened as their rhetoric would suggest: they have often excluded women and racial minorities (among others), in some cases well into the twentieth century. But Miller's finding that access to knowledge played a vital role in the region's political and social evolution is difficult to dispute.

Asia-Pacific
Lanxin Xiang

The Long Game: China's Grand Strategy to Displace American Order
Rush Doshi. Oxford and New York: Oxford University Press,
2021. £21.99/$27.95. 432 pp.

This book alleges that Chinese grand strategy is not only well thought through, but also meticulously planned. The author describes the strategy as a three-part play that has been running since China's opening-up four decades ago. In part one China works to blunt US power (economic, military and political); in part two it builds capacity to catch up with the US; and in part three it embarks on regional and global expansion to displace US hegemony entirely.

This argument is not new. It has been a recurring theme of much American and especially neoconservative analysis for decades, often from writers without serious China expertise. Rush Doshi, a young scholar of a new generation who is now serving in President Joe Biden's National Security Council, has China experience. Still, his claim to have discovered a grand strategy in Chinese-language sources is a dubious one. The texts he cites are highly selective, often taken out of context and frequently misinterpreted. His reading of Deng Xiaoping's strategic concept, for instance, is plainly wrong. The author contends that Deng's formulation 'hiding capabilities and biding time' (韬光养晦), which guided Chinese foreign policy for nearly four decades, reflects a grand strategy of displacing the US, but this interpretation ignores Deng's own admonition to 'never take the lead' (永不出头). The author pointedly rejects the notion that Chinese policy has undergone radical changes under President Xi Jinping (p. 6), when it is clear that Xi has taken Chinese foreign policy in a new direction.

Not surprisingly, Doshi starts the book with a familiar historical analogy: today's China is Wilhelmine Germany before the Great War (p. 16). This analogy gradually gives way to a comparison between contemporary China and Nazi Germany in the 1930s, which provides the logic for the anti-appeasement conclusion. I refuted this logic, then espoused by Paul Wolfowitz, in these pages 20 years ago, in an essay titled 'Washington's Misguided China Policy', but it clearly lives on.

Doshi cites the much-quoted 'Eyre Crowe memorandum' from 1907 on the behaviour of pre-war Germany in a typical misreading of European history. Crowe's argument of no accommodation for Germany proved disastrous and was powerfully rejected by his fellow British diplomat Thomas Sanderson. Of course, the German analogy then needs to be buttressed by a discussion of ideological conflict, or a clash of values. In this characteristically neoconservative view, the important thing is to grasp the 'lessons' of the 1930s, rather than to ponder the events that actually caused war to break out in either 1914 or 1939.

Thinking about contemporary China in terms of Wilhelmine or Nazi Germany is dangerous because it could produce US policies aimed at regime change, or miscalculations that could push the US and China into a war that neither side wants. As Johns Hopkins scholar David Calleo rightly observes on page six of his book *The German Problem Reconsidered* (Cambridge University Press, 1978), 'the proper lesson' to be drawn from the outbreak of the Great War 'is not so much the need for vigilance against aggressors but the ruinous consequences of refusing reasonable accommodation to upstarts'. American foreign policy needs more Sandersons and fewer Crowes. Much like Britain before 1914, the US must choose between two options: accommodate the rising challenger, acknowledge its interests, and accord it status and prestige commensurate with its power; or rigidly defend a fragile status quo, and risk a showdown.

Empire and Constitution in Modern Japan: Why Could War with China Not Be Prevented?
Junji Banno. Arthur Stockwin, trans. London: Bloomsbury Academic, 2021. £85.00. 186 pp.

The late Junji Banno, an eminent Japanese scholar of modern history, has left a thought-provoking and soul-searching opus. The author's purpose in *Empire and Constitution in Modern Japan* is to examine the interrelationship between considerations of empire and constitution in guiding the ambitions of Japanese political and military leaders through to the present. Whereas it has often been argued that the push for 'empire' and the push for 'constitution' have been mutually opposed, Banno argues that the relationship between them in Japan has been 'much more complex' (p. 1).

More than 70 years have elapsed since the end of the Second World War, during which time the Japanese have consistently proclaimed their opposition to war. Many in Japan now believe that war between Japan and China can be avoided. Banno casts doubt on this naive perception. He points out that the Japanese

> have always had in mind 'our last great war', in other words the war against the United States between the end of 1941 and August 1945. But in the 67 years between 1874 and 1941, the targets of expanding military strength were always Korea and China, and with the sole exception of the Russo-Japanese War from 1904 to 1905, the adversary was always China. (p. 3)

He goes on to cite the examples of the Taiwan expedition of 1874, the Sino-Japanese War of 1894, the 21 demands made against China in 1915, the Manchurian Incident of 1931 and the Marco Polo Bridge Incident of 1937.

Indeed, the China Threat has been the only coherent theme of Japanese foreign policy since the Meiji period. General Yamagata Aritomo, the first military leader of modern Japan, pointed out in 1880 that China's territory and population were about ten times larger than those of Japan. 'That is almost exactly the same proportion as it is today, 137 years later', observes Banno (p. 25). To Yamagata, 'Chinese modernization and development as a major power was neither something to be complacent about, nor to rejoice in' (p. 25). The suggestion is that the current Japanese leadership may share similar views.

Banno goes on to observe that the 'road to the Pacific War' with the United States is well understood in Japan, but that the 'road to the Japan–China War' is not (p. 35), even though the history of the Japan–China conflict 'is by no means just a piece of ancient history' (p. 158). He warns that members of Japan's peace movement, of which he was himself a member for more than 70 years, have consistently opposed the idea of becoming embroiled in an American war, but may not necessarily oppose a war with China, having never learned the lessons of history. Among these is the fact that constitutional government is not always able to restrain military behaviour or prevent war.

Great State: China and the World
Timothy Brook. London: Profile Books, 2021. £12.99. 464 pp.

Timothy Brook presents the provocative thesis that 'the fundamental principles guiding the Chinese state today were established not in the late third century BCE, which is where Chinese history usually goes to discover its emergence as a unified state in a long string of dynasties, but in the thirteenth century CE, when China was absorbed into the Mongol world' (pp. xx–xxi). According to the author, Mongol rule replaced China's existing dynastic model with what the author, 'following Mongol usage', calls the 'Great State' (p. xxi). Brook acknowledges that 'Great State' is not a term that would be widely known or accepted in contemporary China. Yet he contends that

> it has hugely shaped Chinese political thinking since the time of Khubilai Khan. Before the 1270s China was a dynastic state in which one family monopolised power at the centre because, so the theory went, Heaven had given that family an exclusive mandate to rule. What changed with the coming of the Mongols was the deeper conviction that this mandate entailed the right to extend the authority of that one family out across the

entire world, incorporating all existing polities and rulers into a system in which military power is paramount. (p. 7)

Based on his understanding of China as a 'Great State', Brook disputes the view that China has never been a colonial power that grew at the expense of other states. 'It is simply not possible', he writes, 'to create a country on this scale without conquering and absorbing territory that was once under other jurisdictions' (p. 379). His argument suggests that China is an expansionist state today because its state system is based on a Mongol model that emphasised territorial conquest. Yet he admits that, unlike the other four permanent members of the Security Council, 'China became a mega-state not by conquering others so much as by being conquered by others' (p. 379). *Great State* is a readable and ambitious work, but is not entirely convincing.

Lion City: Singapore and the Invention of Modern Asia
Jeevan Vasagar. London: Little, Brown & Co., 2021. £18.99.
336 pp.

Jeevan Vasagar, a former journalist who has reported from Singapore for the *Financial Times*, has written a penetrating book about the city-state's remarkable achievements, as well as the dilemmas it faces. The British were first attracted to the island because of its location at the mouth of the Strait of Malacca, through which all manner of goods – silk from China, spices from what is today Indonesia, manufacturing goods from Europe – were transported (p. 7). The opening of the Suez Canal would only increase these flows. The island had strategic importance too: Singapore was built and touted as the key link in an imperial defence line running from the island to Hong Kong and Shanghai. But 'Fortress Singapore' proved no match for the Japanese, who humiliated the British by taking the island after only a week's fighting in February 1942.

Under the leadership of British-educated Lee Kuan Yew, post-war Singapore would develop into a prosperous market economy with a government that the West refuses to recognise as democratic, as seen in President Joe Biden's decision not to invite Singapore to his recent Summit for Democracy. The snub is unlikely to have perturbed Singapore's leaders, however. As Lee Kuan Yew once said, 'Human rights? Are they bankable?' (p. 11). Lee's People's Action Party has faced no serious challengers to date, and the system is based on meritocracy rather than democratic orthodoxy.

Vasagar is a strong advocate for democracy, but he also admires Singapore's spectacular achievements. In 1965, the island's per capita GDP was on par with Jordan's; now, it outstrips Japan's. 'The welfare safety net is narrow in scope but robust. There is no dole for unemployment, but the government ensures there is a state-built home for everyone. There is very little homelessness' (p. 10).

The main threat to today's Singapore, according to Vasagar, lies not in the character of its politics but in its demography. The country's prosperity could be undermined by a severe shortage of labour. The ruling party suffers at the polls when it adopts more receptive immigration policies, but it is hard to see how else it will solve the problem of an ageing society in a country that has one of the world's lowest birth rates (p. 264).

The World Turned Upside Down: A History of the Chinese Cultural Revolution
Yang Jisheng. London: Swift Press, 2021. £35.00. 768 pp.

Yang Jisheng, a leading nonconformist historian in China, has written a history of the Cultural Revolution (1966–76) intended to debunk the official version of events. By holding that the Cultural Revolution was 'internal disorder, erroneously launched by the leader and made use of by cliques' led by Marshal Lin Biao and Jiang Qing (Madame Mao), the official history seeks to legitimise the perpetual rule of the Chinese Communist Party (p. xvi). For Yang, a former government newsman turned political historian, the party is shirking its own collective responsibility for the disorder. He offers a brilliant analysis of this key episode that deserves a wide audience.

Most historical studies prepared outside of China display a fixation on power struggles within the party and Mao Zedong's determination to secure his own supremacy. According to Yang, the Cultural Revolution was a struggle over the road China would take. Mao's principal concern was the decay of China's revolutionary spirit and the corruptive influence of the bureaucratic establishment. He was aware that officials had 'a private side' – a tendency to pursue their own interests and not just those of the party – and had become alarmed that the private side of Chinese bureaucrats was 'steadily swelling' (p. xxv). Determined not to repeat the mistakes of Josef Stalin, whom Mao believed had given too much power to party apparatchiks, Mao sought to break the backbone of the entire bureaucratic class.

During the early stage of the Cultural Revolution, Mao encouraged the rebels to 'roast [bureaucrats] for a while, but not scorch them' (p. xxviii). This balance became difficult to maintain, however, once intense conflict arose between officials and the populace. During the latter stage of the Cultural Revolution, Mao ordered the bureaucrats to contain the rebels, but 'not to attack them' (p. xxviii). 'But how', asks Yang, 'could the newly reinstated bureaucrats not retaliate against their mortal enemies?' (p. xxviii). The author concludes that the Cultural

Revolution was a 'triangular game between Mao, the rebels, and the bureaucratic clique' (p. xxviii).

The Cultural Revolution ended with the victory of the bureaucratic class against the core members of the new class brought to power by Mao, including Madame Mao and her close associates. In that sense, Mao's 'revolution' was an abject failure. Since then, 'China's officials [have] utilized their political power to deflect blame from Mao and the totalitarian system' (p. xxxii). Meanwhile, the 'bureaucratic clique' – which Yang describes as the 'ultimate victor' of the Cultural Revolution (p. 615) – has led the economic reforms that have transformed China, deciding 'who would pay the cost of reforms and how the benefits of reform would be distributed' (p. 615). Anyone expecting this class to lead political reforms in China is sure to be disappointed.

Land and Sea: The Evolving Great-power Contest in Asia

Samir Puri

I

As the United States ended its military presence in Afghanistan, it not only closed the chapter on the wars it started in response to the 9/11 attacks, but also made choices, whether conscious or implicit, about where it would seek to retain and develop geopolitical influence in Asia. US strategic focus there has shifted from inland to maritime, in line with the Biden administration's priority of deterring 'potential Chinese military aggression'.[1] China's drive to expand its maritime influence in Asia is now likely to meet more concerted US resistance. Across swathes of Asian ground, however, China has entered into a close partnership with Russia, which may help to expand its inland influence.

Several recent developments bring these evolving contours into sharp relief. In September 2021, the United States and the United Kingdom announced a security agreement with Australia to help it build nuclear-powered submarines while enhancing cooperation in cyber security, advanced technology and other areas. This tripartite arrangement, known as AUKUS, may help to galvanise the older and more established Quadrilateral Security Dialogue, or 'Quad', comprising Australia, India, Japan and the United States, through which joint naval exercises are run and other cooperative endeavours undertaken. AUKUS and the Quad represent American efforts to engage like-minded nations in overlapping

Samir Puri is IISS Senior Fellow in Urban Security and Hybrid Warfare, based at the IISS–Asia in Singapore.

Survival | vol. 64 no. 1 | February–March 2022 | pp. 227–236   https://doi.org/10.1080/00396338.2022.2033008

coalitions to balance China's growing power and defend a free and open Indo-Pacific region.[2]

Since the chaotic US and allied withdrawal from Afghanistan in August 2021 and the Taliban's swift resumption of power in Kabul, inland Asia has become a more permissive environment for China. China and Russia, in addition to drawing closer together bilaterally, have solidified multilateral arrangements in Central Asia. Notably, at the Shanghai Cooperation Organisation (SCO) summit in September in Dushanbe, Iran's bid to become a full member was approved. Once Iran joins, all but one of Afghanistan's neighbours will belong to the SCO. Across Asia, China is both asserting its maritime power and securing inland influence.

By contrast, the US is reorienting its strategic priorities to compete with China mainly for influence over the Indian and Pacific oceans. Thus, differing spheres of influence are being consolidated in Asia – one involving US-led coalitions of maritime-focused powers, the other constituting Chinese- and Russian-dominated clusters of inland influence. While oceanic and inland Asia are not mutually exclusive, Washington and Beijing are approaching them with strikingly different predilections and priorities.

Singaporean leader Lee Kuan Yew, among others, foresaw a 'contest for supremacy in Asia', warning of China's rising ambition for dominance following President Xi Jinping's ascent to power in 2013. In his 2017 book *Destined for War*, Graham Allison explains that first among China's goals for national rejuvenation under Xi's leadership is 'returning China to the predominance it enjoyed in Asia before the West intruded'.[3] In 1999, Robert S. Ross noted that 'the US is an East Asian maritime power with no strategic imperative to compete for influence on the mainland', whereas China is 'an established regional power' with mainland dominance.[4] Ross was inspired by Nicholas Spykman's *The Geography of the Peace*, originally published in 1944. Spykman envisaged 'a constant struggle between maritime and continental powers to balance their powers and achieve temporary equilibrium'.[5] He cited Halford Mackinder, who in 1904 elucidated the relationship between land and sea power on a truly global scale and distinguished the landmass of the 'heartland' (areas dependent on interior lines of transport) from the coastal 'rimland' (areas more accessible by sea).[6]

These ideas still resonate. Hal Brands and John Lewis Gaddis have noted that 'China will remain chiefly a land power'.[7] 'Chiefly' does not mean 'exclusively'. China has maritime ambitions, indicated by its rising ability and inclination to contend for influence in the South China Sea and in Taiwan, and by the modernisation of the People's Liberation Army Navy.[8] Nevertheless, notwithstanding changes in political geography, the contrast between Asia's rimland and heartland remains relevant due to the permanence of natural geography.

Southeast and Northeast Asia mean more to China in cultural terms than other parts of Asia. Prompted by the United States, nations committed to challenging China's pre-eminence now term the region formerly known as the 'Asia-Pacific' the 'Indo-Pacific' with an eye to enlisting India's geopolitical heft to balance China. But that label also conjures cartographical notions of oceans, islands, coasts and maritime trading routes quite distinct from the steppe, mountain and dessert terrain of 'inner Asia', where China's influence seems to be rising more steeply.[9]

II

Both Donald Trump and Joe Biden were committed to ending the Afghan war – the former in the service of an insular 'America First' foreign policy, the latter in part to help refocus US strategic attention on the contest with China. But in the absence of the US military presence, the region will develop according to local dynamics over which the US has relatively little control.

The SCO has since grown in importance as a diplomatic vehicle for challenging the US and the West in the region. Originally established as an ad hoc grouping called the 'Shanghai Five' (excluding Uzbekistan) in 1996 to resolve border disputes in the wake of the Soviet Union's dissolution, the organisation will include all except Turkmenistan among Afghanistan's neighbouring states once Iran completes its accession and, in terms of political culture, reflects the authoritarian sensibilities of China and Russia. The SCO is not a formal military alliance, but it does encourage and facilitate dialogue and coordination among its members around shared threats. They are especially worried that the Taliban's victory could boost separatist and terrorist factions inside their own borders.

China is particularly concerned that instability could spread into the western Chinese region of Xinjiang, fuelling separatist violence among the Uighur Muslim population. China's aggressive and repressive security policies in Xinjiang in recent years, including the mass detention of Uighurs, reflect, among other things, the strategic importance that Beijing places on this inland area. China also sees opportunity in Afghanistan. Chinese Foreign Minister Wang Yi hosted a Taliban delegation in Tianjin on 28 July, and Chinese mining companies are reportedly exploring Afghanistan for lithium and copper deposits.[10]

Multilateral arrangements like the SCO are only as significant as the bilateral relationships that they undergird. China's relationships with Pakistan, Iran and Russia are crucial. Each of these countries is to some extent at loggerheads with the United States. China has a strong and long-standing relationship with Pakistan. Although Pakistan received significant US military and economic aid after 9/11, the bilateral relationship remained testy and President Imran Khan was quick to applaud the Taliban victory. China bolstered its relations with Iran by signing a 25-year cooperation agreement in March 2021, pledging assistance in the telecommunications, banking and energy sectors in return for big discounts on the purchase of Iranian oil. While there are doubts about how much this deal can deliver, it remains significant that China and Iran have pulled together by virtue of their shared antipathy towards the US and their determination to limit its presence and influence in the region.

China's most important bilateral relationship is with Russia. The two enjoyed a rapprochement after the Soviet Union's collapse, and Moscow looked to Beijing for a deeper economic partnership to offset Western sanctions following Russia's war with Ukraine in 2014. Both countries resent 'the Western ideology of democratism' and see their relationship, though short of an alliance, as an alignment to balance Western influence.[11] China does not have treaty allies except North Korea, instead preferring to informally pursue trade and security relationships with states that are compliant with its world view, ambitions and priorities. Its bilateral ties with Tajikistan may be deepening, as unconfirmed reports of Chinese funding for new police bases there have emerged.[12] In any case, SCO member countries favourably disposed towards China now cover much of inner Asia.

The change of regime in Afghanistan is not itself significant for China's regional stature. The weightier factor is China's position at the centre of numerous diplomatic relationships that add up to rising inland influence. China is, to be sure, building warships, repressing Hong Kong and eyeing Taiwan. Still, some of its biggest security concerns, such as those around Xinjiang, remain inland.

III

The orthodoxy in some Western expert and policy circles is that events in 2021 represent a fair trade, ridding the United States of its draining war in Afghanistan to focus on its maritime-centred rivalry with China.[13] The advent of AUKUS – involving the US and two of its staunchest allies in the Afghan war – barely two weeks after the last US soldiers left Kabul airport reinforces this view.

The overlapping constellations of AUKUS and the Quad encourage a division of labour among US allies to balance China's maritime ambitions across the two oceans. The Quad's roots are in the joint naval exercise *Malabar*, first held in 2002 as a bilateral effort involving US and Indian warships in the Indian Ocean before expanding to include Japan in 2015 and Australia in 2020. Australia's participation that year in manoeuvres off Okinawa elicited an official complaint from China.[14] All the Quad members participated in the 2021 exercise in the Bay of Bengal.

The Quad has also tried to foster non-military influence in the Indo-Pacific. On 24 September, Quad leaders held a summit in Washington, where they made commitments with respect to pandemic response, climate change and other areas. They also highlighted the Build Back Better World (B3W) initiative, which is a planned infrastructure partnership introduced at the G7 summit in June, and pledged to 'rally expertise, capacity, and influence to strengthen ongoing infrastructure initiatives in the region'.[15] They did not earmark funds for B3W projects, however, leaving the initiative languishing in an uphill competition with China's Belt and Road Initiative (BRI), which began funding and building its infrastructure projects in 2013.[16]

The impact of the AUKUS deal on the maritime balance of power will be deferred. The promised fleet of nuclear-powered submarines would allow Australia to project undersea power out of Oceania and closer to China's territorial waters. But the Royal Australian Navy's operational deployment of the subs is not a foregone conclusion, and in any case may take 20 years to be realised.[17] The AUKUS deal drew a wide range of reactions among the allies and partners of its principals, some negative. While Tokyo endorsed the deal, New Delhi's response was guarded and qualified, as it took pains to differentiate AUKUS from the Quad. France was livid that its allies had undercut its own submarine deal with Australia, and the European Union was disappointed that AUKUS had stolen the thunder from the launch of the 'EU Strategy for Cooperation in the Indo-Pacific', which emphasises sustainability, connectivity and digital governance in the region.[18]

On balance, the US seems more preoccupied by its military rivalry with China than by its economic role in Asia. Security calculations, especially over Taiwan, remain integral to the Biden administration's understanding of the great-power contest in Asia. Senior administration officials have explained that 'although Washington should maintain its forward presence, it also needs to work with other states to disperse US forces across Southeast Asia and the Indian Ocean. This would reduce American reliance on a small number of vulnerable facilities in East Asia ... Rather than form a grand coalition focussed on every issue, the US should pursue bespoke or ad hoc bodies focussed on individual problems' to balance and deter China.[19] AUKUS and the Quad appear consistent with that prescription.

In consolidating its inland Asian influence, China is following a historical pattern. In challenging the maritime dominance of Europe, Japan and the United States, however, China is attempting something unprecedented in its history. Maritime dominion in Asia has been mainly a Western prerogative since the age of colonial empire. China's Ming dynasty briefly flirted with its own voyages of exploration under Admiral Zheng He but ceased competing in the naval race after 1433. Imperial China thereafter did not evolve as a dominant naval power. This proved to be a fatal vulnerability in the nineteenth and twentieth centuries. China suffered British naval bombardment and coastal landings in the Opium War that began in 1839. In 1900, soldiers of the Eight Power Alliance landed by sea during the Boxer Rebellion and marched inland to Peking. And in 1931, Japan's army invaded Manchuria by way of a seaborne assault.[20]

Against that background, it is sensible from China's perspective to develop a strong navy. At the same time, it is vital for Beijing to consolidate its inland influence and to reduce its dependence on the rimlands and coastal choke points that the United States and European powers have historically dominated. It is doing so by establishing land-based networks that extend into Europe and the Middle East which obviate heavy reliance on those choke points for moving energy, oil, gas and cargo. Having enlisted both Pakistan and Iran as partners, China can loop both countries into the BRI and potentially open much of Eurasia to beneficial trading links.[21]

Spkyman and Mackinder would surely conclude that the Russia–China partnership is securing influence over large tracts of inland Eurasia. As Spykman wrote, 'special "geopolitical" regions are not geographic regions defined by a fixed and permanent topography but areas determined on the one hand by geography and on the other hand by dynamic shifts in the centres of power'.[22] The US withdrawal from Afghanistan, the announcement of the AUKUS deal and the consolidation of the Quad reflect three such shifts. Nothing can predetermine Asia's strategic destiny, and it remains to be seen whether competing inland and maritime regional hegemonies can stably coexist. China could yet be drawn into a costly commitment in Afghanistan, or into further clashes with India across their mountainous borderlands. A war between China and the United States over Taiwan may yet occur. But if these or comparably disruptive events come to pass, it will be in the context of an inner Asia that is not dominated by the West and an increasingly contested maritime Asia.

Notes

1   US Department of Defense,
     'DoD Concludes 2021 Global
     Posture Review', press release,
     29 November 2021, https://www.
     defense.gov/News/Releases/Release/
     Article/2855801/dod-concludes-2021-
     global-posture-review/.

2   See White House, 'Joint Leaders
     Statement on AUKUS', 15
     September 2021, https://www.
     whitehouse.gov/briefing-room/
     statements-releases/2021/09/15/joint-
     leaders-statement-on-aukus/; and
     White House, 'Joint Statement from
     Quad Leaders', 24 September 2021,
     https://www.whitehouse.gov/briefing-
     room/statements-releases/2021/09/24/
     joint-statement-from-quad-leaders/.

3   See Graham Allison, *Destined for
     War: Can America and China Escape the
     Thucydides's Trap?* (London: Scribe
     UK, 2017), pp. 108-9. Allison also con-
     siders Chinese strategic goals under
     Xi to include 'recovering its historic
     sphere of influence along its borders
     and in the adjacent seas so that others
     give it the deference that great nations
     have always demanded'.

4   Robert S. Ross, 'The Geography of the
     Peace: East Asia in the Twenty-first
     Century', *International Security*, vol. 23,
     no. 4, Spring 1999, pp. 81–118.

5   Or Rosenboim, *The Emergence of World
     Order in Britain and the US, 1939–1950*
     (Princeton, NJ: Princeton University
     Press, 2017), pp. 67–9.

6   Nicholas John Spykman, *The
     Geography of the Peace* (New York:
     Harcourt Brace, 1944).

7   Hal Brands and John Lewis Gaddis,
     'The New Cold War: America, China,
     and the Echoes of History', *Foreign
     Affairs*, vol. 100, no. 6, November/
     December 2021, pp. 10–20.

8   See Brendan Taylor, *The Four
     Flashpoints: How Asia Goes to War*
     (Carlton: La Trobe University Press,
     2018).

9   See Andrew Hurrell, 'Regional
     Powers and the Global System from
     a Historical Perspective', in Daniel
     Flemes (ed.), *Regional Leadership in
     the Global System: Ideas, Interests and
     Strategies of Regional Powers* (Surrey:
     Ashgate, 2010), pp. 15–30.

10   See, respectively, Yew Lun Tian,
     'As Taliban Advances, China Lays
     Groundwork to Accept Awkward
     Reality', Reuters, 16 August 2021,
     https://www.reuters.com/world/
     china/taliban-advances-china-lays-
     groundwork-accept-an-awkward-
     reality-2021-08-14/; and Edward White
     and Fazelminallah Qazizai, 'Chinese
     Mining Groups Scour Afghanistan
     for Opportunities', *Financial Times*, 5
     December 2021, https://www.ft.com/
     content/4c0eb548-3c00-4702-8d43-
     227d80b94a4a.

11   Alexander Lukin, *China and Russia:
     The New Rapprochement* (Cambridge:
     Polity Press, 2018), pp. 5, 27, 64, 84,
     92. Lukin is not sanguine about the
     relationship: 'This does not mean
     Russia is unaware of possible com-
     plications in its cooperation with
     China ... Nobody expects altruism
     from Beijing: everybody knows that
     China would not rescue Russia at
     its own expense or cooperate with
     Moscow against its own interests.'
     See also Nadège Rolland, 'A China–

Russia Condominium over Eurasia', *Survival*, vol. 61, no. 1, February–March 2019, pp. 7–22.

[12] See 'China to Build Base for Tajikistan Police Near Afghan Border, Official Says', *South China Morning Post*, 28 October 2021, https://www.scmp.com/news/china/diplomacy/article/3154065/china-build-base-tajikistan-police-near-afghan-border-official.

[13] See, for example, Oriana Skylar Mastro, 'What US Withdrawal from Afghanistan Means for Taiwan', *New York Times*, 13 September 2021, https://www.nytimes.com/2021/09/13/opinion/china-taiwan-afghanistan.html.

[14] See Shishir Gupta, 'Malabar Exercise that Upsets China Is a Tectonic Shift in Power Balance', *Hindustan Times*, 17 November 2020, https://www.hindustantimes.com/india-news/round-2-of-malabar-war-games-tomorrow-it-represents-a-tectonic-shift-opinion/story-twV1VmPrB56FXLQfP8j27O.html.

[15] White House, 'Fact Sheet: Quad Leaders' Summit', 24 September 2021, https://www.whitehouse.gov/briefing-room/statements-releases/2021/09/24/fact-sheet-quad-leaders-summit/.

[16] See James Crabtree, 'Competing with the BRI: The West's Uphill Task', *Survival*, vol. 63, no. 4, August–September 2021, pp. 81–6.

[17] See, for example, Chris Buckley, 'Nuclear-powered Submarines for Australia? Maybe Not So Fast', *New York Times*, 29 October 2021 (updated 9 November 2021), https://www.nytimes.com/2021/10/29/world/australia/nuclear-powered-submarines.html.

[18] See European Commission, 'Questions and Answers: EU Strategy for Cooperation in the Indo-Pacific', 16 September 2021, https://ec.europa.eu/commission/presscorner/detail/en/QANDA_21_4709.

[19] Kurt M. Campbell and Rush Doshi, 'How America Can Shore Up Asian Order', *Foreign Affairs*, 12 January 2021, https://www.foreignaffairs.com/articles/united-states/2021-01-12/how-america-can-shore-asian-order.

[20] See Samir Puri, *The Great Imperial Hangover: How Empires Have Shaped the World* (London: Atlantic Books, 2020), pp. 171–5.

[21] In distant history, 'the linking up of the steppes into an interlocking and interconnecting world was accelerated by the growing ambitions of China … This expansion of China's horizons linked Asia together.' Peter Frankopan, *The Silk Road: A New History of the World* (London: Bloomsbury, 2015).

[22] Spykman, *The Geography of the Peace*, p. 6.